Unoriginal Genius

Unoriginal Genius

Poetry by Other Means in the New Century

Marjorie Perloff

The University of Chicago Press *Chicago and London*

The University of Chicago Press, Chicago 60637
The University of Chicago Press, Ltd., London
© 2010 by The University of Chicago
All rights reserved. Published 2010.
Paperback edition 2012
Printed in the United States of America

Permission to quote from Jacques Jouet, "Qu'est-ce
qu'un poème de métro" (2000), is gratefully
acknowledged to P.O.L. Éditions. Permission
for Ian Monk's English translation is gratefully
acknowledged.

21 20 19 18 17 16 15 14 13 12   3 4 5 6 7

ISBN-13: 978-0-226-66061-5 (cloth)
ISBN-13: 978-0-226-66062-2 (paper)
ISBN-10: 0-226-66061-3 (cloth)
ISBN-10: 0-226-66062-1 (paper)

Library of Congress Cataloging-in-Publication Data
Perloff, Marjorie.
   Unoriginal genius : poetry by other means in the
new century / Marjorie Perloff.
      p. cm.
   Includes bibliographical references and index.
   ISBN-13: 978-0-226-66061-5 (cloth : alk. paper)
   ISBN-10: 0-226-66061-3 (cloth : alk. paper)
1. Poetry—20th century—History and criticism.
2. Poetry—21st century—History and criticism.
3. Benjamin, Walter, 1892–1940—Criticism and
interpretation. 4. Multilingualism and literature.
I. Title.
PN1271.P47 2010
809.1'911—dc22
                                    2010018363

♾ This paper meets the requirements of ANSI/NISO
Z39.48-1992 (Permanence of Paper).

For Joseph

Contents

Figures

Preface

In 1990, when I was completing *Radical Artifice: Writing Poetry in the Age of Media*, access to the World Wide Web was still a few years away. The "media" then in question were primarily television (as in the Phil Donahue talk show), radio, advertising copy, and signage as in the case of "personalized" license plates. *Radical Artifice* was certainly written on a computer—an old Kaypro, as I recall—but surfing the Web, googling, blogging, viewing or making videos on You Tube, writing on Facebook walls, or Twittering: these were still in the future. There was, it is true, much talk of the possibilities of "E-poetry"—poetry written and formatted for the new electronic screen. But E-poetry never quite got off the ground, the compositional process of an E-poem (however much animation might be used) not being essentially different from that of a "normal" print poem.

The revolution that soon occurred was not in writing *for* the computer screen but writing in an environment of hyperinformation, an environment, moreover, where we are all authors. The first poetry blogs and Web sites, for example, were a novelty; today, those listed in the left-hand column of Ron Silliman's now famous and influential poetry blog number more than twelve hundred! At this writing, Silliman's own poetry blog has received 2.5 million hits—a daunting figure when one thinks that this poet's printed books, *Ketjak* and *Tjanting* and *The Alphabet*, cannot have sold a fraction of this number.

But it is not just a matter of quantity; the fact is that in the blog world or on Facebook just about anything goes. There is usually no editor, no peer review, no critique for which one might be held accountable by anyone outside one's particular community. In this climate, what Hart Crane called the poet's "cognate word" begins to take a back seat to what can be done with other people's words—how already existing words and sentences are framed, recycled, appropriated, cited, submitted to rules, visualized, or sounded. The poetry of 2010 is thus curiously different from that of 1990, even when its authors remain the same.

Paradoxically, this new citational and often constraint-bound poetry—a poetry as visually and sonically formalized as it is semantically charged—is more accessible and, in a sense, "personal" than was the Language poetry of twenty years earlier. Since intertexts are central to this writing, poetry has turned once more to the literary and artistic tradition—whether the poems of Yeats and Stevenson in Susan Howe's *Midnight*, or Heine's Lorelei in Charles Bernstein's *Shadowtime*, or Dante's *Inferno* in Caroline Bergvall's *Via*, whether the reprise of Futurist aesthetic in Brazilian concrete poetry or of Troubadour lyric in Oulipo writing. Then again, the "literary" can now absorb the most curious bits of scientific documentation: think of Christian Bök, the author of the Oulipo *Eunoia*, now writing poetry into the genetic code of bacteria. His project, dubbed *Xenotext*, was, he tells us, "inspired by a previous feat of genetic engineering in which microorganisms were made to carry the tune of Disney's 'It's a Small World (After All)' in their DNA. Information retrieval is this providing a strange new poetic challenge."

: : :

Unoriginal Genius looks at some key exemplars of what we might call poetry by other means, from Walter Benjamin's *Arcades Project* to Kenneth Goldsmith's *Traffic*. Six of the book's seven chapters were delivered as the 2009 Weidenfeld Lectures in European Comparative Literature at Oxford (St. Anne's College) during Trinity Term. A perverse choice for the traditional world of Oxford poetry? No doubt, but perhaps for that very reason the lectureship posed an exciting challenge. I am, in any case, very grateful to Lord and Lady Weidenfeld, who listened so attentively to the first lecture, for making this visiting professorship possible and to St. Anne's principal Tim Gardam for his hospitality. Among my hosts, Michael Sheringham of All Souls, Karen Leeder of New College, Ronald Bush of St. John's, and Jeri Johnson of Exeter were especially gracious. I also had a chance to try out my ideas about constraint, citation, and concretism on lively audiences at the Universities of Warwick, Kent, and Southampton. At these venues, Peter Middleton, Daniel Katz, Andrew Roberts, Anna Schaffner, and Peter Nicholls (then of the University of Sussex) kept me on my toes.

    In an earlier incarnation, the first chapter of *Unoriginal Genius* was given as the keynote address as the 2008 symposium Conceptual Poetry and Its Others at the University of Arizona Poetry Center—a symposium I organized with the then director of the center, Frances Sjoberg. The Arizona symposium was exhilarating in that the poets in attendance—Caroline Bergvall, Charles Bernstein, Christian Bök, Craig Dworkin, Kenneth Goldsmith, Tracie Morris, and Cole Swensen (Peter Gizzi and Susan Howe were on the program but unable to attend)—elicited a very strong response from our roundtables, which included still other important new voices—for example, the poets Vanessa Place and Jesper Olsson and critics ranging from Wyston

Curnow (New Zealand) to Graça Capinha (Portugal). The Arizona Poetry Center is fortunate to be able to draw on experts from the University of Arizona's English Department, including Carlos Gallego, Tenney Nathanson, and the publisher of Chax Press, Charles Alexander.

Earlier versions of some of the book's other chapters were delivered as keynote lectures at international meetings — the Another Language: Poetic Experiments in Britain and North America conference in Bochum Germany (2005), organized by Kornelia Freitag; the 2007 AFEA (L'Association française d'études américaines) in Paris, where Helène Aji, Antoine Cazé, and Christine Savinel were my hosts; the 2007 Colloquium of Comparative Literature in Porto, Portugal, chaired by Ana Luisa Amaral; Eduardo Espina's Poetry of Americas festival at Texas A&M in 2007; and the International Conference on 20th Century American Poetry in Wuhan, China ,overseen by Luo Liangong and Nie Zhenzhao in 2008. International as is this roster, *Unoriginal Genius*, as the Oxford audience made me aware, is at heart a very American book, and its conception was formed in classrooms both at Stanford and, more recently, at the University of Southern California, where Marie Smart and Amaranth Borsuk gave much help with my own Web site and the figures for the book. It is impossible to cite the many former students, colleagues, and friends who helped me articulate my ideas. When I think about my own poetic-critical community (online and off), I feel truly blessed. Here I wish to thank only my two no-longer-anonymous readers for the University of Chicago Press: Gerald Bruns and Adelaide Russo. No one could ask for more thorough and perceptive readers than these, and their unflagging support, as well as that of my longtime Chicago editor Alan Thomas, have meant the world to me.

This book is dedicated to the person with whom I most often discuss poetry even if — or precisely because — he often expresses deep skepticism about the contemporary poetry landscape and much prefers Kipling's "The Buddha at Kamakura," Poe's "The Raven," or Eliot's *The Waste Land*, the poem with which I begin here, to their later incarnations. If I can convince Joseph that a particular text is a work of genius — and he made this claim for Georges Perec's *Life, a User's Manual,* before I did — then I know I'm on the right track. But as Joseph loves to say, citing Charles Bernstein's *Shadowtime,*

Just a-

round the corner is another corner.

Marjorie Perloff
Pacific Palisades, 2009

Acknowledgments

An earlier version of chapters 1 and 2 in combination was published as "Unoriginal Genius: Benjamin's Arcades as Paradigm for the New Poetics," *Études Anglaises* 61, no. 9 (April-June 2008), 229–52.

A short version of chapter 3 appeared as "From Avant-Garde to Digital: The Legacy of Brazilian Concrete Poetry," *Interdisciplinary Humanities*, Spring 2008, 66–89. A portion of the chapter was also published in *Do modernismo a contemporaneidade* (Porto, 2008), 11–45.

An earlier version of chapter 4, "Constraint, Concrete, Citation: Refiguring History in Charles Bernstein's *Shadowtime*," was published in *Poetics Today: Constrained Writing I*, ed. Jan Baetens and Jean-Jacques Poucel, 30, no. 4 (Winter 2009): 693–718. A short version also appeared in *Foreign Literature Studies* (Wuhan), 2008, 12–30.

An earlier version of chapter 5, "The Rattle of Statistical Traffic: Constraint and Citation in Susan Howe's *The Midnight*," was published in *boundary* 2, special issue, "American Poetry after 1975," ed. Charles Bernstein, 36, no. 2 (Fall 2009): 205–28.

1

Unoriginal Genius: An Introduction

We are in the midst of a mighty recasting
of literary forms, a melting down in which
many of the opposites in which we have
been used to think may lose their force.
Walter Benjamin

I love originality so much I keep copying it.
Charles Bernstein[1]

Récriture

The publication in 1922 of *The Waste Land*—surely the most famous poem
in English of the twentieth century—met with a largely negative reception,
even on the part of admirers of T. S. Eliot's earlier poetry like Edgell Rickword, who reviewed *The Waste Land* for the *Times Literary Supplement*.[2] A
World War I poet, student of French poetry (he published one of the first
critical studies in English of Rimbaud), and founding editor of the *Calendar
of Modern Letters* (1925–27), which took a strong stand against the Edward-
ians in the name of Modernism,[3] Rickword expressed admiration for Eliot's
"sophistication" but could not condone *The Waste Land*'s extensive use of
citation:

> [Mr. Eliot's] emotions hardly ever reach us without traversing a zig-zag of allu-
> sion. In the course of his four hundred lines he quotes from a score of authors and
> in three foreign languages, though his artistry has reached that point at which it
> knows the wisdom of sometimes concealing itself. There is in general in his work
> a disinclination to awake in us a direct emotional response. . . . He conducts a
> *magic-lantern show*; but being too reserved to expose in public the impressions

stamped on his own soul by the journey through the Waste Land, he employs the slides made by others, indicating with a touch the difference between his reaction and theirs.[4]

As for the vegetation myths that Eliot cites as his key source in the infamous notes, this "cultural or middle layer" of the poem "is of no poetic value in itself. We desire to touch the inspiration itself, and the apparatus of reserve is too strongly constructed." True, there are a few direct expressions of feeling, like the "concluding confession 'These fragments I have shored against my ruins,'" but on the whole, the poet's method is "reticence itself":

> Here is a writer to whom originality is almost an inspiration borrowing the greater number of his best lines, creating hardly any himself. It seems to us as if "The Waste Land" exists in the greater part in the state of notes. This quotation is a particularly obvious instance:

> London Bridge is falling down falling down falling down
> *Poi s'ascose nel foco che gli affina*
> *Quando fiam uti chelidon*—O swallow swallow
> *Le Prince d'Acquitaine à la tour abolie*[5]

This collage of nursery rhyme, Dante's *Purgatorio*, the *Pervigilum Veneris*, and Gerard de Nerval prompts the following assessment:

> Perhaps if the reader were sufficiently sophisticated he would find these echoes suggestive hints, as rich in significance as the sonorous amplifications of the romantic poets. None the less, we do not derive from this poem as a whole the satisfaction we ask from poetry. Numerous passages are finely written; there is an amusing monologue in the vernacular [the Lil passage in "The Game of Chess"] and the fifth part is nearly wholly admirable. The section beginning "What is that sound high in the air . . ." has a nervous strength which perfectly suits the theme; but he declines to a mere notation, the result of an indolence of imagination.
>
> Mr. Eliot, always evasive in the grand manner, has reached a stage at which he can no longer refuse to recognize the limitations of his medium; he is sometimes walking very near the limits of coherency.

And Rickword concludes with the hope that the poet will soon "recover" from this "ambitious experiment."

This *TLS* review is an important document for anyone who wants to understand the poetry emerging in the twenty-first century. Rickword's basic charge is quite clear: *citation*, especially citation that draws on other languages, undermines and destroys the very essence of poetry, which is (or should be) the expression of personal emotion—emotion conveyed, of course, in the poet's *own words*, invented for this express purpose. The "zigzag of allusion" thus bodes ill; one's "magic-lantern show"—a term Rickword no doubt derived from Proust[6]—should not consist of "slides made by others." A poem as a "set of notes," most of them "borrowed" from other texts: such "mere notation" can only be "the result of an indolence of the imagination."

It is one of the nice ironies of literary history that Eliot himself, having produced his "ambitious experiment," never used its citational mode again. Was he listening to his critics? *The Waste Land* was, after all, partly the product of Ezra Pound's extensive cuts: did Eliot come to think better of Pound's collagist method? Whatever the reason, his most important later poems, "Ash Wednesday" and the *Four Quartets*, are lyric meditations, oblique and dense in their communication of emotion but certainly reliant almost wholly on *the poet's own words*. "We do sometimes wish to hear the poet's full voice," says Rickword, and in *Ash Wednesday* and the *Quartets* we hear it, however carefully Eliot avoids the particulars of his actual life.

It is *The Waste Land*, however, that, almost a century after it was written, remains Eliot's most celebrated poem—the poem that has given most readers "the satisfaction we ask from poetry." The immediacy of the pub scene, for example, with its "borrowed" lines—

HURRY UP PLEASE ITS TIME
HURRY UP PLEASE ITS TIME
Goonight Bill. Goonight Lou. Goonight May. Goonight—

where the refrain, a crossing of the barman's nightly last call with the warning of Isaiah ("A little one shall become a thousand, and a small one a strong nation: I the LORD will hurry it in its time," 61:22), modulates into the routine words of the pub crawlers (which will in turn modulate into the "mad" Ophelia's "Goodnight sweet ladies"), has itself become an appropriated text, cited by many later writers for its suggestibility and ironic potential.

In his important study *La seconde main ou le travail de la citation* (*The Second Hand or the Work of Citation*), Antoine Compagnon writes:

> Blessed citation! Among all the words in our vocabulary, it has the privilege of simultaneously representing two operations, one of removal, the other of graft, as well as the object of these operations—the object removed and the object grafted on, as if the word remained the same in these two different states. Is there known elsewhere, in whatever other field of human activity, a similar reconciliation, in one and the same word, of the incompatible fundamentals which are disjunction and conjunction, mutilation and wholeness, the less and the more, ex-

port and import, decoupage and collage? The dialectic of citation is all-powerful: one of the vigorous mechanisms of displacement, it is even stronger than surgery.[7]

The "doubling" function of citation is characterized even more dramatically by Walter Benjamin, himself a great citational writer, in this instance talking about a fellow appropriationist, Karl Kraus:

> In the quotation that both saves and punishes, language proves the matrix of justice. It summons the word by its name, wrenches it destructively from its context, but precisely calls it back to its origin. It appears, now with rhyme and reason, sonorously, congruously, in the structure of a new text. As rhyme, it gathers the similar into its aura; as name, it stands alone and expressionless. In citation the two realms—of origin and destruction—justify themselves before language. And conversely, only where they interpenetrate—in citation—is language consummated.[8]

The language of citation—Compagnon appropriately calls it *récriture*—has found a new lease on life in our own information age. It is a commonplace that in the world of digital discourse, of the Internet, e-mail, cell phone, and Facebook, communication has been radically transformed both temporally and spatially. The speed whereby the sender's message reaches its destination has obviously created a new sense of simultaneity even as space has become increasingly indeterminate. Neither telephone area codes nor e-mail addresses tell us where caller and recipient are actually located at the moment of communication, nor do most e-mail addresses (e.g., AOL or Gmail) provide vital statistics about their possessors: they reveal neither nationality nor ethnicity, race nor religion, age nor even gender. And even when, as on Facebook, such information is given, how do we know it is accurate? Then, too, forwarded e-mails can be altered without the recipient's knowledge so that the sender's identity actually merges with that of the writer whose text is being forwarded. And poets' blogs, heavily dependent as most are on recycled material, are further framed by viewer responses, producing a curious amalgam of voices that begins to take on a life of its own.

Under these circumstances, communication is likely to shift from a specific geographic location (for example, the New York of Frank O'Hara) or one's particular local circle (e.g., the Beats) to those, wherever and whoever they are, who share a particular set of interests and allegiances. The word *community* thus takes on an entirely new meaning: the community now exists on particular websites or in the blogosphere—a situation whose far-reaching implications we have not even begun to understand.

Consider the following message sent to me on Facebook (June 6, 2009):

Dear MP,

My name is Ina Serdarevic and I'm a poet, artist and student at the University of Copenhagen, Denmark.

I just finished reading *Soliloquy* by Kenny G (the whole thing, well, sort of). I'm working on an article about Contemporary Literature and Conceptual Poetry in USA, and it hit me that *Soliloquy* is even funnier and more groundbreaking today than it was in the 90's when it was first published. Because of the new technology; I mean, yes there was internet back then but things—such as myspace, blogspot, twitter, flickr, youtube and most importantly FACEBOOK are casting a new kind of light on Goldsmith's book that reveal new layers of importance and new possibilities. Like for instance, look at this very message I'm sending you: you are one among many CHARACTERS in the book, I call you characters because Kenny G earlier described *Soliloquy* as POETRY, and a lot of these characters that I'm reading about in my book are directly available and accessible to me on Facebook. I type your name and Voilà!—a second later I've established contact. How many writers can actually take credit for building up a secret network between his readers and book characters?? I mean, this is truly amazing, and by taking advantage of the various search engines on the net, along with Facebook contacting, it's in fact possible to create a map of the world within *Soliloquy*. I can look up people and talk to them about their personal experience beyond the frame that Goldsmith is creating, I can disprove and invalidate certain situations in the book and get multiple angles on them by addressing the different characters. People like John Post Lee, Karin Bravin, Carter Kustera, Alix Pearlstein, Steve Clay, Charles Bernstein and yourself, are all presented in the book and connected to their own proper equivalents of flesh and blood, they are all to be found on Facebook by anyone who wishes to find them. This awareness gives an odd feeling while reading the book but is also creating a cool and interesting fuzz about it. It's almost like reading *Finnegans Wake* and having access to all its characters and a key to all the allusions and covert indications.

With this message, I'm simply trying to establish contact with a prominent figure from the book.

What to make of this ingenious and engaging e-mail from a total stranger? Its address (MP) and reference to Kenneth Goldsmith by his disc jockey name (Kenny G) is nothing if not casual and certainly irreverent. And Serdarevic's recipients (of whom I am one) could easily take umbrage at the idea that an overseas student is using a poetic text along with Facebook as a way to make contact with the American artists or critics she wants to know. But her letter does argue persuasively that *Soliloquy* (1997) curiously anticipates our own moment. A conceptualist text that transcribes every word its author spoke during an entire week in New York City (while omitting all the words of those he spoke to), *Soliloquy* blurs the distinction between "real" people—people with Internet profiles and publications—and fictional characters. In doing so, it prompts the reader to investigate more fully to what extent Goldsmith's portraits, of himself as well as of others, are reliable, the poet's "actual" speech notwithstanding. On the one hand, *Soliloquy* has the air of a urban documentary; on the other, its submission to a rigid set of constraints—the Aristotelian unities of time, place, and action, as well as its governing rule that only the narrator is to be heard—gives the book an aura of hyperreality. Reading such a text, one must negotiate between inside and outside in ways that are still unfamiliar. As in the case of *Finnegans Wake*, each reading yields new connections. The mirrors, as Serdarevic understands, keep multiplying.[9]

But how did this student happen to hear about Goldsmith's work in the first place? Copenhagen, like Stockholm or Helsinki or Olso—for that matter, like São Paulo, Brazil, and Wuhan, China—has become in recent years a center for avant-garde poetics, hosting festivals at which poets from the United States have joined others from around the world. Partly this shift in literary venues has been brought about by the changing relationship between majority and minority literatures. As recently as the 1980s, US anthologies had titles like *In the American Tree*, Ron Silliman's important compendium of Language poetry, which divided its contributors into two sections, West and East—eighteen West Coast poets (mostly from San Francisco) and twenty from the East (mostly from New York).[10] *In the American Tree* excluded such leading Language poets as Steve McCaffery (Canadian) and Tom Raworth (British) and made no attempt to bring poets from other regions of the United States into the Language fold. Two decades later, the notion of a "new American poetry" restricted to those who dwell and work in the United States seems increasingly anachronistic. Where poets actually live is much less important than what they do, and mobility—whether of texts, now eminently movable, or of their authors—is the status quo. In the Scandinavian countries, where English is a strong second language and where Modernist avant-gardes have found a receptive audience, Internet sites now have a broadly global reach.

Consider the electronic journal of international contemporary poetry and poetics *nypoesi* (*New Poetry*), which is edited from Norway by Paal Bjelke Andersen.[11] *nypoesi* regularly features poetry, both in the original and in translation, from the United States, the United Kingdom, France, and Germany, as well as from Scandinavia. It also publishes intriguing theoretical essays like Alexandr Skidan's "Poetry in the Age of Total Communication" (November 2007), translated from Russian into both Norwegian and English.[12] In the same vein, the Brazilian journal *Sibila*, founded and edited by Régis Bonvicino in São Paulo, carried in issue 11 an exciting roundtable on "poésia em tempo de guerra e banalidade" (poetry in a time of war and banality), in which the Finnish poet-translator Leevi Lehto has an essay, also reproduced on the *Sibila in English* website, called, with a nod to T. S. Eliot, "Plurifying the Languages of the Trite," with its partly tongue-in-cheek "central claim . . . for an *absolute and global pluralism of forms, contents, and languages*."[13] When I was searching for Lehto's essay on Google, I got the prompt "Did you mean: 'Purifying the Languages of the Tort'?" Clarifying the language of torts: a poet like Lehto could have a marvelous time making connections between the trite and the tort, the relation of the pure to the plural.

Invention

Reading *nypoesi* or *Sibila* or the French-English website and electronic journal *Double Change*,[14] one is struck by how different the new poetics is, not just from the mainstream poetry of print journals like *The New Yorker* or *American Poetry Review* but also from the first wave of Language poetry in the 1980s. Here are some representative extracts:

(1) were I idiom and
    the portray
    what on
    idiot you remarking
    cessed to only up
    opt hope this
    was soundly action
    more engineer
    taut that the

    Bruce Andrews, from "While" (1981)

(2) at the end of delight, one
    who or that which revolves

    more than chests have
    to heave ". . . where gold,

dirt, and blood flow
together"! : margins

the family, not personal
fallibility leads

to instrumentality
in self-restraint

Diane Ward, from "Limit" (1989)

(3) morrow every listen
   ago potato who have a paper voice
   the hole where the effort went
   tome is crayern
   a fasten into trance, necklace some awake of notes, floorer
   as classed some follow

Peter Inman, from "Colloam" (1986)[15]

Different as these three selections are, theirs is a period style that exhibits specific features. First, this is a poetry of programmatic nonreferentiality, words and phrases refusing to "add up" to any sort of coherent, much less transparent, statement. Syntactic distortion is the key: in Andrews's "While," articles modify verbs rather than nouns ("the portray" where we expect "portrait"), infinitive slots contains adverbs ("to only"), syllables are elided as in "cessed" (processed? recessed? accessed?), and it is not clear whether "this" in line 6 is the direct object of "hope" or the subject of "was" in the following line. Similarly in Diane Ward's "Limit," the agent ("one / who or that which") is indeterminate, and nouns in apposition ("margins / the family") don't form a sequence. Inman's "Colloam" (the title word is not in the OED; it seems to be a neologism formed of *colophon* and *loam*), the verb "fasten" does not have "necklace" as its object; rather, we are given the phrase "a fasten into trance," where "fasten" and "trance" relate phonemically rather than semantically. All three poems use predominantly abstract language, and the pronouns have no discernible referents. Who is Ward's "one / who . . . revolves"? Or Inman's "who" with the "paper voice"? In each case, linkage is produced by sound rather than signification: in Andrews's poem, "idiom" is related to "idiot" (see line 5), the words "up / opt hope" alliterate, and "taut" (pun on *taught*) in the last line visually echoes "that" and "the." Inman rhymes "ago" and "potato," "floorer" leads to "follow," and "crayern" seems to be a phonetic spelling of "crayon" or a reference to *crayer*, an obsolete word meaning "small vessel."

"Tome" and "crayon" can be related metonymically, but why and how would a large, heavy book be equated to a small vessel?

The defeat of reader expectation—a kind of cognitive dissonance—is central to these poems. Ward's "At the end of" anticipates a noun phrase like "the day" or "the journey" but not "the delight"; in Inman, the "hole" promises to contain something tangible rather than "effort," and although "morrow" (as in *tomorrow*) and "ago" are related temporally, neither the potato nor the neologism "crayern" fits into its syntactic slot. Reading these lines, one has to make one's way through a maze, with no guidance from a controlling voice or a context. "The family / not personal," as Ward puts it.

At the same time, it is important to note that the words, morphemes, syntactic units, and sound patterns in each of these examples have been *chosen* by the poet in question. Even the jagged free verse (or "new sentence" in the case of much Language-centered prose), designed to obstruct the very possibility of pattern or ordering principle, underscores the primacy of the poet's *inventio* as constructive principle. This is a poetry that conceives of the poem as meaning-making machine and takes its motive from what Adorno termed *resistance*: the resistance of the individual poem to the larger cultural field of capitalist commodification where language has become merely instrumental.

Central to such resistance is the drive to Make It New, to avoid dependence on earlier poetic models. Allusions to Modernist lyric, let alone Romantic ode or Renaissance elegy, give way to a rapprochement with the language of theory, references to Derrida and Deleuze, Foucault and Baudrillard, cropping up in epigraph or wordplay. Form, in this scheme of things, is (in Robert Creeley's phrase, though not in his practice) never more than the extension of content. Thus the look of the poem as well as its sound structure are primarily instrumental, used to emphasize the poem's semantic density and verbal originality.

Verbal originality: it is this criterion that links the "language poems" in question to the lyric of the 1960s and '70s. Now that the much-fabled poetry wars of that era have receded into the distance, we can see that however different, the poems of Elizabeth Bishop and Allen Ginsberg, Sylvia Plath and James Wright, Denise Levertov and A. R. Ammons, all are, to put it most concisely, Originals. Here are the openings of some famous American poems of the period:

> This is the time of year
> when almost every night
> the frail, illegal fire balloons appear,

climbing the mountain height,
rising toward a saint
still honored in these parts,
the paper chambers flush and fill with light
that comes and goes, like hearts.

Elizabeth Bishop, "The Armadillo"

What thoughts I have of you tonight Walt Whitman, for I walked down the sidestreets under the trees with a headache self-conscious looking at the full moon.

In my hungry fatigue, and shopping for images, I went into the neon fruit supermarket, dreaming of your enumerations.

What peaches and what penumbras! Whole families shopping at night! Aisles full of husbands! Wives in the avocados, babies in the tomatoes!—and you, García Lorca, what were you doing down by the water-melons?

Allen Ginsberg, "A Supermarket in California"

What a thrill—
My thumb instead of an onion.
The top quite gone
Except for a sort of a hinge—

Of skin,
A flap like a hat,
Dead white.
Then that red plush.

Sylvia Plath, "Cut"

Just off the highway to Rochester, Minnesota,
Twilight bounds softly forth on the grass,
And the eyes of those two Indian ponies
Darken with kindness.
They have come gladly out of the willows
To welcome my friend and me.

James Wright, "A Blessing"

The ache of marriage:

thigh and tongue, beloved,
are heavy with it,

it throbs in the teeth

We look for communion
and are turned away, beloved,
each and each

Denise Levertov, "The Ache of Marriage"

I went for a walk over the dunes again this morning
to the sea,
then turned right along
      the surf
              rounded a naked headland
              and returned
along the inlet shore

A. R. Ammons, "Corson's Inlet"[16]

Whether in rhyming stanzas (Bishop, Plath), free verse (Ammons, Levertov, Wright), or rhythmical prose (Ginsberg), whether explicitly first-person (Plath, Ammons, Ginsberg) or more outer-directed (Bishop, Wright, Levertov), whether speech-based (Plath, Ammons), self-consciously literary (Bishop, Wright), or even surreal (Ginsberg, Levertov), these are poems of strong individualistic cast: each has its own voice, its own discourse radius, that connects it to other poems by the same author.

Language poetry had as its explicit aim to oppose such "natural" expressivist speech, such individual voicing and accessible syntax. But for the most part—and this has been insufficiently recognized—the poets represented in, say, Ron Silliman's *In the American Tree* did accept their predecessors' trust in invention, in the poet's power to create a unique *parole* from the language pool of the culture—a *parole* framed to *resist* what Adorno had defined as the culture industries. In the climate of the new century, however, we seem to be witnessing a poetic turn from the resistance model of the 1980s to dialogue—a dialogue with earlier texts or texts in other media, with "writings through" or *ekphrases* that permit the poet to participate in a larger, more public discourse. *Inventio* is giving way to appropriation, elaborate constraint, visual and sound composition, and reliance on intertexuality. Thus we are witnessing a new poetry, more conceptual than directly expressive— a poetry in which, as Gerald Bruns puts it with reference to Cage's "writings through" *Finnegans Wake*, the shift is "from a Chomskyan linguistic competence, in which the subject is able to produce an infinite number of original sentences from the deep structure of linguistic rules, to the pragmatic discourse that appropriates and renews what is given in the discourse that constitutes a social and cultural world."[17]

Poetry by Other Means
In this new poetic climate, *The Waste Land*, with its "zig-zag of allusion," to use Edgell Rickword's dismissive phrase, its "unoriginal" lines and borrowed "magic lantern slides," can be seen as a foundational text. Together with Pound's *Cantos*, with their amalgam of citation and found text, it looks ahead not only to the mosaic of borrowings found in Louis Zukofsky's *"A"* but also to the impacted pastiche of John Ashbery's later poems, where almost every line has an intertextual referent. Both Susan Howe and Steve McCaffery, who began their poetic careers under the sign of Concrete poetry, have always devised complex uses of citation and constraint, intertext and intermedia: Howe's *The Defenestration of Prague* (1983) is a classic example of "writing through," in this case, Jonathan Swift's "Journal to Stella," while constraint is exemplified in such McCaffery sequences as *Evoba* or the more recent *Dark Ladies*, a dazzling, rule-generated writing through Shakespeare's *Sonnets*.

All the same, nothing quite prepared the poetry world for the claim, now being made by conceptual poets from Kenneth Goldsmith to Leevi Lehto, Craig Dworkin to Caroline Bergvall, that it is possible to write "poetry" that is entirely "unoriginal" and nevertheless qualifies as poetry. In fall 2007, for example, Kenneth Goldsmith, in a set of short manifesto statements for the blog of the venerable Poetry Foundation of America, announced his advocacy of conceptual or "uncreative" writing—a form of copying, recycling, or appropriation that "obstinately makes no claim on originality." Indeed, "at a reading I gave recently," Goldsmith recalls wryly, "the other reader came up to me and said incredulously, 'You didn't write a word of what you read.'"[18]

Incredulous as that "other reader" may have been, let's remember that Edgell Rickword made almost the same complaint about *The Waste Land*: "Here is a writer [Eliot] . . . borrowing the greater number of his best lines, creating hardly any himself." Indeed, the poetics of "unoriginality," now hotly debated in journals like *Poetry* and on the blogosphere, can be traced back to a number of movements and paradigms that antedate Language writing by decades. One such was the concretism of the 1950s and '60s (itself a bridge to the great avant-garde projects of the early twentieth century)—a movement associated with the smaller or marginalized nations of the postwar: Sweden (Oyvind Fahlström), Switzerland (Eugen Gomringer), Scotland (Ian Hamilton Finlay), Austria (Ernst Jandl), and especially Brazil (Augusto and

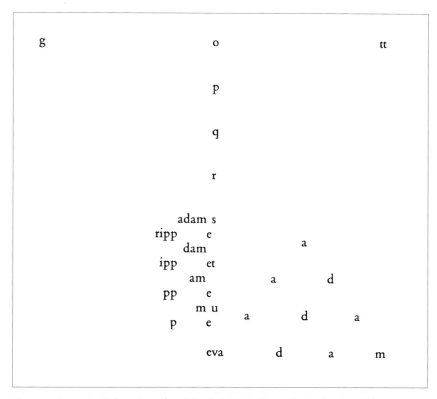

Figure 1.1. Ernst Jandl, "creation of eve." *Poetische Werke* © 1997 by Luchterhand Literaturverlag, Munich, a member of Verlagsgruppe Random House GmbH.

Haroldo de Campos). The concretist program is best understood as a revolt against the transparency of the word, which had dominated the discourse of the 1950s and '60s; in Ernst Jandl's "creation of eve" (fig.1.1), for example, the breath of life is viewed as issuing from the *o* in "Gott"—God's mouth, so to speak—in an alphabetical sequence (*opqrstu*) that culminates in the *v* of "eva," even as, on the left, the word "adam" (Adam alone) disappears, while his rib (*Rippe*) is reduced, step by step, to its final letter, *e*, which yields the name "eva," its last letter—*a*—providing the ground for Adam's diagonal reemergence to Eve's right.[19]

Such concretist texts—texts in which lettristic or morphemic form is inextricable from meaning—anticipate contemporary digital poetics, where letter, font, size, spacing, and color are used to generate complex verbovisual configurations. The German-Finnish digital poet Cia Rinne, for example, has recently produced a work called *archives zaroum*, the title fusing the Russian *zaum* (transrational) with the German word *warum* for "why" and *darum* (because).[20] *Archives zaroum* consists of twenty-nine animated and interactive multilingual visual poems, emerging from a set of seven tabbed file folders, each with a title typed in black and red. Clicking on the tabs and on the diagrams—boxes, lines, circles, flow charts—within each file, one makes repeated discoveries. Take, for example, a still version of animated text from the first file called "1, 2, 3, Soleil" (fig.1.2), with its tension between verticals and horizontal possibilities of "on" and "no," between circle and point, its couplet

> i am what i am what i ami
> a mia mi ami a miami amen

and the love theme qualified by the ambivalence between the words "TO," "GET," and "HER," in their separate boxes, and the parenthesis containing "together," as well as the juxtaposition of "a part" and "apart." But of course in the animated version, where every word, letter, and pictogram turns out to be clickable, these "simple words and phrases yield further puns, rhymes, and anagrams, complicated by the layering of languages used."[21]

A second precursor of twenty-first-century poetics was the Oulipo (Ouvroir de littérature potentielle), founded in Paris in 1960 and still going strong. The aim of Oulipo, as one of its founders, Jacques Roubaud, puts it in an introductory essay, is "to invent (or reinvent) restrictions of a formal nature [*contraintes*] and propose them to enthusiasts interested in composing literature." The *potential* of constraints is more important than their actual execution. But the constraint is not just some arbitrary rule, randomly chosen and imposed on a given text. On the contrary, in Roubaud's words, "a text written according to a constraint describes the constraint."[22] Thus Georges Perec's *La disparition*, a lipogrammatic novel written without using the vowel *e* (in French the most frequent letter of the alphabet), tells the story of a group of people who disappear or die, one after the other, their deaths being occasioned by their inability to name the unnamable—the letter *e* in *eux* (them), for example, *eux* being the "undesirables" who "disappeared" in World War II.

Like concretism, Oulipo thus insists that the verbal cannot be separated from its material representation and vice versa. In such recent incarnations as Jan Baetens's *Vivre sa vie* (2005), a "poeticization" of Jean-Luc Godard's well-known film, source material for the poet's "writing-through" is often drawn from popular culture—film, comic strip, newspaper column, how-to manual. But at its best, the constrained text never just replicates source mate-

Figure 1.2. Cia Rinne, page from *zaroum* (Helsinki, Finland, 2009). Reprinted by permission of the author.

rial; rather, the submission to a chosen rule becomes, as Baetens says, a way of freeing oneself "from the burden of the stereotypes of one's own culture," of calling one's own identity "radically into question."[23]

A third poetic mode now prominent is what might be called *translational poetics*—a poetics for the twenty-first century that has two poles: multilingualism on the one hand, exophonic writing on the other.[24] Ezra Pound's *Cantos*, with their insertion of Chinese characters, Greek and Latin phrases, lines from Guido Cavalcanti, or passages of American dialect and phonetic spelling, provide a paradigm for the former, which has recently given us such works as Caroline Bergvall's French-English "About Face" and her syncretist Middle/Modern English version of Chaucer's "Wife of Bath's Tale," *Alyson Singes*. The *exophonic*, familiar to us from the French poems of Paul Celan or the English lyrics of Fernando Pessoa, has become much more common today, thanks to the current state of mobility and migration, in which the use of English (or French or German or Dutch) as a second language has become almost normative.[25] Consider the writing of Yoko Tawada, who composes in the German of her adopted nation—a German made strange both phonemically and syntactically by the overt *mise en question* to which it is subjected by this native Japanese speaker. Homophonic translation, now practiced by many poets—for example, Charles Bernstein in "Laurel's Eyes," based on Heine's *Lorelei*—is a form of exophonic poetry, whereas the dialect and hip-hop poems of Tracie Morris exemplify multilingualism.

Writing poetry in a second language is, of course, itself a major constraint. In a discussion of sound and poetry, for example, the Finnish poet-translator Leevi Lehto remarks on the difficulties of translating Charles Bernstein's poem "Besotted Desquamation," in which every line contains four words beginning with the same letter:

> When I sat down to translate Charles's poem into Finnish, I was disappointed, confused even, to find that the words my dictionary suggested for replacement seemed to begin with just about any letter. I began to have doubts as to the very fundaments of the profession of translation. I mean, how can we imagine how to translate anything, when we cannot even get the first letters right? Eventually, I think I did find a problem to the solution. What I did was to put the original away—for good, I never looked at it again. . . . I then proceeded, not to translate, not even to rewrite, but to write the poem, exactly the way Charles had done before me.[26]

Haroldo de Campos called this practice "transcreation." A multilingual poet like Lehto—and there are now many such poets, especially in the Scandinavian countries or in South America—can recreate another's poem with great finesse. At the same time, more and more poets and their readers in the English-speaking world cannot read any language but their own and so rely on translation as if it were the primary text. Again, Lehto has an apt comment:

> I tend to see translation—and the translation of poetic sound in particular—as part of a larger dynamics of cultural development and interaction. In a sense, I don't think of translation as having anything to do with interlingual communication, and I'm all for inverting the currently dominant paradigm where the languages are seen as something primary, translation as a secondary, ensuing "problem." To me, "in the beginning was translation." Translation, not languages per se, forms the *basis* of cultures—meaning, among other things, that translation is always also (already) political.

In the beginning was translation: the layering of languages is one variant of the citational or intertextual poetics I spoke of earlier. From the Eliot of *The Waste Land*, the Pound of *The Cantos*, or the Marcel Duchamp who reproduced his early ready-mades and notecards in *The Green Box*,[27] to Charles Bernstein's "writing-through" Walter Benjamin in the opera-libretto *Shadowtime*, and the use of appropriated text, including archival material, documentary, informational manual, and, most recently, the discourse of the Internet from hypertext to blog to database, *citationality*, with its dialectic of removal and graft, disjunction and conjunction, its interpenetration of origin and destruction, is central to twenty-first-century poetics. Indeed, *récriture*, as Antoine Compagnon calls it, is the logical form of "writing" in an age of literally mobile or transferable text—text that can be readily moved from one digital site to another or from print to screen, that can be appropriated, transformed, or hidden by all sorts of means and for all sorts of purposes. This is not Pound's "Make it New!" but Jasper Johns's "Take an object. Do something to it. Do something else to it."[28] In his *Introduction* to the *UbuWeb Anthology of Conceptual Writing*, Craig Dworkin puts it this way:

> What would a non-expressive poetry look like? . . . One in which substitutions at the heart of metaphor and image were replaced by the direct presentation of language itself, with "spontaneous overflow" supplanted by meticulous procedure and exhaustively logical process? In which the self-regard of the poet's ego were turned back onto the self-reflexive language of the poem itself. So that the test of poetry were no longer whether it could have been done better (the question of the workshop), but whether it could conceivably have been done otherwise.[29]

The rejection of the "lyrical interference of the ego," aggressively formulated by Marinetti in his 1912 *Manifesto of Futurist Literature*, has, of course, been with us at least since Charles Olson's "Projective Verse" (1950), and it was a major theme in language poetics: witness Charles Bernstein's *Content's Dream* (1986), with its strong critique of "voice" models and the "natural look" in poetry.[30] But appropriation, as manifested in Bernstein's own later works, goes much further than the earlier constructivist model, advocating, in Goldsmith's words, "uncreativity, unoriginality, illegibility, appropriation, plagiarism, fraud, theft, and falsification as its perceptions: information management, word processing, databasing, and extreme process as its methodologies" ("Conceptual Poetics"). "You didn't write a word of what you read!"—the fabled Death of the Author has, in recent poetry, finally become a fait accompli.

Or has it? Here it will be helpful to look more closely at that "death," as formulated by Roland Barthes, Michel Foucault. and, closer to home, Fredric Jameson.

Whose Death?

"Writing," Barthes declared famously in "The Death of the Author" (1968), "is the destruction of every voice, every origin. Writing is that neuter, that composite, that obliquity into which our subject flees, the black-and-white where all identity is lost, beginning with the very identity of the body that writes."[31] Barthes was countering, of course, the still popular belief in the Author as origin—as the "past of his own book" and hence its supreme expositor—as well as the corollary claim that we must look to biography or autobiography for the necessary explanation of the work. "To assign an Author to a text," Barthes wrote, "is to impose a brake on it, to furnish it with a final signified, to close writing" (53). He wanted, instead, to give the authority over a text to its reader—"that *someone* who holds collected into one and the same field all of the traces from which writing is constituted" (54). The reader, freed of interference by the author, can make his or her own way through the text, allowing its multiple and subliminal meanings their full play. "The birth of the reader must be requited by the death of the Author" (55).

When Barthes made this somewhat grandiose pronouncement, he was hardly devaluating the genius of a Balzac, a Proust, a Mallarmé—the writers he alludes to in his essay. On the contrary, he takes the greatness of Balzac's and Proust's novels as such a given that he longs for a subtler, deeper, more nuanced reading of these texts than any biographical explanation or source study would allow. In essence, he is carrying to its extreme the Modernist notion contained in D. H. Lawrence's aphorism "Never trust the author, trust the tale." For Barthes, as for the Foucault of "What Is an Author"(1969), to *read* critically is to understand that "writing is primarily concerned with creating an opening where the writing subject endlessly disappears."[32]

But what would Barthes, or the Foucault who declared that "the writing of our day has freed itself from the necessity of 'expression' . . . the confines of interiority" (116), have made of the conceptual poems and fictions of our own time? What role, they would have asked, can the individual imagination play in a work like Caroline Bergvall's *Via*, a sequence, in alphabetical order, of the forty-seven English translations archived at the British Library of the first tercet of Dante's *Inferno*? An opening where the writing subject endlessly disappears into the words of some unknown and some famous Dante translators from the mid-nineteenth century to the present? A black-and-white text where all identity is lost?

The problem is compounded in the historicist turn such formulations as the "Death of the Author" were given in the 1980s and '90s. In the conclusion to his seminal *Postmodernism, or The Cultural Logic of Late Capitalism* (1991), Fredric Jameson is less concerned with the disappearance of the subject in the interstices of a writing that "speaks" its author than in the contrast between a Modernist epoch of Great Authors, of "demiurges and prophets," and a postmodernist ethos in which the very concept of "genius" is irrelevant.

"If the poststructuralist motif of the 'death of the subject' means anything socially," writes Jameson, "it signals the end of the entrepreneurial and inner-directed individualism, with its 'charisma' and its accompanying categorical panoply of quaint romantic values such as that of the 'genius' in the first place." The new order "no longer need prophets and seers of the high modernist and charismatic type. . . . Such figures no longer hold any charm or magic for the subjects of a corporate, collectivized, post-individualistic age."[33] Jameson goes on to spell out how, in the age of the simulacrum, genius theory is simply passé. Indeed, the Modernists themselves have now been reified as classroom "classics"—and hence become safe and largely unread and uninteresting.

Or have they? Jameson himself returns to the Modernist masters in his more recent collection of essays *The Modernist Papers* (2007). The critic who had asked dismissively, 'Whatever happened to Thomas Mann and André Gide?" and "Is T. S. Eliot recuperable?" (*Cultural Logic*, 303), is now writing trenchant analyses of works by Baudelaire and Rimbaud, Kafka and Joyce, Yeats and Mallarmé, William Carlos Williams, Gertrude Stein, and Wallace Stevens—and yes, Thomas Mann. *The Modernist Papers* contains two essays on Mann, the first on the dialectical irony of *The Magic Mountain*, the second on rereading *Dr. Faustus*. If, as Jameson posits, these "great" and now classical writers failed in their attempt to transform the institutional system in which they produced their work, they were also notable for their willingness to "believe success is somehow possible."[34] Following Adorno, Jameson rejects the simplistic equation of the Modern with "the new and innovation and analogized by comparisons with scientific discovery," in favor of a negative dialectic:

> What drives modernism to innovate is not some vision of the future or the new, but rather the deep conviction that certain forms and expressions, procedures and techniques, can no longer be used, are worn out or stigmatized by their associations with a past that has become conventionality or kitsch, and must be creatively avoided. Such taboos then produce a desperate situation in which the nature of the innovation, to continue to use such language, is not traced or given in advance; rather what emerges then determines the form by which the blocks and taboos of the next generation will be governed (and in this sense, postmodernity and its pluralisms have been seen as a final turn of the screw in which it seems to be just such taboos and negative restrictions that have themselves become taboo). (*Modernist Papers*, 5)

Given this — and Jameson often implies this — our own literature can only be a kind of end run: its "final turn of the screw" (but why final?) can produce a "postmodern" art significant only for its overturning of previous taboos and negative restrictions in what is held to be a "desperate situation." That art, as Jameson made clear in his earlier essay "The Cultural Logic of Late Capitalism," is characterized by "the 'death' of the subject itself — the end of the autonomous bourgeois monad or ego or individual," the dissolution of "the high-modernist conception of a unique *style*, along with the accompanying collective ideals of an artistic or political vanguard" (*Cultural Logic*, 15). And in this new culture of pastiche, talk of "great writers" and artistic genius is obviously meaningless. *Après* Modernism, *le déluge*.

But of course no turn is the *final* turn. In a series of studies made in the 1920s, the Russian Formalist critic Juri Tynyanov gave, like Jameson, a dialectical account of literary change but one that is less teleologically driven.[35] "Evolution," Tynyanov held, "is caused by the need for a ceaseless dynamics. Every dynamic system inevitably becomes automatized and an opposite constructive principle dialectically arises."[36] A device obsolete in one period can be restaged and reframed at a different moment and in a different context and once again made "perceptible." The poetry of Velimir Khlebnikov is a case in point. "Transrational language" [*zaum'*]," writes Tynyanov, "always existed in the language of children and mystics, but only in our time did it become a literary fact. And, on the other hand . . . charades [and] logogriphs are children's games for us, but in [Nikolai] Karamzin's period [the 1790s], in which verbal trifles and the play of devices were foregrounded, they were a literary genre" (*Russian Formalism*, 106–7). An example closer to home would be the turn in Language poetry from the ubiquitous short free-verse line of mainstream poetry in the 1960s and '70s to the "New Sentence" as a way of calling attention to a poeticity that does not rely on lineation as marker. And the New Sentence has been in its turn replaced by citational or documentary prose, drawn from a variety of source texts, high and low, as well as by the use of visual layout on page or screen, used to defamiliarize poetic material.

Once we grant that current art practices have their own particular momentum and *inventio*, we can dissociate the word *original* from its partner *genius*. If the new "conceptual" poetry makes no claim to originality—at least not originality in the usual sense—this is not to say that *genius* isn't in play. It just takes different forms.

Make It (Not) New

Original genius: the common phrase is, at heart, a tautology. The *Oxford English Dictionary* tells us that *original* comes from the Latin verb *oriri*, to arise, to be born; the Latin *genius*, like *genesis*, derives from *gen*, the root of *gignere* (to beget), which comes from the Greek *gignesthai*, to be born. In classical pagan belief, a *genius* was "the tutelary god or attendant spirit allotted to every person at his birth, to govern his fortunes and determine his character, and finally to conduct him out of the world; also the tutelary and controlling spirit similarly connected with a place (*genius loci*), an institution, etc." (OED). Until the later seventeenth century, good and evil geniuses controlled our fates; the first occurrence of *genius* in the modern sense of "natural ability or capacity; quality of the mind, the special endowments which fit a man for his [sic] peculiar work" is in Milton (1649), and although men might have a genius for this or that, the notion of an individual person being *a genius* was a nineteenth-century invention, especially in Germany in the age of Sturm und Drang. And of course the genius of Beethoven or Goethe had to be *original*: the noun *originality*, defined by the OED as "the fact or attribute of being primary, first hand: authenticity, genuineness," made its first appearance in 1776 (H. Swinburne's *Travels in Spain*): "One of the most valuable pictures in the world. I do not know how Amiconi came to doubt its originality."

In this example, *originality* refers to the "real" work as opposed to a copy or simulation. In this sense *originality* is, of course, an important legal concept with respect to intellectual property. In Walter Benjamin's famous formulation in *The Work of Art in the Age of Mechanical Reproducibility*, "The presence of the original is the prerequisite to the concept of authenticity," and it is the original, not its reproduction. that has full *aura*. But in the looser sense, *originality* means (OED, 4b) "made, composed, or done by the person himself (not imitated from another), first-hand." Originality is often defined by what it is *not*—not derivative, not arising from or dependent on any other thing of the kind, underived. And further: originality, whether in the arts or the sciences, is synonymous with novelty, invention, creativity, and independence of mind. Plato, according to Benjamin Jowett (1875), was "a great *original genius* struggling with unequal conditions of knowledge" (OED 5b).

The "death of the author" in the years of poststructuralism meant, of course, the death of genius theory as well, with social theorists like Pierre Bourdieu turning their attention to the way culture creates the illusion of "genius" for the evidently gullible masses. "It is this ideology [that a work of art has value]," Bourdieu posits, "which directs attention to the *apparent producer*, the painter, writer, or composer, in short, the 'author,' suppressing the question of what authorizes the author, what creates the authority with which authors authorize." And again, "The ideology of creation, which makes the author the first and last source of the value of his work, conceals the fact that the cultural businessman . . . by putting it on the market, by exhibiting, publishing, or staging it, consecrates a product which he has 'discovered' and which would otherwise remain a mere natural resource."[37]

But Bourdieu was himself by no means immune to the attraction of that "otherwise . . . natural resource." The whole second section of *The Field of Cultural Production* is devoted to Flaubert, whose fiction is taken to exemplify the "literary field and *habitus*" of his time. The opening lecture begins with this comment on Flaubert's *Sentimental Education*: "I believe that this fascinating and mysterious work condenses all those enigmas that literature can put to those who wish to interpret it. A true example of the absolute masterpiece, the novel contains an analysis of the social space in which the author was himself located, and thus gives us the instruments we need for an analysis of him" (145). *Absolute masterpiece*: what enabled Flaubert, rather than, say, the Goncourt brothers, to produce such a "fascinating and mysterious," such an emblematic work? And if masterpieces were produced in the mid-nineteenth century, is it really plausible to believe that it is no longer possible to produce a "fascinating and mysterious work" today? Or is it just that our own "masterpieces" no longer make the claim to be "original"?

Appropriation, citation, copying, reproduction—these have been central to the visual arts for decades: one thinks of Duchamp, whose entire oeuvre consists of "copies" and found materials; of Christian Boltanski, whose "artworks" treated photographs of his actual childhood classmates; or of the carefully staged auto-images of Cindy Sherman. In the poetry world, however, the demand for original expression dies hard: we expect our poets to produce words, phrases, images, and ironic locutions that we have never heard before. Not words, but My Word. As Hart Crane puts it in the concluding stanza of his great lyric sequence "Voyages":

> The imaged Word, it is, that holds,
> Hushed willows anchored in its glow,
> It is the unbetrayable reply
> Whose accent no farewell can know.[38]

Despite the bravado of that conclusion, within six years of "Voyages," Crane's last published poem, "The Broken Tower," contains this passage:

> My word I poured. But was it cognate, scored
> Of that tribunal monarch of the air
> Whose thigh embronzes earth, strikes crystal Word
> In wounds pledged once to hope,—cleft to despair?

(Complete Poems, 106–7)

Was the crystal Word "cognate"? For Modernist poets from Crane to Robert Lowell or Sylvia Plath, and well into the present, the drive to "pour" out one's *own* Word was assumed to be the poet's primary mission. But as the various avant-garde movements demonstrated as early as the 1910s—think of Khlebnikov's *Tables of Destiny*, Pound's *Cantos*, the *Merz*-works of Kurt Schwitters—there were other ways of Making It New. In the year Crane published "Voyages," Walter Benjamin, living in exile in Paris, began a project called *Das Passagen-Werk*—a huge collage-text/commonplace book, made up in large part of the words of others. This encyclopedic set of handwritten notes, not published in anything like complete form until 1983 (and in English not until 1999), is not, strictly speaking, a poem, certainly not a lyric one. Nor is it a narrative or even a fiction. And yet, as I shall argue in my next chapter, its juxtaposition of poetic citation, anecdote, aphorism, parable, documentary prose, personal essay, photograph, diagram—indeed every genre—makes Benjamin's assemblage a paradigm for the poetry of "unoriginal genius" to come.

2

Phantasmagorias of the Marketplace: Citational Poetics in Walter Benjamin's *Arcades Project*

Only the meeting between two different street *names* makes for the magic of the "corner."

Walter Benjamin[1]

Walter Benjamin's monumental *Passagen-Werk*, begun in 1927 and still in progress at the time of his death in 1940, reproduces the encyclopedic collection of notes the writer made over thirteen years of reflection on the Paris Arcades (*Passages*)—the glass-covered, marble-walled shop-lined walkways that were built through entire blocks of buildings in the early nineteenth century and that look ahead to our own indoor shopping malls (figures 2.1–2). Drawing on the archives at the Bibliothèque nationale and other libraries, Benjamin assembled his observations and reflections, along with citations from an astonishing variety of sources, into sets or sheafs of papers, known in German as *Konvoluts*.[2] Originally conceived as an essay of fifty pages, the project grew and grew into an elaborate network of entries, numbering well over a thousand pages. Benjamin's German editor Rolf Tiedemann lists some 850 sources consulted between 1934 and 1940.[3]

Benjamin's original intention was to use these notes to produce a coherent book called *Paris, Capital of the Nineteenth Century*—the French translation of the *Passagen-Werk* bears that title, and the two synoptic essays (1935, 1939) by that name now constitute the prelude to *The Arcades Project*[4]—but the plan kept shifting. The material, as it was presented in the first German

Figure 2.1. *Passage Choiseul* (Paris, 1908). Photographer unknown (from Walter Benjamin, *The Arcades Project*, p. 927).

edition (1982), is described by Benjamin's English translators as having "the form of montage—with its philosophic play of distances, transitions, and intersections, its perpetually shifting contexts and ironic juxtapositions" (*Arcades*, xi). But the term *montage* implies a continuity absent here: as the translators admit, "what is distinctive about *The Arcades Project* . . . is the working of quotations into the framework of montage, so much so that they eventually far outnumber the commentaries" (xi).

The astonishing piling up of quoted passages dismayed the *Passagen-Werk*'s first readers, most notably Benjamin's close friend, collaborator, and prospective editor, Theodor Adorno. In May 1949, the latter wrote to Gershom Scholem:

> At the beginning of last year I finally received the Arcades material hidden in the Bibliothèque Nationale. During last summer I worked through the material in the most detailed fashion, and some problems then arose. . . . The most significant is the extraordinary restraint in the formulation of theoretical thoughts in comparison with the enormous treasure of excerpts. This is explained in part by the (for me, already problematic) idea, which is formulated explicitly in one

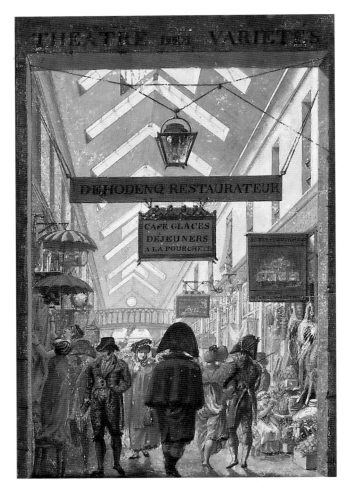

Figure 2.2. Philibert Louis Debucourt, *Passage des Panoramas à Paris* (1807). Gouache, 24.5 × 16.5 cm. Musée de la Ville de Paris, Musée Carnavalet, Paris. Photograph: Erich Lessing / Art Resource, New York.

place, of the work as pure "montage," that is, created from a juxtaposition of quotations so that the theory springs out of it without having to be inserted as interpretation. (Buck-Morss, 73; *Passagen*, 1042)

The reference is to a remark Benjamin made early in the assemblage of the *Arcades*: "Method of this project: literary montage. I needn't *say* anything. Merely show. I shall appropriate no ingenious formulations, purloin no valuables. But the rags, the refuse—these I will not describe but put on display" (*Arcades*, 860; *Passagen*, 1030). Adorno was always skeptical of his friend's predilection for such montage, but when, in 1938, Benjamin sent him the completed manuscript of the "Baudelaire" essay, to be published, as stipulated, by the Institute for Social Research in New York, Adorno exploded. In a long and famously devastating letter (November 10), he complained that "Panorama and 'trace,' flaneur and arcades, modernism and the immutable *without* theoretical interpretation—is this 'material' that can patiently wait for interpretation without being consumed by its own aura?" And again, "Bypassing theory affects the empirical evidence. . . . the theological motif of calling things by their proper name reverts tendentially to a wide-eyed presentation of the bare facts."[5]

Rolf Tiedemann, working with Adorno, had similar reservations about the insufficiently dialectical argument of the *Passagen-Werk*. The quotations, he posits, are like the building blocks of a house: "Next to the foundations we find the neatly piled excerpts, which would have been used to construct the walls; Benjamin's own thoughts would have provided the mortar to hold the building together. The reader now possesses many of these theoretical and interpretive reflections, yet in the end they almost seem to vanish beneath the very weight of excerpts. It is tempting to question the sense of publishing these oppressive chunks of quotations" (*Arcades*, 931). Yet Tiedemann does respect Benjamin's own explanation that the cited passages serve "to discover in the analysis of the small individual moment the crystal of the total event. And therefore to break with vulgar historical naturalism."[6] However boring and annoying these "oppressive chunks of quotations" may be, they are, Tiedemann concludes reluctantly, necessary to the whole.

But such "necessity" hardly accounts for the fact that, as Richard Sieburth notes in his seminal "Benjamin the Scrivener," "of the quarter of a million words that comprise Tiedmann's edition, at least 75 per cent are direct transcriptions of texts Benjamin collected over thirteen years. The amount of source material he copied so exceeds anything he might conceivably need to adduce as documentary evidence in an eventual book that one can only conclude that this ritual of transcription is less a rehearsal for his *livre à venir* than its most central *rite de passage*."[7] Indeed, however earnestly Benjamin may have tried in his later years to produce the historical /philosophical study of nineteenth-century capitalism and the role of the commodity fetish that would have accorded with Frankfurt School principles of dialectical materialism, the *Passagen-Werk* is less interested in representing the realities of life in nineteenth-century Paris or in establishing the motive of Baudelaire's poetic production than in creating its own textual "arcade," at once historical/geographical and yet, in Sieburth's words, "the book of a dream (*Finnegans Wake*) and the dream of a book (like Mallarmé's *Livre*), in its most

Utopian conception *a text without author, speaking entirely by quotation*" (32, my emphasis). As such, the *Passagen-Werk* could hardly have been brought to any kind of satisfactory conclusion, even if Benjamin had lived to "complete" it, because the citational material took on a life of its own—a life, not of historiography or of philosophical treatise but of poetic construct. There is now a whole library on the philosophical/political perspective of the *Arcades Project*,[8] but its *literary* appeal—an appeal evident in the response of its avid readers over the past few decades—remains less clearly understood.[9]

To begin with—and this central aspect of the work is distorted in the English edition, which translates both the French citations and Benjamin's commentary into one uniform language[10]—the *Passagen-Werk* is a bilingual text, constantly shifting between French citation (whether nineteenth-century popular song, extract from Baudelaire, old Paris guidebook, or 1930s newspaper) and German commentary. A given page may also include diagrams, as in the replication of signage (e.g. "ANGELA, 2d floor, to the right") in the *A Konvolut* (*Arcades* 40; figure 2.3). Then too, Benjamin used small black squares to signal cross-references, and in the original thirty-six Konvoluts or sheafs, "a further system of thirty-two assorted symbols (squares, triangles, circles, vertical and horizonal crosses—in various inks and colors) to refer the editor to related papers" (*Arcades*, 958). The editors of *Benjamin's Archive* observe:

> Benjamin often applied much care to the graphic form, the physical arrangement, of his manuscripts. While he worked extremely carefully on the structure and layout of his essays and books, equally important to him were the proportions of the architecture of the page. Part of the writing's sense of form involved the need to create something for the eye to do. Topographical relationships, spatial organization, optical alignments and divisions are not only apparent on the drafts and the pages that include calligraphic elements. Countless scraps and sheets in the bequest are evidence of a sensibility attuned to graphic elements, spatial dimensions, and design. (Marx, 231)

Figure 2.4, for example, is a manuscript page from the "Baudelaire" (*J*) Konvolut.[11] Benjamin's pages were folded down the middle, "making of them double sheets, and in each case, he wrote on the first and third side in the left-hand column. . . . Each side with writing on it bears an alphanumeric classmark in the top left corner"[12] (J 68; see Marx, 253).

The Frankfurt edition makes no attempt to replicate this format, but it does retain the black squares, so that the opening section of the *A Konvolut* ("Passagen, Magasins de Nouveauté(s), Calicots") looks like this (figure 2.5).[13] The configuration of the page, in any case, is hardly that of "normal" prose.

readers will be disturbed by this), it passes from lips to ear, passes almost imperceptibly from pen to paper, and finally from writing desk to nearby letterbox. The good *dame du bureau* has a friendly smile for all, and papers and envelopes for correspondents. The early mail is dispatched, Cologne and Augsburg have their news; and now—it is noontime!—to the tavern." Rodenberg, *Paris bei Sonnenschein und Lampenlicht* (Leipzig, 1867), pp. 6–7. [A2a,8]

"The Passage du Caire is highly reminiscent, on a smaller scale, of the Passage du Saumon, which in the past existed on the Rue Montmartre, on the site of the present-day Rue Bachaumont." Paul Léautaud, "Vieux Paris," *Mercure de France* (October 15, 1927), p. 503. [A3,1]

"Shops on the old model, devoted to trades found nowhere else, surmounted by a small, old-fashioned mezzanine with windows that each bear a number, on an escutcheon, corresponding to a particular shop. From time to time, a doorway giving onto a corridor; at the end of the corridor, a small stairway leading to these mezzanines. Near the knob of one of these doors, this handwritten sign:

> The worker next door
> would be obliged if,
> in closing the door,
> you refrained from slamming it.

[A3,2]

Another sign is cited in the same place (Léautaud, "Vieux Paris," *Mercure de France* [1927], pp. 502–503):

> ANGELA
>
> 2nd floor, to the right

[A3,3]

Old name for department stores: *docks à bon marché*—that is, "discount docks." ⟨Sigfried⟩ Giedion, *Bauen in Frankreich* ⟨Leipzig and Berlin, 1928⟩, p. 31. [A3,4]

Evolution of the department store from the shop that was housed in arcades. Principle of the department store: "The floors form a single space. They can be taken in, so to speak, 'at a glance.'" Giedion, *Bauen in Frankreich,* p. 34. [A3,5]

Giedion shows (in *Bauen in Frankreich,* p. 35) how the axiom, "Welcome the crowd and keep it seduced" (*Science et l'industrie,* 143 [1925], p. 6), leads to corrupt architectural practices in the construction of the department store Au Printemps (1881–1889). Function of commodity capital! [A3,6]

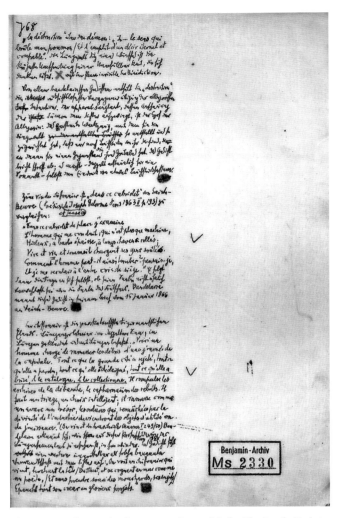

Figure 2.4. Walter Benjamin, notes and materials for *The Arcades Project* (1928–1940) (10.4). Akademie der Künste, Berlin. Walter Benjamin Archiv [WBA Ms 2330]. © Hamburger Stiftung zu Förderung von Wissenschaft und Kultur / Suhrkamp Verlag.

In the German edition, the typeface of the citations is smaller than that of the author's commentary; in the English, citation and commentary are the same size but, again, rendered in different fonts, and the cross references are given in outline rather than as black squares.[14] Translations into other languages no doubt proceed in still other ways.

But of course the "original" German (more properly German/French)

>De ces palais les colonnes magiques
A l'amateur montrent de toutes parts,
Dans les objets qu'étalent leurs portiques,
Que l'industrie est rivale des arts.«
    Chanson nouvelle cit Nouveaux tableaux de Paris ou
    observations sur les mœurs et usages des Parisiens au
    commencement du XIXᵉ siècle Paris 1828 I p 27

>A vendre les Corps, les voix, l'immense opulence inquestio-
nable, ce qu'on ne vendra jamais.«
    Rimbaud

>Wir haben«, sagt der illustrierte Pariser Führer, ein vollständiges
Gemälde der Seine-Stadt und ihrer Umgebungen vom Jahre
1852⟨,⟩ »bei den inneren Boulevards wiederholt der Passagen
gedacht, die dahin ausmünden. Diese Passagen, eine neuere Erfin-
dung des industriellen Luxus, sind glasgedeckte, marmorgetäfelte
Gänge durch ganze Häusermassen, deren Besitzer sich zu solchen
Spekulationen vereinigt haben. Zu beiden Seiten dieser Gänge, die
ihr Licht von oben erhalten, laufen die elegantesten Warenläden
hin, so daß eine solche Passage eine Stadt, eine Welt im Kleinen ist
■ Flaneur ■, in der der Kauflustige alles finden wird, dessen er
benötigt. Sie sind bei plötzlichen Regengüssen der Zufluchtsort
aller Überraschten, denen sie eine gesicherte, wenn auch beengte
Promenade gewähren, bei der die Verkäufer auch ihren Vorteil
finden.« ■ Wetter ■
Diese Stelle ist der locus classicus für die Darstellung der Passagen,
denn aus ihr entspinnen sich nicht allein die divagations über den
Flaneur und das Wetter, sondern auch was über die Bauweise der
Passagen in wirtschaftlicher und architektonischer Hinsicht zu
sagen ist, könnte hier seine Stelle finden.   [A 1, 1]

Namen von Magasins de Nouveautés: La fille d'honneur / La Vestale / Le
page inconstant / Le masque de fer / Le petit chaperon rouge / La petite
Nanette / La chaumière allemande / Au mamelouk / Au coin de la rue –

Figure 2.5. Walter Benjamin, manuscript list from "A Konvolut," *Das Passagen-Werk* (Erster Band, p. 83). © Suhrkamp Verlag.

version is not really "original" or definitive: who knows how Benjamin would
have used his fragments had he lived to see the project into print? Where, for
example, would the visual images—scientific drawings, lithographs, photographs—that Benjamin had gathered into a separate album have been placed
in a given Konvolut?[15] In the end perhaps it doesn't matter, for the project is
best understood as an ur-hypertext: the numerical classification of the notes

(e.g., A3, 1, A3, 2, . . . A3a, 1) providing ready passage from link (black square) to link in this *Passagen-Werk*—a passage that would be even easier in a hypothetical digital version of the whole, which would allow the reader to follow particular threads (hyperlinks) from text to text, indeed to rearrange them. Benjamin's *Arcades* is thus literally a *movable* feast: its hypertextual mode looks ahead to such filing projects as Cia Rinne's *archives zaroum* for *nypoesi*.

Consider, to begin with, Benjamin's use of lists. When he first set up his classification system in 1934, so Susan Buck-Morss tells us (50), he used the motifs assembled in early notes to create an alphabetical list of his files (figures 2.6–7). But the twenty-six capital letters listed here (figure 2.8; see *Arcades*, 29; *Passagen*, 81), followed by a second sequence in lowercase, the majority of whose entries are missing, are curiously nonparallel. Take the first four:

A Arcades, *Magasins de Nouveautés,* Sales Clerks
B Fashion
C Ancient Paris, Catacombs, Demolitions, Decline of Paris
D Boredom, Eternal Return

First the arcades themselves, then the shops inside them, and then the clerks who work in those shop—all under one category, *A*. Second, "fashion," which is sold under the first rubric. Third, a temporal and spatial shift to the old Paris and the history of its underground life. And fourth, a state of mind—boredom, *cette tristesse diserte et plate qu'on appelle l'ennui*, as Louis Veuillot called it in 1914 (D2, 5, *Passagen*, 161)—ennui broken now and again by the dream of eternal return.[16]

But this very gap between expectation and fulfillment replaces sequential exposition and coherent argument with what looks like web-page design, the *A* file connecting just as readily with *K* (Dream City) or with *Z* (the Doll, the Automaton) as with *B*. The technique of the *Konvoluten* is thus less montage than sampling, literally defined as the act of taking a portion, or sample, of one sound recording and reusing it as an instrument or element of a new recording. The sampling form, moreover, nicely mimes the *flâneur*'s own movement through the "masquerade of space" (M1a, 4), which is the world of the Arcades themselves: one moves at will from toy shop to skating rink to pub to Oriental carpet merchant, from cited poem to photograph to travel-guide documentation, without bounded map or master plan.

The *A* Konvolut (*Passagen*, 83; *Arcades*, 31), for example, begins with two epigraphs, one from a popular Parisian song of the early nineteenth century, the other being the opening of Rimbaud's prose poem "Solde," from the *Illuminations*:

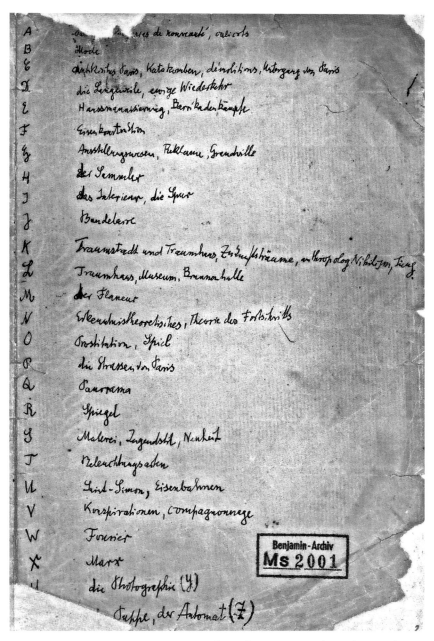

Figure 2.6. Walter Benjamin, manuscript page from *The Arcades Project* (convolutes, 10.5). Akademie der Künste, Berlin. Walter Benjamin Archiv [WBA Ms 2001]. © Hamburger Stiftung zu Förderung von Wissenschaft und Kultur / Suhrkamp Verlag.

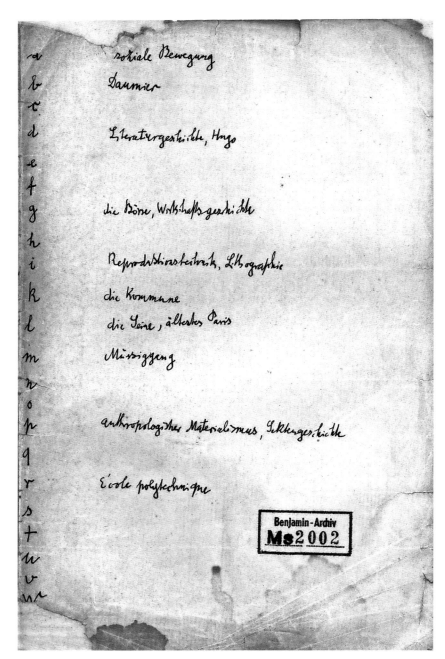

Figure 2.7. Walter Benjamin, overview of *The Arcades Project* (convolutes, 10.5). Akademie der Künste, Berlin. Walter Benjamin Archiv [WBA Ms 2002]. © Hamburger Stiftung zu Förderung von Wissenschaft und Kultur / Suhrkamp Verlag.

Overview

A Arcades, *Magasins de Nouveautés,* Sales Clerks 31
B Fashion 62
C Ancient Paris, Catacombs, Demolitions, Decline of Paris 82
D Boredom, Eternal Return 101
E Haussmannization, Barricade Fighting 120
F Iron Construction 150
G Exhibitions, Advertising, Grandville 171
H The Collector 203
I The Interior, The Trace 212
J Baudelaire 228
K Dream City and Dream House, Dreams of the Future, Anthropological Nihilism, Jung 388
L Dream House, Museum, Spa 405
M The Flâneur 416
N On the Theory of Knowledge, Theory of Progress 456
O Prostitution, Gambling 489
P The Streets of Paris 516
Q Panorama 527
R Mirrors 537
S Painting, Jugendstil, Novelty 543
T Modes of Lighting 562
U Saint-Simon, Railroads 571
V Conspiracies, *Compagnonnage* 603
W Fourier 620
X Marx 651
Y Photography 671
Z The Doll, The Automaton 693
a Social Movement 698
b Daumier 740
c .....
d Literary History, Hugo 744
e .....
f .....
g The Stock Exchange, Economic History 779
h .....
i Reproduction Technology, Lithography 786
k The Commune 788
l The Seine, The Oldest Paris 796
m Idleness 800
n .....
o .....
p Anthropological Materialism, History of Sects 807
q .....
r Ecole Polytechnique 818
s .....
t .....
u .....
v .....
w .....

Figure 2.8. Walter Benjamin, "Overview" (1908). Reprinted by permission of the publisher from THE ARCADES PROJECT by Walter Benjamin, translated by Howard Eiland and Kevin McLaughlin (Cambridge, MA: The Belknap Press of Harvard University Press), p. 29. Copyright © 1999 by the President and Fellows of Harvard College.

De ces palais les colonnes magiques
A l'amateur montrent de toutes parts,
Dans les objets qu'étalent leurs portiques,
Que l'industrie est rivale des arts.

A vendre les corps, les voix, immense opulence inquestionable, ce qu'on ne vendra jamais.[17]

The magic columns of these palaces
Show to the amateur on all sides,
In the objects their porticos display,
That industry is the rival of the arts.

For sale the bodies, the voices, the tremendous unquestionable wealth, what will never be sold.

The cited passages are not quite opposites. Rimbaud's mysterious "Solde" expresses a deep yearning for those *splendeurs invisibles* and *délices insensibles* one longs to purchase—those palaces with magic columns, so to speak, of the popular song. But it also casts a jaundiced eye on the notion that everything—even bodies and voices—is for sale in the new commodity culture of the nineteenth century. The stage is thus set for Benjamin's own quite ambivalent presentation of the luxury and phantasmagoria—a favorite Benjaminian term—of the *magasins de nouveautés*.

The *A* file opens with Benjamin's quotation from a nineteenth-century guidebook. In the English translation,[18] it reads:

"In speaking of the inner boulevards," says the *Illustrated Guide to Paris*, a complete picture of the city on the Seine and its environs from the year 1852, "we have made mention again and again of the arcades which open onto them. These arcades, a recent invention of industrial luxury, are glass-roofed, marble-paneled corridors extending through whole blocks of buildings, whose owners have joined together for such enterprises. Lining both sides of these corridors, which get their light from above, are the most elegant shops, so that the arcade is a city, a world in miniature. ■ Flâneur ■, in which customers will find everything they need. During sudden rainshowers, the arcades are a place of refuge for the unprepared, to whom they offer a secure, if restricted promenade—one from which the merchants also benefit." ■ Weather ■

And the author now adds his brief commentary: "This passage is the locus classicus for the presentation of the arcades; for not only do the divagations on the flâneur and the weather develop out of it, but, also, what there is to be said about the construction of the arcades in an economic and architectural vein, would have a place here."

Benjamin thus introduces his subject matter and points to the cross-references or links: "The Flâneur" (*M*) and "Weather." The latter never became a separate file; its notes were accommodated under "Boredom" (*D*), which has entries like D2, 8, a reference to Émile Tardieu's "humorous book" *L'ennui* (Paris, 1903), where weather is called "one among many factors supposedly causing boredom" (105). And the *D* link also thickens the poet's plot with cautionary tales like the following (*D* 3a, 4):

> Boredom began to be experienced in epidemic proportions during the 1840s. Lamartine is said to be the first to have given expression to the malady. It plays a role in a little story about the famous comic Deburau. A distinguished Paris neurologist was consulted one day by a patient whom he had not seen before. The patient complained of the typical illness of the times—weariness with life, deep depressions, boredom. "There's nothing wrong with you," said the doctor after a thorough examination. "Just try to relax—find something to entertain you. Go see Deburau some evening, and life will look different to you." "Ah, dear sir," answered the patient, "I *am* Deburau."

A single page of *Arcades* thus gives us citations of popular song from the Napoleonic era, lyric poem, documentary prose (the travel book), and authorial commentary, as well as literary narrative. And finally—we are now at the bottom of the first *A* page—the list:

> Namen von Magasins de Nouveautés: La fille d'honneur / La Vestale / Le page inconstant / Le masque de fer / Le petit chaperon rouge / La petite Nanette / La chaumière allemande / Au mamelouk / Au coin de la rue—Namen die meist aus erfolgreichen Vaudevilles stamen. ■ Mythologie ■ Ein gantier: Au ci-devant jeune homme; ein confiseur: Aux armes de Werther. (*A*1, 2)

> Names of *magasins de nouveautés: La Fille d'Honneur, La Vestale, Le Page Inconstant, Le Masque de Fer* <The Iron Mask>, *Le Petit Chaperon Rouge* <Little Red Riding Hood>, *Petite Nanette, La Chaumière allemande* <The German Cottage>, *Au Mamelouk, Le Coin de la Rue* <On the Streetcorner>—names that mostly come from successful vaudevilles. ■ Mythology ■ A glover: Au Ci-Devant Jeune Homme. A confectioner: Aux Armes de Werther. (*A*1, 2)

Here the seemingly sober catalog of names looks ahead to the cataloging of such recent long poems as Kenneth Goldsmith's *No. 111 2.7 93–10.20.96*, with its constraint-generated alphabetically organized syllable lists.[19] Benjamin's ambiguous *fille d'honneur* (the term means "maid of honor," but the word *fille* itself designates a girl of the streets or prostitute) stands next to the Vestal Virgin, and that figure, in turn, next to the inconstant page, the iron mask, and Little Red Riding Hood. The ironies multiply: German cottages are juxtaposed to Persian cavalry, the glove shop is designed for the *ci-devant* (would-be aristocratic) young man, and the confectioner named for the pistols of Goethe's suicidal lover, Young Werther, or its vaudeville version in Massenet's dramatic operetta.

The resonance of such lists—and they recur throughout the *Arcades*—is enormous. Take the *gantier* or glove shop Au Ci-Devant Jeune Homme. The Arcades are, of course, the emblem of the new bourgeois Paris of the Second Empire, in which the glove of the pre-Revolutionary aristocrat has been replaced by the commercial glove shop. Juxtaposed to Aux Armes de Werther, moreover, the glove becomes the dueling glove, thrown down in the moment of challenge. Romantic dueling, romantic love, *Liebestod*: all these have become, in midcentury Paris, grist for the commerce of the shopping arcade. No more *grand amour*, only pastries and sweets. No wonder this catalog of shop names has a link to "Mythology," which was never assigned its own file but is a major thread throughout the entire book.

In the next paragraph of this entry (*A1, 2*), Benjamin's list of shops modulates into a set of citations:

> "The name of the jeweler stands over the shop door in large *inlaid letters*—inlaid with fine imitation gems." Eduard Kroloff, *Schilderungen aus Paris* (Hamburg 1839), vol. 2, p. 73. "In the Galerie Vero-Dodat there is a grocery store; above its door, one reads the inscription: 'Gastronomie Cosmopolite.' The individual characters of the sign are formed, in comic fashion, from snipes, pheasants, hares, antlers, lobsters, fish, bird kidneys, and so forth." Kroloff, *Schilderungen aus Paris*, vol. 2, p. 75. ■ Grandville ■ (*A1, 2*)

A minor social commentator of the 1830s, Eduard Kroloff here characterizes the commercial sleight-of-hand that corrodes the very language of nineteenth-century Paris. The jeweler's name is cast in large letters carved from fake stones (*täuschend nachgeahmten Edelsteinen*); an even more egregious sign, this time on an elegant grocery store, boasts letters, spelling *Gastronomie cosmopolite*, made out of animal and fish parts—even bird kidneys. Here urban signage is implicitly presented as an assault on nature—an assault ingenious yet troubling, with animals and birds surviving only as so many dead and stuffed remnants.

The paragraph concludes with the one-word link "Grandville," a reference to the great French caricaturist and illustrator J. J. Grandville (the nom de plume of Jean Ignace Isidore Gérard), whose lithographic fantasies (see figure 2.9) "confer," so Benjamin observes, "a commodity character on the universe" (*Arcades*, 8). Grandville's "sybilline books of *publicité*" (853) get a Konvolut of their own, "Exhibitions, Advertising, Grandville" (*G*), but the link also connects *A* to "Fashion" (*B*), "The Flâneur" (*M*), and, perhaps most ingeniously, to "Iron Construction" (*F*), where we find such entries as this:

> Gußeiseisenzauber: "Hahbble put se convaincre alors que l'anneau de cette planète n'était autre chose qu'un balcon circulaire sur lequel les Saturniens viennent le soir prendre le frais." Grandville, *Un autre monde* (Paris 1844), p. 139 ■ Haschisch ■

> Magic of cast iron: "Hahbble was able then to convince himself that the ring around this planet was nothing other than a circular balcony on which the inhabitants of Saturn strolled in the evening to get a breath of fresh air." Grandville, *Un autre monde* (Paris, 1844), p. 139. ■ Hashish ■ (*F1, 7*)

The curious name "Hahbble" is not a misprint but Grandville's own slang for *hâbleur* or "boastful chatterbox," a character in Grandville's book of illustrations *Un autre monde* (see *Arcades* 963, note 2). The "magic" of cast iron that allows the planet Saturn to appear like a giant "circular balcony" (see figure 2.10) connects, via the link that concludes the paragraph, not to a folder by that name—for a "Hashish" file does not exist—but to the largest and most important Konvolut, "Baudelaire," with its drug motif taken from the poet's *Le vin et le haschisch* (e.g., *J*68, 4).[20] We can thus make our way spatially from the shop sign "Gastronomie cosmopolite," assembled from animal components (*A1*, 2), to the magic of cast-iron balconies (*F1,7*), then to the trance or phantasmagoria induced by hashish, and thereby to the folder central to Benjamin's entire enterprise—the one called "Baudelaire."

This, the *J* Konvolut, which takes up roughly one-fifth of the *Passagen-Werk*, appears to be more of a piece than the others, and there are fewer black squares signaling links to other folders. But the technique is the same: the analysis of Baudelaire's oeuvre is composed not in any linear or logical fashion but out of small fragments—citations from Baudelaire, whether from his poems, critical writings, letters to his mother, or diaries; citations from other writers of the period, ranging from Victor Hugo's *La légende des siècles* to Félix Pyat's drama *Le chiffonier de Paris;* quoted statements specifically about Baudelaire made by other writers, ranging from Baudelaire's contemporaries (e.g., Alfred de Vigny, Edgar Allan Poe) to the Modernists Proust, Gide, and Valéry as well as scholars and commentators who are Benjamin's contemporaries; descriptions of the Paris of the Second Empire by travel writers, journalists, sociologists, and memoirists of the period—and so on. What Adorno bemoans as Benjamin's "refusal of interpretation," his "wide-eyed presentation of the bare facts," actually produces a composite image of Baudelaire that is as vivid as it is complex and contradictory. Consider, for example, the following entry:

Figure 2.9. J. J. Grandville, "The marine life collection." From *Un autre monde* (1844), in Susan Buck-Morss, *The Dialectics of Seeing: Walter Benjamin and the Arcades Project* (Cambridge, MA: MIT Press, 1989), p. 156.

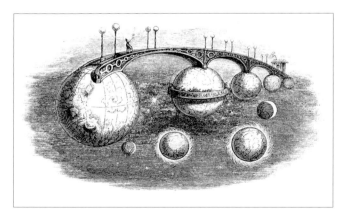

Figure 2.10. J. J. Grandville, "An interplanetary bridge; Saturn's ring is an iron balcony." From *Un autre monde* (1844), in Susan Buck Morss, *The Dialectics of Seeing* (Cambridge, MA: MIT Press, 1989), p. 153.

Nadar beschreibt das Kostüm von Baudelaire dem er in der Nähe von dessen Woh-
nung dem Hotel Pimodan beg(eg)net. "Un pantaloon noir bien tiré sur la botte vernie,
une blouse—blouse roulière bleue bien raide en ses plis neufs—pour toute coiffure
ses longs cheveux noirs, naturellement bouclés, le linge de toile éclatante et stricte-
ment sans empois, quelques poils de barbe naissante sous le nez et au menton, et les
gants roses tout frais . . . Ainsi vêtu et non coiffé, Baudelaire parcourait son quartier
et la ville d'un pas saccadé, nerveux et mat à la fois, comme celui du chat, et choisis-
sant chaque pavé comme s'il eût à se garer d'y écraser un oeuf." cit Firmin Maillard;
La Cité des intellectuels Paris (1905) p 362

Nadar describes the outfit worn by Baudelaire, who is encountered in the vicinity of
his residence [of 1843–45], the Hôtel Pimodan. "Black trousers drawn well above his
polished boots; a blue workman's blouse, stiff in its new folds; his black hair, naturally curly, worn long—his only coiffure; bright linen, strictly without starch; a faint
moustache under his nose and a bit of beard on his chin; rose-colored gloves, quite
new. . . . Thus arrayed and hatless, Baudelaire walked about his *quartier* of the city
at an uneven pace, both nervous and languid, like a cat, choosing each stone of the
pavement as if he had to avoid crushing an egg." Cited in Firmin Maillard, *La Cité des
intellectuels* (Paris, <1905>), p. 362 ($\mathcal{J}$ 1a, 3)

Nadar, who was one of Baudelaire's close friends, photographed the poet
many times; indeed, Nadar's visual image of Baudelaire has become ours
today. But of course the photographs were black and white, and so we don't
see the poet's "bright" linen or "rose-colored gloves." Indeed, Nadar's verbal
sketch of the *flâneur* as a nervous yet languid cat, calculating its movements
along the pavement as if to "avoid crushing an egg," has a Baudelairean cast,
as if the visual artist might here capture the poet's words as readily as he had
rendered his physical appearance. The shift from the German of the explan-
atory note to the French of the citation underscores the weight Benjamin
gives to Nadar's own words. But rather than elaborating on Nadar's portrait
or relating it to *Les Fleurs du mal* itself, Benjamin soon shifts gears:

Zum allegorischen Element. "Dickens . . . parlant des cafés dans lesquels il se faufilait
aux mauvais jours . . . dit de l'un qui se trouvait dans Saint-Martin's Lane: 'Je me souviens que d'une chose, c'est qu'il était situé près de l'église et que, dans la porte, il y
avait une enseigne ovale en verre avec ce mot Coffee Room peint à l'adresse des pas-
sants. S'il m'arrive, encore maintenant, de me trouver dans tout autre café, mais où il y
a aussi cette inscription sur une glace, et si je la lis à l'envers (moor eeffoc) comme je les
faisais souvent alors dans mes sombres rêveries, mon sang ne fait qu'un tour. Ce mot
baroque moor eeffoc est la devise de tout vrai réalisme." G. K. Chesterton: Dickens
(Vies des hommes illustres No 9) Traduit de l'anglais par Laurent et Martin-Dupont
Paris 1927 p. 32 ($\mathcal{J}$ 3, 2, ellipses Benjamin's)

On the allegorical element. "Dickens . . . mentions, among the coffee shops into which he crept in those wretched days, one in St. Martin's Lane, 'of which I only recollect that it stood near the church, and that in the door there was an oval glass plate with COFFEE ROOM painted on it, addressed toward the street. If I ever find myself in a very different kind of coffee room now, but where there is such an inscription on glass, and read it backwards on the wrong side, MOOR EEFFOC (as I often used to do then in a dismal reverie), a shock goes through my blood.' That wild word, 'Moor Eeffoc,' is the motto of all effective realism." G. K. Chesterton, *Dickens* (series entitled *Vie des hommes illustres*, no. 9), trans. from the English by Laurent and Martin-Dupont (Paris, 1927), p. 32 (*J3,2*)

Baudelaire's Second Empire Paris here gives way, as in film montage, to a parallel London, specifically Dickens's London, with the further twist that Benjamin is citing Dickens not directly but through Chesterton, and Chesterton in a French reference book series, *Vie des hommes illustres*, at that. The link seems random, as when today one jumps from one Google item to another, often not certain where the search will lead. In this case, it leads to the eerie mirror image of the coffee-room inscription—*MOOR EEFOC*—which provides a perfect counterpart to the Baudelairean "shock" experience in Second Empire Paris. Two pages later, we read:

Baudelaire über den im Kreise der Ecole païenne großgewordenen: "Son âme, sans cesse irritée et inassouvie, s'en va à travers le monde, le monde occupé et laborieux; elle s'en va, dis-je, comme une prostituée, criant: Plastique! Plastique! La plastique, cet affreux mot me donne la chair de poule." Baudelaire: *L'Art romantique* Paris p 307

Baudelaire on the child raised in the company of the Pagan School: "His soul, constantly excited and unappeased, goes about the world, the busy, toiling world; it goes, I say, like a prostitute, crying *Plastique! plastique!* The plastic—that frightful word gives me goose flesh." Baudelaire, *L'Art romantique* (Paris), p. 307. (*J4,7*)

Neoclassical art with its call for plasticity—the sculpturesque—was the bête noire of Baudelaire, the proponent of Delacroix and Romantic painting.[21] Here, in a nice sleight-of-hand, the word *plastique* shifts from aesthetic criterion to synthetic product peddled by the harlot, whose cry, reminiscent of Blake's "London," gives the narrator "goose flesh"—again, a shock experience. Throughout the text, the phantasmagoria at the heart of Baudelaire's poetic is presented metonymically in every possible representation, so that when individual poems like *À une passante* or *Le Mauvais Vitrier* are cited or discussed by this or that critic, the reader already has familiarity with the context and texture of Baudelairean lyric. Benjamin's text, that is to say, far from being a critical exposition of Baudelaire's ethos, forces us to enter the poetic universe itself, in all its multiplicity. Indeed, the *J* Konvolut becomes a kind of theater on whose stage Baudelaire's actual writings, verse and prose, can be reenacted as if their presence were of immediate interest to all concerned.

"Baudelaire" thus exhibits the tension between authenticity and artifice, disclosure and impenetrability that we have witnessed on those very first pages of the *A* Konvolut, whose elaborate textile network juxtaposes citation and commentary, image and scholarly material so as to dramatize the attraction—yet also a kind of horror—of the Paris Arcades. In *A*1.4 we read: "It was the time in which Balzac could write, 'The great poem of display chants its stanzas of color from the Church of the Madeleine to the Porte Saint-Denis.'" ("Es war die Zeit in der Balzac schreiben konnte: 'le grand poème de l'étalage chante ses strophes de couleur depuis la Madeleine jusqu'a la porte Sainte-Denis.'") The reference is to Balzac's *Le diable à Paris* (1846), and it is startling to see *le grand poème de la mer* of Rimbaud's *Le bateau ivre* replaced by *le grand poème de l'étalage*—display. Signage—here made from antlers or pheasants, from fake diamonds and rubies—is all. And yet, in Eliot's phrase, such signs are taken for wonders, not only by the *flâneurs* of the *passages* but by Benjamin himself. A true hall of mirrors, as enticing as it is chilling, the realm of the arcades becomes the poet's phantasmagoria.

Page after page of Benjamin's astonishing text contains movable passages that can (and do) reappear in altered contexts; the repeated juxtapositions, cuts, links, shifts in register, framing devices, and visual markings conspire to produce a poetic text that is paradigmatic for our own poetics. The most sober documentation—for example, F. A. Beraud's account of police edicts regulating prostitution in 1830 in the *O* Konvolut—is placed side by side with an extract from Baudelaire or Rimbaud, from popular song, tall tale, comic anecdote, cartoon, legend, or myth.

But there is a further resonance Benjamin's book permits, this time an intertextual—and potentially digital—one made possible by the *Arcades Project*'s exfoliating references. Consider Konvolut *E*, "Haussmannization, Barricade Fighting," which splices together fascinating yarns, observations, and images, detailing the painful process of Baron Georges-Eugène Haussmann's construction of the Paris boulevards—a construction-demolition project that figures so largely in Baudelaire's *Fleurs du mal*. Here is a French citation from Le Corbusier's *Urbanisme*:

"Le baron Haussmann fit dans Paris les plus larges trouées, les saignées les plus effrontées. Il semblait que Paris ne saurait supporter la chirurgie d'Haussmann. Or, Paris, ne vit-elle pas aujourd'hui de ce que fit cet homme téméraire et courageux? Ses moyens? La pelle, la pioche, le charroi, la truelle, la brouette, ces armes puériles de

Figure 2.11. Anon., Tools used by Haussmann's Workers. Artist unknown. From Walter Benjamin, "E Konvolut," in *The Arcades Project*, p. 134.

Figure 2.12. Marcel Duchamp, *Coffee Mill* (*Moulin à café*) (1911). Oil on cardboard. 33 × 12.5 cm. Tate Gallery, London. © 2009 Artists Rights Society, New York.

Figure 2.13. Marcel Duchamp, *Chocolate Grinder* (*Broyeuse de chocolat*), no. 1 (1913). Oil on canvas. 62 × 65 cm. Philadelphia Museum of Art. The Louise and Walter Arensberg Collection. © 2009 Artists Rights Society, New York.

tous les peuples . . . jusqu'au machinisme neuf. C'est vraiment admirable ce que sut faire Haussmann." Le Corbusier: *Urbanisme* (Paris <1925>,) p 149.

"Haussmann cut immense gaps right through Paris, and carried out the most startling operations. It seemed as if Paris would never endure his surgical experiments. And yet, today, does it not *exist* merely as a consequence of his daring and courage? His equipment was meager; the shovel, the pick, the wagon, the trowel, the wheelbarrow— the simple tools of every race . . . before the mechanical age. His achievement was truly admirable." Le Corbusier, *Urbanisme* (Paris <1925>), p. 149. (*E* 5 a, 6)

In the Harvard edition, this passage is accompanied by an illustration from Benjamin's files of the "Tools used by Haussmann's workers" (figure 2.11). Here are those "simple tools" Corbusier is talking about: the shovel, the pick, the wagon, the trowel, the wheelbarrow. But what does that not-so-simple machine with the crank depicted in the lower right remind us of? Those familiar with the ready-mades of Marcel Duchamp will recognize its affinity to the painted *Coffee Mill* of 1911 (figure 2.12) and to its offshoot the 1914 *Chocolate Grinder* (figure 2.13), which was, in turn, to become an important property of *The Large Glass*.

Moulins : 1. A eau ; 2. A vent ; 3. A huile ; 4. A café ; 5. A légumes ; 6. A fromage ; 7. A poivre ; 8. A sel.

Figure 2.14. "Moulins," from *Nouveau petit Larousse illustré: Dictionaire encyclopédique* (1912).

Figure 2.15a. Marcel Duchamp, *Nude Descending a Staircase* (*Nu descendant un escalier*), no. 2 (1912). Oil on canvas. 146 × 89 cm. Philadelphia Museum of Art. The Louise and Walter Arensberg Collection. © 2009 Artists Rights Society, New York.

Figure 2.15b. Marcel Duchamp, *Nude Descending a Staircase (Nu descendant un escalier)*, no. 3 (December 1937). Pochoir-colored reproduction with attached postage stamp.
© 2009 Artists Right Society, New York.

Surely the *Chocolate Grinder* has nothing to do with Le Corbusier's references to the tools and machines of Haussmann's Paris, as illustrated here. Or does it? We know that Duchamp based this and related ready-mades on current illustrations of mechanical drawings, not unlike those reproduced in the *Passagen-Werk:* for example, one of *moulins* (mills) from the *Petit Larousse illustré* of 1912 (figure 2.14). But there is a more specific link. In late spring 1937, when Benjamin was working away at the notes for his *Arcades* project, he wrote in his diary, "Saw Duchamp this morning, same Café on Blvd. St. Germain. . . . Showed me his painting: *Nu descendant un escalier* in a reduced format, colored by hand en pochoir, breathtakingly beautiful, maybe mention."[22] The reference is to Duchamp's *pochoir* (one of a series), replicating in miniature (35 × 20 cm, approximately one-quarter of the original size) his famous *Nude Descending a Staircase* of 1912 (see figure 2.15a-b). The *pochoir* was made by taking a black-and-white reproduction of the painting and then "colorizing" it by applying ink and gouache using stencils or templates cut from a thin sheet of metal. Duchamp called the resulting pictures *coloriages originaux* and signed them "Marcel Coloriavit"; on some of the sheets, he pasted below the illustration a five-centime French revenue stamp, over which he wrote his signature.[23]

Original or copy? Benjamin's enthusiasm for Duchamp's "breathtakingly beautiful" *pochoir* reflects the aesthetic that governs the entire *Arcades Project*: to copy and reproduce one's own earlier words or the words of others can be a very fruitful exercise. If the 1912 *Nude* was "shocking," Duchamp asks, what about this miniature produced twenty-five years later? Has its delicately altered color substantially changed it? And if not, why not? In Wittgenstein's words, "But isn't the same at least the same?"

The lesson here is that context always transforms content. Suppose the mirror image of the sign for Coffee Room—*MOOR EEFFOC*—that Benjamin cites from a French translation of Chesterton, who in turn is citing Dickens, appeared in a film noir or a Susan Howe poem, or perhaps in stenciled letters on the bottom of a painting by Jasper Johns. Clearly, it would function quite differently from the way it does here, in a set of intricately metonymic notes designed to pinpoint the particularity of Baudelaire's poetics. In the context of Konvolut *E* with its Haussmann story—a story hardly as sanguine for Benjamin as for Le Corbusier, whom he cites—the image of the workers' tools produces nostalgia for a time when Paris was not yet sliced up by boulevards. In the context of Duchamp's ready-mades, on the other hand, these tools are understood as entering the new industrial age, the age of mechanical reproduction.

: : :

"The power of a country road," remarked Benjamin in his essay-memoir "One-Way Street" (1928), "is different when one is walking along it from when one is flying over it by airplane. In the same way, the power of text is different when it is read from when it is copied out. . . . Only the copied text commands the soul of him who is occupied with it, whereas the mere reader never discovers the new aspects of his inner self that are opened by the text."[24] These words anticipate in an uncanny way the turn writing would take in the twenty-first century, now that the Internet has made copyists, recyclers, transcribers, collators, and reframers of us all. Benjamin's Passages become the digital passages we take through websites and Youtube videos, navigating our way from one Google link to another and over the bridges provided by our favorite search engines and web pages. In this new arcade-world, writing a poem is no easier than it ever was. Just different.

3

From Avant-Garde to Digital: The Legacy of Brazilian Concrete Poetry

In the spring of 2001, the poet Kenneth Goldsmith participated in a panel on Brazilian concrete poetry with, among others, one of the movement's founders, Decio Pignatari.[1] Goldsmith recalls:

> I was stunned. Everything [Pignatari] was saying seemed to predict the mechanics of the internet . . . delivery, content, interface, distribution, multi-media, just to name a few. Suddenly it made sense: like de Kooning's famous statement: "History doesn't influence me. I influence it," it's taken the web to make us see just how prescient concrete poetics was in predicting its own lively reception half a century later. I immediately understood that what had been missing from concrete poetry was an appropriate environment in which it could flourish. For many years, concrete poetry has been in limbo: it's been a displaced genre in search of a new medium. And now it's found one.[2]

The limbo Goldsmith refers to was quite real: in the 1980s and '90s, the going view, especially in Anglo-America, where concrete poetry had never really caught on, was that the 1950s experiment in material poetics was ideologically suspect—too "pretty," too empty of "meaningful" content, too much like advertising copy. In the university this estimate still prevails. To this day, one would be hard put to find an English or comparative literature department that offers courses in concrete poetry. Doesn't the subject belong more properly, if at all, in the art department, my colleagues ask, specifically in courses on graphic design?

Even books *about* concrete poetry have raised this issue. Consider Caroline Bayard's sophisticated theoretical study *The New Poetics in Canada and Quebec: From Concretism to Post-modernism* (1989). Bayard begins with a survey of the midcentury poetics of Oyvind Fahlström, Eugen Gomringer, and

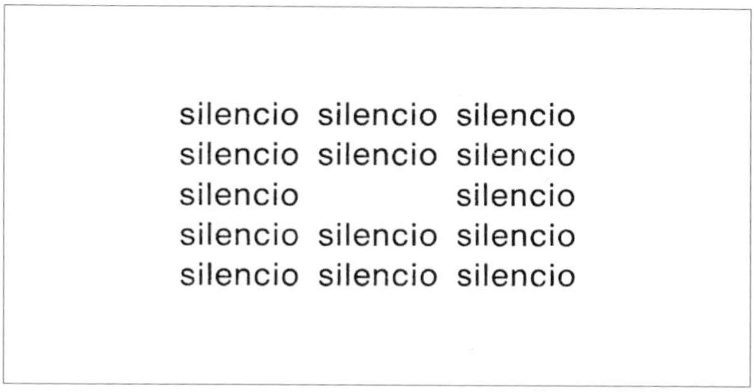

```
silencio silencio silencio
silencio silencio silencio
silencio         silencio
silencio silencio silencio
silencio silencio silencio
```

Figure 3.1. Eugen Gomringer, "silencio" (1953). Reprinted by permission of the author.

```
sem um numero
    um numero
       numero
         zero
          um
           o
          nu
        mero
      numero
    um numero
  um sem numero
```

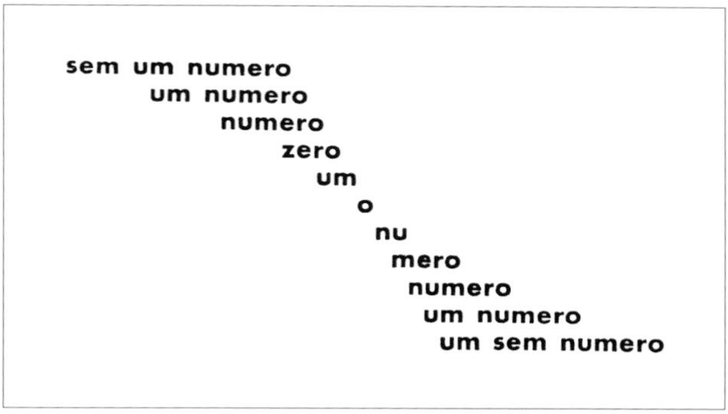

Figure 3.2. Augusto de Campos, "sem um numero" (1957). From *Antologia Noigandres* 5 (São Paulo, 1962). Reprinted by permission of the author.

Augusto and Haroldo de Campos, only to conclude that the "fusion of expression and content" being advocated by the concretists was an instance of what Umberto Eco had termed the "iconic fallacy"—the fallacy that "a sign has the same properties as its object and is simultaneously similar to, analogous to, and motivated by its object."[3] At its most naive "naturalizing" level the iconic fallacy manifests itself, Bayard argues, in poems like Gomringer's *"silencio"* (figure 3.1), where the empty rectangle at the center of the composition is presented as the equivalent to the "silence" conveyed by the verbal sign. But even where the motivation is much subtler, as in Augusto de Campos's "sem um número" (without a number), which makes no reference to an external object but uses graphic space structurally so as to dramatize the central **o** (zero) status of the peasant (figure 3.2), concrete poetry, Bayard contends, is bedeviled by a lingering Cratylism—the doctrine put forward by Plato's Cratylus in the dialogue by that name, that the sound and visual properties of a given word have mimetic value, and that, by extension, concrete poetry equates "graphic-typographical form with semantic function" (Bayard, 23). This is, Bayard believes, a dangerous doctrine. "Typographical and calligraphic aesthetics were most striking in the 1960s, but also the least durable. They corresponded to the Cratylian phase of the experience, and while they inserted into texts typefaces hitherto unknown to literature, the experiment was short-lived" (163). For—and here ideology comes in— "changing the sign system does not in any way imply that one is modifying the political system" (171). And Bayard refers us to Herbert Marcuse's argument that far from representing a breakthrough, the innovative typographic devices of the concretists "dissolve the very structure of perception in order to make room . . . for what?" (171).

This "for what?" functions as a battle cry. Visual poetry and with it sound poetry, as in the case of Henri Chopin (Bayard, 27–28), are thus both judged to be questionable practices. Indeed, Bayard argues, it was only when the "form=content" assumption of concretism was abandoned, as it was in the 1970s and '80s by poets like bpNichol, bill bissett, and Steve McCaffery, who turned their attention to the anagrammatic and paragrammatic play *inherent in language* rather than on such concretist elements as font, color, and spacing, that a more adequate poetics was born.

It is a compelling argument: in my own *Radical Artifice: Writing Poetry in the Age of Media*, written in the late '80s, I was persuaded, as was Caroline Bayard, that post-concrete poetics was providing a needed "corrective" to the purported mimeticism and aestheticized composition of the earlier work.[4] But now that, in Goldsmith's words, "an appropriate environment in which [concrete poetry] could flourish" has become available, the texts in question have recovered their place in the larger poetic field. To understand how this process of recovery works and how concrete poetry itself perceived its role as the renewal of the avant-garde practices of the early twentieth century, it may be useful to take up the concept of the *arrière-garde*, now gaining currency.[5] We need, in other words, to ground concretism in its history, to understand, for example, its relation to the two world wars as well as to the varying cultures that produced it. And further: from the vantage point of the twenty-first century, we can begin to discriminate between the various manifestations of what once seemed to be a unified movement. Not all concretisms, after all, are equal.

Bringing Up the Rear

As William Marx makes clear in the introduction to *Les arrière-gardes au xxe* siècle, the concept of the avant-garde is inconceivable without its opposite. In military terms, the rear guard of the army is the part that protects and consolidates the troop movement in question; often the army's best generals are placed there. When an avant-garde movement is no longer a novelty, it is the role of the *arrière-garde* to complete its mission, to ensure its success. The term *arrière-garde,* then, is synonymous neither with reaction nor with nostalgia for a lost and more desirable artistic era; it is, on the contrary, the "hidden face of modernity" (Marx, 6). As Antoine Compagnon puts it in his study of Barthes in the Marx collection, the role of the *arrière garde* is to save that which is threatened. In Barthes's own words, "Être d'avant-garde, c'est savoir ce qui est mort; être d'arrière garde, c'est l'aimer encore."[6]

The proposed dialectic is a useful corrective, I think, to the usual conceptions of the avant-garde, either as one-time rupture with the bourgeois art market, a rupture that could never be repeated—the Peter Bürger thesis— or as a series of ruptures, each one breaking decisively with the one before, as in textbook accounts of avant-gardes from Futurism to Dada to Surrealism to Fluxus, to Minimalism, Conceptualism, and so on. This second or progress narrative, ironically, continues to haunt the academy even when the avant-garde is by no means at issue: I am referring to the unstated premise of critical theory that the perspective of enlightened globalists, postcolonialists, or multiculturalists on a given artwork or movement is inherently more "advanced" than what came before. But as Haroldo de Campos points out in a blistering attack on Third World studies, it is condescending—indeed, as he says, *overaltern*—to assume, as does, for example, Fredric Jameson in his "theory of a cognitive aesthetics of third-world literature," that subaltern fiction, "having as a necessary goal the achievement of a 'national allegory,' will not offer the satisfaction of a Proust or Joyce." At the current stage of development, Jameson posits, a given novel—his example is Guimarães Rosa's *Grande Sertão: Veredas*—may be understood as "a *high literary* variant of the Western." To which Haroldo responds:

> The first thing that occurs to me, before a somewhat deprecating label like this one, is that the author of *The Political Unconscious* ignores the Brazilian Portuguese language and has built a fake, oversimplified image of the complex Faustian, metaphysical struggle between God and Devil embedded in the deep structure of Rosa's masterpiece. . . . The Anglophone master's discourse of the overaltern "salvationist" critics works as a rhetorical by-product of unconscious imperial-

ism by effacing the *sub*altern "minor" languages and by underrating their creative verbal power.[7]

The "new realism," Haroldo insists, has not shed the language of Joyce and Borges as readily as it might seem.

This commentary provides us with a useful entry into the discourse of the concretism of the 1950s. In 1953, the Brazilian-born Swedish poet Oyvind Fahlström published a "Manifesto for Concrete Poetry" under the title "Hipy papy bithithdthuthda bthuthdy," a version of "Happy Birthday" he took from A. A. Milne's *Winnie-the-Pooh*.[8] The second epigraph for this manifesto—the first announces that Fahlström has shifted from "normal" writing to the creating of *worlets* (words, letters)—is in French and declares, "Remplacer la psychologie de l'homme par L'OBSESSION LYRIQUE DE LA MATIÈRE." The citation is from Marinetti's *Technical Manifesto of Literature* (1912)—the famous manifesto, first printed as a leaflet in French and Italian, supposedly spoken by the propeller of the airplane in which Marinetti finds himself. The *Technical Manifesto*, the modernist reader will recall, advocates the destruction of syntax, of adjectives, adverbs, and all verbs forms except the infinitive, and of punctuation, in favor of "tight networks of analogies" between disparate images," as in "trench= orchestra" or "machine gun=femme fatale." Such strings of unrelated nouns—what Marinetti called *parole in libertà*—would replace the tedious lyric "I," which is to say all psychology: "the man who is damaged beyond redemption by the library and the museum, who is in thrall to a fearful logic and wisdom, offers absolutely nothing that is any longer of any interest." For psychology, Marinetti insisted, we must substitute *matter*, specifically such categories as noise, weight, and smell. And Marinetti exemplifies this "new" poetry by reciting from his onomatopoeic battle poem *Zang tumb tuuum* with its cataloging of such items as "lead + lava + 300 stinks + 50 sweet smells paving mattress debris horseshot carrion flick-flack piling up camels donkeys TUMB TUUUM."[9]

Like Marinetti, Fahlström has little time for the conventional pieties of his day: his manifesto begins with a satiric thrust at the Sigtuna lakefront art colony (rather like our Yaddo and McDowell summer colonies), whose cultural hero was the neo-Romantic poet Bo Setterlind, the author of a long poem called *Mooncradle*. Like Marinetti, Fahlström senses that words "have lost their luster from constant rubbing on the washboard" (110) and believes that "changing the word order is not enough; one must knead the entire clause structure. Because thought processes are dependent on language, every attack on prevailing linguistic forms ultimately enriches worn-out modes of thought" (117). And just as Marinetti dismisses ego psychology, Fahlström dismisses the fixation on "CONTENT" as the chief "unifying element" of the poetic text:

> The situation is this: e v e r s i n c e t h e W A R, [there has been] a l o n g, a b j e c t, d o o m s d a y m o o d, a feeling that all experimental extremes have been exhausted. For those of us unwilling to drift into the world of alcoholic or heavenly sustenance, all that remains is to use what means we have at our disposal to
> Analyse
>
>
> analyse
> analyse our wretched predicament.
> Today with laboured symbolic cryptograms, silly romantic effusions or desperate grimaces outside the church gate being propounded, as the only healthy options, the concrete alternative must also be presented. (Fahlström, "Hipy papy," 110–11)

But as the reference above to the postwar doomsday mood makes clear, there are, of course, also enormous differences between the avant-guerre Futurist Marinetti and the post–World War II Fahlström—differences that similarly define the relationship of Pound and Joyce to the Noigandres group. The Utopian avant-garde, of which Marinetti was very much of a representative, believed in definitive rupture with the stultifying past. "A roaring motorcar," Marinetti declared famously in the First Manifesto (1909), "is more beautiful than the Winged Victory of Samothrace" (Marinetti, 13). And one of his best-known manifestos is *Contro Venezia passatista* (1910), which insists, partly tongue-in-cheek, that the famed Venetian canals should be drained and filled with cement so that factories might rise up to replace the "dead' museum culture of this *passéist* city, whose abject citizens are little better than *cicerones*, guiding the wealthy foreign tourists from one museum or church to another.

Or again, there is the manifesto called *Down with Tango and Parsifal*, with its diatribe against Wagner and those who dance like "hallucinated dentists." For the Italian Futurists, as for their Russian counterpart and the Cabaret Voltaire, the past is not only dead but deadly. Avant-garde means to make it new. Accordingly, there is no homage to the poets and artists of the preceding century. The 1912 manifesto "Slap in the Face of Public Taste" (signed by David Burliuk, Velimir Khlebnikov, Alexei Kruchenykh, and Vladimir Mayakovsky) declared that "the past is too tight. The Academy and Pushkin are less intelligible than hieroglyphs," and exhorted fellow poets to "throw Pushkin, Dostoevsky, Tolstoy, etc., etc. overboard from the Ship of Modernity."[10]

The new technology, it seems, has changed everything. "If all artists were to see the crossroads of these heavenly paths," says Kasimir Malevich, referring in 1915 to the "brilliance of electric lights" and "growling of propellers" of the modern city, "if they were to comprehend these monstrous runways and intersections of our bodies with the clouds in the heavens, then they would not paint chrysanthemums."[11] Who was it that did paint chrysanthemums? Monet for one, Renoir for another: artists of the great Impressionist movement who were now considered passé. Indeed, Duchamp went further and rejected retinal art *tout court*—dismissing Courbet, not to mention the Impressionists, as devoid of any real ideas.

The *arrière-garde*, in contrast, treats the propositions of the early twentieth-century avant-garde with a respect bordering on veneration. One can't imagine Marinetti or Malevich using the words of his late nineteenth-century precursors as epigraphs, but Fahlström certainly does so. And the Brazilian Noigandres group specifically derives its names from a passage in Pound's *Cantos*. Thus concretism, cutting-edge (literally!) as it was vis-à-vis the normative verse or painting of its own day, transformed the Utopian optimism and energy of the pre–World War I years into a more reflective, self-conscious, and complex project of recovery.

Consider the curious triangulation that occurs when we read Fahlström or the Brazilian concretists against such of their postwar North American contemporaries as Elizabeth Bishop or Robert Lowell. "They are doing something in Rio now called 'concretionist,'" Bishop, then a resident of Brazil, tells Lowell in April 1960. "It seems like pre-1914 experiments, with a little 'transition' & Jolas, and a dash of Cummings. It's awfully sad. I was interviewed about it in Belém and said ferociously that perhaps it had 'A certain nostalgic charm.'" And in the next paragraph she remarks, "How is THRONES? I refused to buy ROCKDRILL. Pound criticism is wildly confused, don't you think, but I agree with D. Fitts that poetry is not to be drilled into you, nor is music and that's one of P's—oh well—I'll skip it."[12]

It may seem remarkable that both Lowell and Bishop, poets who came of age under the sign of Pound, could be so indifferent to the late Cantos. But for them, as for most poets of the midcentury, Pound remained the poet of Imagism, of the Vorticist *Lustra* epigrams and the satiric *Homage to Sextus Propertius*, even as the radical late Cantos, with their collocation of Latin and Provençal phrases, American slang, numbers, symbols, and Chinese ideo-

LXXXVI

WITH   solicitude

IV. xvi. 18

that mirroured turbationem,
Bismarck forgotten, fantasia without balance-wheel,
"No more wars after '70" (Bismarck.)
"Dummheit, nicht Bosheit," said old Margherita
    (or Elenor? dowager)
"Sono tutti eretici, Santo Padre,
    ma non sono cattivi."
Mind (the Kaiser's) like loose dice in a box.
Ballin said: "If I had known,
    wd/ indeed have stuffed all Hamburg with grain."
Bülow believed him. But Talleyrand set up Belgium,
Two dynasties, two buffer states,
    wd/ have set Poland.
So that Belgium saved Frogland; Svizzera neutral.
xvi.20: only two of us who will roll up our sleeves.
And Brancusi repeating: je peux commencer
    une chose tous les jours, mais
                  fiiniiiir

詳   hsiang²   xvii, 7

Lost the feel of the people   靈   xviii, 5

xviii, 19

典

580

Figure 3.3. Ezra Pound, from "Canto 86." From THE CANTOS OF EZRA POUND, copyright © 1934 by Ezra Pound. Reprinted by permission of New Directions Publishing Corp.

grams (see figure 3.3) set the stage for the "concretionism" Bishop found so "awfully sad." *Rock-Drill, Thrones*: the newly reconfigured page layout of these Cantos was dismissed as some sort of elaborate game, a collocation of unrelated fragments not worth reading, much less purchasing. Lowell, who found even the "loveliness and humor" of the *Pisan Cantos* (1948) spoiled by a severe disjunction—"the drift must be cut somewhere," he told Pound[13]—had by 1959 returned to the Romantic lyric paradigm, as his *Life Studies* of that year testifies.

The *arrière-garde*, then, is neither a throwback to traditional forms—in this case, the first-person lyric or lyric sequence—nor what we used to call *postmodernism*. Rather, it is revival of the avant-garde model—but with a difference. When, for example, Oyvind Fahlström makes his case for the equivalence of form and content, his argument amalgamates Khlebnikov's *zaum* poetics of the Russian avant-garde with principles developed by the French *lettristes* who were his contemporaries. The basic axiom, developed by Khlebnikov in his examination of etymologies, is that, as Fahlström put it, "l I k e—s o u n d i n g   w o r d s   b e l o n g   t o g e t h e r" ("Hipy papy," 115). "Myths," for example, "have been explained in this way: when Deukalion and Pyrrha wanted to create new human beings after the Flood, they threw stones and men and women grew from them: the word for stone was 'laas,' for people 'laos.' . . . Figs are related to figment, pigs to pigmentation" (115).

Here is the Cratylian or iconic "fallacy" so regularly called into question by critics of concretism. From an *arrière-garde* perspective, however, there is an important precedent for Fahlström's formulation, which also covers rhythm ("metrical rhythms, rhythmic word order, rhythmic empty spaces"), homonyms, syllepsis, which "unites words, sentences, and paragraphs" ("Hipy papy," 114–15), anagram, paragram, and the "arbitrary attribution of new meanings to letters, words, sentences, or paragraphs." "We might," for example, "decide that all 'i's in a given worlet signify 'sickness.' The more there are, the more serious the illness" (116).

Khlebnikov, whom Roman Jakobson considered the great poet of the twentieth century, expended much labor on tracing the relationships of meanings produced by such words and syllables. In a short essay (1913) on cognates of the word *solntse* (sun), Khlebnikov observes: "Here is the way the syllable *so* [with] is a field that encompasses *son* [sleep], *solntse* [sun], *sila* [strength], *solod* [malt], *slovo* [word], *sladkii* [sweet], *soi* [clan—Macedonian dialect], *sad* [garden], *selo* [settlement], *sol'* [salt], *slyt'* [to be reputed], *syn* [son]."[14] And to make the relationships more vivid, Khlebnikov sketches them as the rays of a sun bearing the key word "SO" (figure 3.4). Logically, the relationship between these verbal units is largely arbitrary—what does salt have to do with sun?—but poetically, Khlebnikov shows, they can be made to inhabit the same universe: "Although the refined tastes of our time distinguish what is *solenyi* [salty] from what is *sladkii* [sweet], back in the days when salt was as valuable as precious stones, both salt and salted things

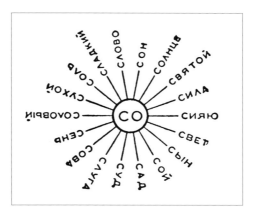

Figure 3.4. Velimir Khelbnikov, "Here is the way the syllable SO is a field" (1912–13).

were considered sweet; *solod* [malt] and *sol'* [salt] are as close linguistically as *golod* [hunger] and *gol* [the destitute]." And the analysis continues in this vein.

Khlebnikov's poetic etymologies recall Plato's *Cratylus*, where despite Socrates's arguments against the representability of the sign, he is the one to come up with ingenious meanings for letters and syllables. The noun for truth, αληθεια (*aletheia*), is shown to be an "agglomeration of θεια αλη (thea alé, divine wandering), implying the divine motion of existence." Or again, Ψευδος (*pseudos*) is "the opposite of motion; here is another ill name given by the legislator to stagnation and forced inaction, which he compares to sleep (ευδειν, *eudein*), but the original meaning of the word is disguised by the addition of ψ (*ps*)."[15] If, as Rosmarie Waldrop put it neatly, "concrete poetry is first of all a revolt against the transparency of the word," making "the sound and shape of words its explicit field of investigation,"[16] the Plato of the *Cratylus* and Khlebnikov after him are certainly involved with concrete Poetry. For the link between stagnation and sleep or between truth and a divine wandering are precisely the links that intrigue poets.

This, then, is the force behind Fahlström's *worlets* and his fascination with complex forms. In his own case, the early concrete experiments were only a first step in the elaborate language games we find in his collages, installations, musical compositions, and especially the radio plays, which I shall consider later vis-à-vis sound poetry. In all these instances, materiality and medium are central: Fahlström had dissociated himself early from the Surrealists who were his contemporaries, remarking that his aesthetic differed from theirs in that "the concrete reality of my *worlets* is in no way opposed to the concrete reality of real life. Neither dream sublimates nor myths of the future, they stand as an organic part of the reality I inhabit."[17]

In its inattention to sound and syntax, Fahlström implies, Surrealism should be understood as a deviation from the true avant-garde path. The new poetics thus positions itself elsewhere—as the *arrière-garde* of Italian and Russian Futurism, of the "destruction of syntax" (Marinetti) and the "word set free" (Khlebnikov). The question remains why such concretism as Fahlström's, with its marvelous recovery of *zaum*, sound poetry, innovative typography, and appropriated text, came into being when and where it did. And what did the two World Wars have to do with it?

The Gomringer Variant

In *The Geography of the Imagination* (1981), Guy Davenport made a comment that sheds much light on the relation of concrete poetry to the avant-gardes of the early century:

> Our age is unlike any other in that its greatest works of art were constructed in one spirit and received in another.
>
> There was a Renaissance around 1910 in which the nature of all the arts changed. By 1916 this springtime was blighted by the World War, the tragic effects of which cannot be overestimated. Nor can any understanding be achieved of twentieth-century art if the work under consideration is not kept against the background of the war which extinguished European culture. . . . Accuracy in such matters being impossible, we can say nevertheless that the brilliant experimental period in twentieth-century art was stopped short in 1916. Charles Ives had written his best music by then; Picasso had become Picasso; Pound, Pound; Joyce, Joyce. *Except for individual talents, already in development before 1916, moving on to full maturity, the century was over in its sixteenth year.* Because of this collapse (which may yet prove to be a long interruption), the architectonic masters of our time have suffered critical neglect or abuse, and if admired are admired for anything but the structural innovations of their work.[18]

Extreme though Davenport's assessment may sound—surely many avant-garde works were produced *after* 1916—his basic premise is, I think, correct. Pound, for example, had not yet begun the *Cantos*, but the ideogrammic technique that made them so famous—their fragmentation, collage, multilingualism, and use of citation—were already in place in "Cathay." Duchamp had already produced his first ready-mades, and Malevich had exhibited his black-and-white squares at the O.10 show in St. Petersburg.

The interwar years witnessed the refinement of these early innovations—

El Lissitsky's of Malevich's abstractions, Duchamp's incorporation of his ready-mades into the *Large Glass*, Gertrude Stein's permutations in *How to Write* of her early prose technique—but the rupture that caused such widespread shock and consternation in art circles had already occurred. And in the 1930s and '40s, as Socialist Realist writing came to the fore, avant-garde innovation was considered suspect. When revival came after World War II, it occurred not in Paris, where the postwar ethos was one of existentialist introspection as to how France had taken such a terribly wrong turn in the pre-Hitler years, and certainly not in the war capitals, Berlin, Rome, Moscow—but on the periphery: in Sweden (Fahlström), Switzerland (Eugen Gomringer), Austria (Ernst Jandl), Scotland (Ian Hamilton Finlay), and especially São Paulo, Brazil.

The periphery, as we have seen in Fahlström's case, defined itself by its resistance to the dominant aesthetic of its day, turning instead to the avant-gardes of the early twentieth century. But the rear flank of the army can't protect the troops without understanding the moves the front-runners have made—a situation that makes *arrière-garde* activity much more than mere repetition. Eugen Gomringer, generally considered the father of concrete poetry,[19] is a case in point. Gomringer differed from Fahlström, as from the Campos brothers, in coming out of an artistic rather than a literary milieu.[20] As early as 1944 he had seen the international exhibition of concrete art organized by Max Bill in Basel, and in 1944–45 he made the acquaintance of Bill and Richard Loehse at the Galerie des eaux vives in Zurich.[21] Soon he was collaborating with two graphic artists, Dieter Rot and Marcel Wyss, to create a new journal called *Spirale*. Bauhaus, Hans Arp, Mondrian, and *De Stijl*—these were Gomringer's chief visual sources.

At the same time he had a taste for poetry, having begun as a student to write sonnets and related lyric forms in the tradition of Rilke and George, many of them on classical subjects, like the dramatic monologue "Antinous" (1949) or the Petrarchan sonnet "Paestum," which begins:

Am Strand und in der Dünen Einsamkeit
Läßt sich von kleinen Händen nichts bewegen,
Da scheinen Sonne, Mond und fallen Regen
Und Winde wehn im alten Maß der Zeit.[22]

On the shore in the loneliness of the dunes
Nothing can be moved by small hands,
Here shines the sun, the moon, and rain falls
And winds blow, as they did in ancient times. (my translation)

The poem moves through neatly rhyming quatrains and sestet, tracking the poet's contemplation of the stones of Paestum and their testimony to the human potential for greatness.

The turn to concrete poetry, based on the abstract art (called "concrete" because of its emphasis on the materials themselves) exhibited in the Zurich and Basel galleries, thus came without a working out of the problems of iconicity and representation that we find in Fahlström and the Noigandres poets. Gomringer merely turned from the conventional lyric to Concrete art-inspired "constellation." Here is the 1952 "avenidas," written in Spanish in homage to Gomringer's birthplace, Bolivia:

avenidas
avenidas y flores

flores
flores y mujeres

avenidas
avenidas y mujeres

avenidas y flores y mujeres y
un admirador

This minimalist poem, divided into four couplets, repeats the three nouns *avenues, flowers,* and *women* with six repetitions of the conjunction *and* (*y*), in the following pattern: a, a + b; b, b + c; a, a + c; a + b + c +; the final line introduces a fourth noun modified by an indefinite article—*un admirador*—thus bringing the poet, discreetly referred to in the third person, into the picture.

Structurally, "avenidas" is not yet a "concrete" poem: the stanza breaks, for example, could be elided and the spacing between couplets could be changed without appreciably altering the lyric's meaning. Within the year, however, Gomringer had written "silencio" (see figure 3.1), "ping pong," "wind," and the "o" poem (figures 3.5–7), poems whose typography is clearly constitutive of their meaning.[23] The motivation of these "constellations," as Gomringer called them, was closely related to the situation of Switzerland in the immediate postwar era. In the 1930s and '40s there had been much talk of German Switzerland's becoming a separate nation and adopting a written German variant of its own. Although the plan was abandoned, the war further isolated Switzerland, turning it into a neutral island surrounded by warring power blocs. After the war, a unified but still multilingual Switzerland once again opened its borders to the larger European world, but that world (including Germany itself) was now newly divided by the Iron Curtain. Con-

```
ping pong
    ping pong ping
    pong ping pong
            ping pong
```

Figure 3.5. Eugen Gomringer,
"ping pong" (1953). Reprinted
by permission of the author.

```
          w    w
       d      i
     n     n     n
   i    d    i    d
 w              w
```

Figure 3.6. Eugen Gomringer,
"wind" (1953). Reprinted by
permission of the author.

Figure 3.7. Eugen Gom-
ringer, the "o" poem (1953).
Reprinted by permission of
the author.

```
                                    o
                                    bo
                                    blow
                                    blow blow
                                    blow blow blow
                                    blow blow
                                    blow
                                    bo
           o                        o
           go                       so
           grow                     show
           grow grow            show show
           grow grow grow o show show show
           grow grow            show show
           grow                     show
           go                       so
           o                        o
           lo
          flow
        flow flow
      flow flow flow
        flow flow
          flow
           lo
           o
```

crete poetry, Gomringer insisted, could break down the resultant linguistic and national borders by transcending the local dialects associated with *Heimatstil*, the endemic Swiss nativism. In using basic vocabulary as in the short poem beginning "sonne man / mond frau" (sun man / moon woman), poetry could avoid the local.[24]

But such globalism was not without its problems. From his first manifesto, "From Line to Constellation" (1954), Gomringer emphasized the need for reduction, concentration, and simplification as "the very essence of poetry." "Headlines, slogans, groups of sounds and letters," he wrote, "give rise to forms which could be models for a new poetry just waiting to be taken up for meaningful use." The "new poem" should be "simple" and could be perceived "visually as a whole as well as in its parts. It becomes an object. . . . Its concern is with brevity and conciseness." Such a poem is called a "constellation" in that "it encloses a group of words as if it were drawing stars together to form a cluster."[25]

Reduction, compression, simplicity, objecthood: note that these are not equivalent to Fahlström's call for "verbivocovisual" language and paragrammicity. In his second major statement on the subject in 1956, Gomringer declared that "Concrete poetry is founded upon the contemporary scientific-technical view of the world and will come into its own in the synthetic-rationalistic world of tomorrow."[26] This functional definition of a "universal poetry" brings Concretism dangerously close to industrial design and conformity to the political-ideological status quo. And indeed by 1958, in "The Poem as Functional Object," Gomringer is talking about "reduced language" as necessary to "the achievement of greater flexibility and freedom of communication." "The resulting poems," he wrote, "should be, if possible, *as easily understood as signs in airports and traffic signs.*"[27]

But what happens when the identity of poem and industrial sign is complete? How, then, is art different from commerce, poetry from good design? In 1967 Gomringer took on the position of chief design consultant for Rosenthal, the famous china and glass manufacturer, and increasingly his work involved consolidation rather than innovation. Perhaps the difficulty was that his concept of poeticity set itself against the traditional model of Goethean—or Rilkean—lyric without absorbing the Italian *parole in libertà* and Russian *zaum* works that had performed such a similar role. He had, in other words, no useful paradigm to revive and adjust, believing that his "simple" and "direct" constellations were something entirely new. In 1965, in his last major poem, with its Rilkean title *das stundenbuch* (the book of hours), Gomringer turned from visual "constellation" to the normal page, producing fifty-eight pages, most with five couplets each, containing permutations of twenty-four short conceptual nouns (e.g., *Geist, Wort, Frage, Antwort*—mind, word, question, answer), each modified by *mein* and *dein* ("my" and "your") in a latter-day meditation on the relationship of life to death. Here the role of graphic space has become much less significant:

> deine frage
> mein geist
>
> deine frage
> mein wort
>
> deine frage
> meine antwort
>
> deine frage
> mein lied
>
> deine frage
> mein gedicht[28]

Iconicity, anagram, paranomasia—these now give way to the accessibility of the sign: Gomringer's is a poem readable by anyone with a minimum of German. True, the elegantly produced 1980 edition provides not only the text but also four complete translations, into English (Jerome Rothenberg), French (Pierre Garnier), Spanish (Jaime Romagosa), and Norwegian (Jan Östergren), respectively. But the very fact that *stundenbuch* translates so nicely shows that the materiality of the signifier no longer plays the central role in the poem's production. The lines "deine frage / mein wort" inevitably become "your question / my word": the translator need only follow the score.

Pós-Tudo, Pós-Utopico

The Brazilian concretists, to whom I now turn, had a close relationship to Gomringer at the inception of the movement, but their work soon took a different direction.[29] The very name Noigandres, chosen by the Campos brothers and Decio Pignatari for their movement, launched in 1952, is revealing. Noigandres, Augusto has explained, was taken from Ezra Pound's Canto XX, in which the poet seeks out the venerable Provençal specialist Emil Lévy, a professor at Freiburg, and asks him what the word *noigandres* (used by the great troubadour poet Arnaut Daniel) means, only to be told by Lévy that for six months he has been trying without success to find the answer: "Noigandres, NOIgandres! / You know for seex mons of my life / Effery night when I go to bett, I say to myself: / Noigandres, eh *noigandres*, Now what the DEFFIL can that mean!"[30] But despite this colorful disclaimer with its phonetic spellings, "Old Lévy" had, in fact, gone on to crack the difficult nut in question: the word, he suggested, could be divided in two—*enoi* (ennui) and *gandres*, from *gandir* (to ward off, to remove)—and in its original troubadour context the word referred to an odor (probably of a flower) that could drive ennui away. Other Provençalists have suggested that *noigandres* might also refer to *noix de muscade* (nutmeg), which is an aphrodisiac—a reading that is plausible given that Arnaut's poem is a love poem. And since the nutmeg plant is prickly on the outside and silky on the inside, *noigandres* may also be a sexual metaphor.[31]

For our purposes here, it matters less what the word *noigandres* actually means than that the Brazilian concretists took a word of complex etymology from Pound's *Cantos* to name their movement and journal. This was an unusual move: in the Brazil of the early 1950s Pound was barely known. Incarcerated in St. Elizabeth's Hospital for his wartime activities, he was at best a controversial figure—one whose reception of the 1948 Bollingen Prize, awarded by a panel of distinguished fellow poets, had aroused the ire of most critics and journalists. Then, too, he had long been an exile, living in obscurity in Rapallo, Italy, so that the interwar literary world of Europe had largely forgotten him.

Why, then, *The Cantos* and Joyce's controversial *Finnegans Wake* rather than models closer to home? As Augusto de Campos explained it in a 1993 interview with me:

> In the fifties . . . there was a very important demand for change, for the recovery of the avant-garde movements. We had had two great wars that marginalized, put aside for many many years, the things that interested us. You see, the music of Webern, Schoenberg and Alan Berg, for example, was not played because it was condemned both in Germany and in Russia, the two dictatorships. You could say that all experimental poetry, all experimental art, was in a certain sense marginalized. Only in the fifties began the rediscovery of Mallarmé, the rediscovery of Pound. Pound suffered at that time from the charge of fascism. His work was very much condemned. We participated in an international movement . . . that tried to rescue Pound, who was excluded from American anthologies.[32]

The war, Augusto observes, had put all artistic experiment on hold. "It was a traumatic situation . . . [in] all the arts. Duchamp was rediscovered in the sixties by the Pop movement and by Cage, and then he balanced the influence of Picasso. . . . There was a great movement in music, in Europe as in the

U.S.—the revival of Charles Ives, Henry Cowell and Cage. So, I think it was a necessity to recover the great avant-garde movements." And now Augusto adds a comment that is significant for our understanding of concrete poetics today. It is the need for recovery of the avant-garde, he argues, that has prompted him to turn a critical eye on postmodernism: "There is inside the discussion of post-modernism *a tactic of wanting to put aside swiftly the recovery of experimental art and to say all this is finished!*"[33]

Here is the important distinction between avant- and arrière-garde. The original avant-garde was committed not to recovery but discovery, and it insisted that the aesthetic of its predecessors—say, of the poets and artists of the 1890s—was "finished." But by midcentury the situation was very different. Because the original avant-gardes had never really been absorbed into the artistic and literary mainstream, the "postmodern" demand for total rupture was always illusory. Haroldo de Campos, following Augusto's lead, explains that the concrete movement began as rebellion—"We wanted to free poetry from subjectivism and the expressionistic vehicle" of the then-dominant poetic mode. But it is also important to appreciate continuity. Thus Haroldo praises Paul Celan's work, which has "the contemporaneity of concrete poetry. He was a poet who was . . . influenced by the syntax of Hölderlin, by some devices of Trakl, but on the other side, there are visual elements in his poetry, there is a reduction and fragmentation of language typical of concrete poetry." Indeed, the "German tradition" in concrete poetry is criticized for being "much less interested in the field of semantics than, for instance, Brazilian poetry." "The Gomringer poetry," Haroldo adds, "is very interesting, but very limited."[34]

What about Surrealism? For the Brazilian *arrière-garde*, as for Oyvind Fahlström, Surrealism was distraction rather than breakthrough. In Latin America, Augusto de Campos declares, Surrealism, with its "normal grammatical phrases' and the "very conventional structure" that belies its reputed psychic automatism (170), had "a traumatic influence as a kind of avant-garde of consummation!" Haroldo adds, "A kind of conservative avant-garde . . . all the emphasis on the unconscious and on figurality. I think French poetry did not free itself from surrealism until now. They did not understand *Un coup de dés.* . . . No poet after Mallarmé was as radical as Mallarmé. Not even Apollinaire. Apollinaire is decorative where Mallarmé is structural." And Augusto cites Pignatari as quipping, "Brazil never had surrealism because the whole country is surrealist."[35]

The point here is that whereas the Surrealists were concerned with "new" artistic content—dreamwork, fantasy, the unconscious, political revolution—the concrete movement always emphasized the transformation of materiality itself. Hence the chosen pantheon included Futurist artworks and *Finnegans Wake*, Joaquim de Sousandrade's pre-Modernist collage masterpiece *The Inferno of Wall Street* (1877), and the musical compositions of Anton Webern, Pierre Boulez, Karlheinz Stockhausen, and John Cage.

How, then, did this recovery project work in practice? The concrete poems in Augusto's first book *Poetamenos* (Poetminus), were, interestingly, not iconic at all but fused Mallarméan spacing, Joycean pun and paragram, and the Poundian ideogram with Webern's notion (in *Klangfarbenmelodie*) that musical notes have their own colors. Plate 1, from *Poetamenos* (1953), shows the third color poem, "Lygia Fingers."[36]

This love poem juxtaposes the "red" title word with green, yellow, blue, and purple word groups to create a dense set of repetitions with variations and contrasts. The need for translation is minor here, since Augusto himself has invented a multilingual poetics that curiously anticipates twenty-first-century "translational" poetics. "Lygia" contains English, Italian, German, and Latin words and phrases, and it bristles with puns and double entendres. Thus *finge* ("feints" or "tricks") in line 1 becomes *finge/rs* (line 2). Do Lygia's fingers play tricks? The third and fourth lines confirm this possibility with the anagram *digital* and *dedat illa[grypho]*. As Sergio Bessa has explained, in lines 3–4 Augusto deconstructs the Portuguese verb *datilografar* (to typewrite) in order to insert his beloved's name into the scene of writing: *grypho*, moreover, can be read both as "glyph" and "griffin."[37] By the time we reach line 5, Lygia has morphed into a *lynx*, a feline creature (*felyna*), but also a daughter figure (*figlia*), who makes, in a shift from Italian to Latin, *me felix* (me happy). Note too that "Lygia" contains as paragram the English suffix *-ly* (repeated five times, twice color coded so as to stand out from the word in which it is embedded)—a suffix that functions as teaser here, given that the adjective it modifies (happily? deceptively? treacherously? generously?) is wholly indeterminate. The German phrase *so lange so* in line 8 puns on Solange Sohl, whose name Augusto, as he tells it, had come across in a newspaper poem and had celebrated as the ideal beloved in the Provençal manner *ses vezer* (without seeing her) in his 1950 poem "O Sol por Natural."[38] In line 10, the second syllable of Lygia morphs into Italian to give us *gia la sera sorella*—"already evening, sister," where *sorella* may be the addressee or an epithet for *sera*, the longed-for evening. The poem then concludes with the English words *so only lonely tt-* and then the solitary red letter *l*, recapitulating the address to Lygia, but this time reduced to the whisper or tap of *tt* and a single liquid sound.

```
lygia          finge
       rs      ser
               digital
               dedat  illa(grypho)
lynx lynx                              assim
          mãe  felyna   com    ly
          figlia  me  felix  sim  na  nx
       seja:      quando   so  lange  so
ly
gia     la      sera     sorella
                         so  only lonely tt-

l
```

Plate 1. Augusto de Campos, "Lygia" (1953). From *Poetamenos* (São Paulo: Edições Invenção 1973). Reprinted by permission of the author.

PORTA-RETRATOS:

GERTRUDE STEIN
AUGUSTO DE CAMPOS

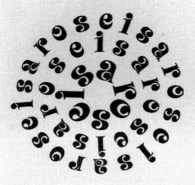

EDITORA NOA NOA

Plate 2. Augusto de Campos, cover from *Gertrude Stein's Porta-Retratos* (Santa Catarina: Editora Noa Noa, 1989). Reprinted by permission of the author.

To recapitulate: in this and related poems in *Poetamenos*, what Umberto Eco called the "iconic fallacy" continues to be operative, but here it is made reflexive and subversive—as if to say that representation must itself be called into question. And indeed, issues of iconicity or even spatial design—striking as that design surely is—are subordinated to the poem's overall verbivocovisual composition, all of whose materials have a signifying function. Pound's familiar distinction between *melopoeia, phanopoeia,* and *logopoeia* is applicable here, but note that *phanopoeia* is transferred from the realm of representation (e.g., the word or word group as effective "image" of X or Y) to that of the materiality of the poem: its sound (emphasized by color) and its visual appearance on the page. *Logopoeia,* the dance of the intellect among words, occurs throughout, and it is *melopoeia* that dominates: I have already talked of the *lygia–finge–digital–illa gryphe–lynx lynx–figlia* thread; consider also the echo of *so lange so* in *sorella* and then in *so only lonely,* the spacing further drawing out these word-notes. "Lygia" thus emerges as a troubadour lyric made new: the time frame of the *aubade* or *planh* gives way to the spatial-aural construct of this amorous *Klangfarbenmelodie.* The love song, moreover, nicely ironizes its conventional subject matter: Lygia, both lynx and digital, has her own tricks, and in any case the figure of Solange Sohl looms in the background.

The next step—and we find it in the work of both Augusto and Haroldo de Campos—was the large-scale translation, more properly, in Haroldo's words, *transcreation,*[39] that included works from the *Iliad* (Haroldo) and Arnaut Daniel (Augusto), from Goethe and Hölderlin to August Stramm and Kurt Schwitters (Haroldo and Augusto), to Rimbaud, Hopkins, and e. e. cummings (Augusto), from essays on Hegel, Christian Morgenstern, and Bertolt Brecht (Haroldo), to the "rhythmic criticism," as Augusto calls it, the "ventilated prose" or *prosa porosa* used in Augusto's riffs on Lewis Carroll, Gertrude Stein, Duchamp, and Cage in *O Anticritico* (1986). Together, Haroldo and Augusto have given us an artist's book called *Panaroma do "Finnegans Wake,"* which contains translations of selected fragments from the *Wake,* together with critical and scholarly commentary and artwork.[40]

The poetics of such "translation" has been described by Haroldo as follows:

> Writing today in the Americas as well as in Europe will mean, more and more, as far as I can see it, rewriting, remasticating. Writers of a monological, "logocentric" mentality—if they still exist and persist in that mentality—must realize that it will become more and more impossible to write the "prose of the world" without considering at least some reference point, the differences of these "ex-centrics," in the same time Barbarians (for belonging to a peripheral so-called underdeveloped

world) and Alexandrians (for making "guerilla" incursions into the very heart of the Library of Babel).[41]

The texts that come out of this program are very much artworks in their own right. The *Panaroma*, for example, takes as one of its epigraphs the phrase "to beg for a bite in our bark Noisdanger" from the *Wake* and provides an anagram on *Noigandres*, thus reminding readers of the link between Joyce and Pound. The translated fragments, many of them quite short, emphasize the linguistic and poetic side of Joyce's work at the expense of its narrative, mythic analogues. And the illustrations sprinkled throughout the text are themselves like abstractions from concrete poems, letters and ideograms arranged in new ways (figure 3.8). As a result, *Panaroma* is less a translation *of* Joyce than it is a found text, a transposition taking on its own life. Indeed, from here, it is a short step to Haroldo's own *Galaxias*.

Another example of such transcreation may be found in Augusto's version of Gertrude Stein's *Porta-Retratos* (Santa Catarina, Brazil: Editora Noa Noa, 1989). The portrait on the cover (reprinted as the frontispiece), *uma rosa para Gertrude* (plate 2), was made in 1988.[42] In his preface, Augusto admits that he came to Stein rather late, that in his youth he accepted Joyce's and Pound's hostile estimate of her work and has only recently come to realize how astonishing her verbal compositions really are. What interests him especially, Augusto notes, is Stein's emphasis, in "Composition as Explanation," on the "continuous present." His red "rose," made of three concentric circles, beautifully enacts this concept. The sentence "A rose is a rose is a rose . . ." does not begin or end anywhere: begin reading the concentric circles wherever you like and the clause is read as continuing. Then, too, the sequence "roseisarose" contains a paragram on *eis*—Portuguese for "here is." Here, indeed, is the rose itself. In English Stein's sentence remains linear, a one-directional sequence followed by a period. In his visual variant Augusto has found a way to apply Stein's two other two principles from "Composition as Explanation" as well: "beginning again and again" and "using everything." His cover ideogram thus provides the needed context for the translations inside: "A Portrait of One: Harry Phelan Gibb," "If I Told Him," "Georges Hugnet," and "Identity: A Tale."

Meanwhile—and this is another form of transcreation—Haroldo was engaging in theoretical projects that similarly consolidated the position of the *arrière-garde*. In *Ideograma*, a book that has gone through three editions since its first appearance in 1977, Haroldo gives us a translation of Ernest Fenollosa's famous "The Chinese Written Character as a Medium for Poetry,"

Figure 3.8. Augusto de Campos, page from *Panaroma do "Finnegans Wake"* (São Paulo: Editora Perspectiva, 1971), 36–37. Reprinted by permission of the author.

which had such a decisive influence on Ezra Pound. Haroldo's purpose, however, is not merely to reproduce or enlarge on Fenollosa's argument but, on the contrary, to submit it to theoretical scrutiny. Indeed, his own long chapter, "Poetic Function and the Ideogram," is perhaps a more cogent critique than any we have to date in English of a notion that Pound himself accepted at face value: namely, that in the Chinese language words are much closer to things than in English, that the "pictorial appeal" of the ideogram makes Chinese a more "poetic" language than the Western ones, characterized as they are by a high degree of abstraction.

Haroldo counters that, first of all, "in ordinary use Chinese readers treat ideograms in the same way as users of alphabetical languages treat script, as conventionalized symbols, without any longer seeing in them the visual metaphor—the visible etymology—which so impressed Fenollosa." More important, "The Chinese Written Character," at least as adapted by Pound, displays an improper understanding of what Roman Jakobson called the *poetic function*:

> Whereas for the referential use of language it makes no difference whether the word *astre* ("star") can be found within the adjective *desastreux* ("disastrous") or the noun *desastre* ("disaster") . . . for the poet this kind of "discovery" is of prime relevance. In poetry, warns Jakobson, any *phonological coincidence is felt to mean semantic kinship* . . . in an overall fecundating process of pseudoetymology or poetic etymology. . . .
>
> What the Chinese example enhanced for Fenollosa was the homological and homologizing virtue of the *poetic function*.[43]

Haroldo will later complicate his theory of meaning by incorporating Charles Peirce and Derrida, but for our purposes here, the Jakobson reference is central for an understanding not only of Fenollosa but of concrete poetry itself. The Cratylian argument, we can now see, is not a "fallacy" in the sense Caroline Bayard took it to be one, for the whole point is that poetry *is* that discourse in which *astre* and *desastre* belong together, even if in ordinary discourse there is no meaningful relationship between the two. Both Augusto and Haroldo de Campos, like Oyvind Fahlströhm and such other concretists as Ian Hamilton Finlay and Ernst Jandl, understood this distinction. The iconic aspect of concrete poetry, emphasized in the early stages by Gomringer and Max Bense, was always subordinate to the necessity for relational structure, whereby, to enlarge on Jakobson's thesis, any phonological or visual coincidence is felt to mean semantic kinship. In this sense the material is the meaning. Fenollosa—or at least Fenollosa-Pound, as Haroldo recognizes—was onto something important, but by naturalizing the ideogram, and thus the image, he assumed that word and thing could be one.

Haroldo's "rear-guard" operation vis-à-vis the early twentieth-century avant-garde is thus pivotal: indeed, it paves the way for Haun Saussy's 2008 critical edition of *The Chinese Written Character*, an edition that demonstrates incontrovertibly that Pound largely—and willfully—misread Fenollosa, even as that "misreading" of Chinese ideogrammicity became the gospel that guided many later poets in Pound's wake.[44] More important, Haroldo's understanding of how the materiality of the signifier really could work in the new poetics made it possible for him to write his long hypnotic poem *Galáxias* (1984), which the poet himself described as follows:

> An audiovideotext, videotextogram, the *galaxies* situate themselves on the border between prose and poetry. In this kaleidoscopic book there's an epic, narrative—mini-stories that articulate and dissolve themselves like the "suspense" of a detective novel . . . but the image remains, the vision or calling of the epiphanic. . . . This permutational book has, as its semantic backbone, a recurrent yet always varied theme all along: travel as a book and the book as travel. . . . Two *formants*, in italics, the initial one (beginning-end: "and here I begin") and the final one (end-beginning-new beginning), encompass the game of moveable pages, interchangeable in their reading, where each fragment introduces its "difference," but contains, in itself, like a watermark, the image of the entire book.[45]

Haroldo's dense network of verbal and sonic echoes, whose first "galaxy" begins with the words *e começo aqui e meço aqui este começo e recomeço e remeço e arremess*o (translated into French as *et ici je commence et ici je me lance et ici j'avance ce commencement*), marks, as critics, myself included, have noted,[46] a major bridge between Khlebnikov's "Invocation by Laughter," with its variations on the morpheme *smekh* on the one hand and the bravura morphemic variations of Ernst Jandl and later Christian Bök on the other,[47] with *Finnegans Wake* and Gertrude Stein's *How to Write* providing additional models for the text's larger articulation.

Galáxias is thus, as Haroldo himself put it, a limit text—the logical culmination of the concretist program. The other possibility—and I come back now to my beginning—is the electronic. In 1997, when digital poetry was still in its infancy, Augusto began to produce, for the Casa das Rosas in São Pãolo, electronic constellations in which meaning is produced both spatially and temporally, both kinetically and musically. The most elaborate of these is probably "SOS," his 1983 "expoema" now set, so to speak, to digital music.[48] In his *Anthologie despoesia* Jacques Donguy has produced the 1983 text in both Portuguese and French and provided a transcription of the Portuguese, which I give here in English:

ego eu ya ich io je yo I	ego eu ya ich io je yo I
sós pós nós	alone after we
que faremos apos?	what will we do afterwards?
sem soi sem mãe sem pai	without sun without mother without father
a noite que anoitece	in the night that becomes night
vagaremos sem voz	we will go roaming without voice
silencioso	silently
SOS	SOS

Augusto's note reads, "A centripetal voyage toward the dark hole of the unknown. From the ego-trip (the personal pronoun of the first person singular in different languages) to the SOS-trip. To the enigma of the after-life."[49]

The stationary concrete poem is extremely effective as the eye moves from the outer circle of those first-person pronouns into the eye of the storm "SOS." But it cannot compare to the electronic version, which uses animated text and sound. In "SOS" the words first appear as stars in the black night, against the background of discordant musical phrases and ambient sounds, and then disappear again as Augusto declaims the words, bringing in, in time for the third visual circle, a second reader, his son Cid, the two voices producing a kind of counterpoint in a series of verbal rounds of repetition and variation as the wheel of words starts turning, circle by circle. The sounds become more and more ominous until in the final moment of the "bomb" explodes in the center, the yellow circle spreads out to the margins, *SOS* appearing in huge black letters on yellow ground. Quickly the image bursts and dissolves into a black hole. What will we, who are alone, do afterward? Then, too, "SOS" contains a pun on *eso es* (that is): that, so to speak, is the human condition.

As an electronic poem, SOS, like such related works as "cidade-city-cité" and "ininstante" (both 1999), obviously has an iconic dimension. The spinning circles of words represent the planets spinning out of control as doomsday nears. But the poem's iconicity would not add up to much were it not for that central pun on *SOS*—at once the classic distress symbol as relayed in Morse Code and, with an accent over the *o*, the Portuguese adjective, in plural form, for *only* or *alone. Sós*, moreover, rhymes with *pós* (after). The black hole that awaits us in Augusto's poem is a terrifying image, especially in its verbivocovisual dimension.

Like "Lygia," "SOS" retains such traditional poetic features as pun, symbol, and rhyme: its language, moreover, is the poet's invention. But many of the "clip-poems" and later digital experiments are essentially found texts—a word, say, seen on a billboard or computer screen is reconstructed to pro-

Figure 3.9. Augusto de Campos, "REVƎЯ" (1970).
From *Equivocábulos* (São Paulo, 1970). Reprinted
by permission of the author.

duce poetic effect. Figure 3.9 shows Augusto de Campos's one-word poem
"REVƎЯ."[50]

The title means "to see again" or "to review," with a pun on the French
rever, to dream. But far from containing dream imagery, visual or verbal, Augusto's digital poem consists of no more than the word *REVƎЯ*, a mirror
image around the central *V*, itself alternately silhouetted in black against
a double blue and green band and a larger red and green one. The red and
green bands move to fill the whole screen, first one and then the other, but
the word REVƎЯ shoots out like a noisy rocket, one letter at a time, repeatedly demanding our attention. The piece continues indefinitely until the
reader clicks it to stop. No undisturbed sleep, it seems, for the viewer, who
is forced to watch the formation of the single word REVƎЯ. No escape from
the eternal WORD, noisily intruding on our contemplation of "pure" color.
REVƎЯ: will it NEVER go away, will it play out for-EVER? A Cratylist, moreover, could hardly help noticing the presence of EVE in the poet's green garden.

In dreams begin responsibilities. "REVƎЯ" positions itself against all
those avant-garde dream poems from Rimbaud's "Le bateau ivre" to John
Berryman's *Dream Songs*, abjuring the semantic density of these lyrics even
as it slyly spins out its own. Then, too, Augusto's recent digital poems cast
an ironic eye on the poet's earlier stationary works: "REVƎЯ" does so by its
very title, and "SOS" makes use of the *pós/vós/sós* rhyme to call into question
the poet's earlier concrete book *Pós-Tudo* (Post-everything).[51] To view these
and the whole corpus of concrete poems, sound recordings, debates, manifestos, interviews, broadsides, book designs at the newly founded site of the
Academy of Culture (Basel), called *poesia concreta o projecto verbivocovisual*,
is to have the sense that this particular poetic movement is only now, half a
century after its inception, coming into its own.

4

Writing through Walter Benjamin: Charles Bernstein's "Poem including History"

The events surrounding the historian, and
in which he himself takes part, will underlie
his presentation in the form of a text written
in invisible ink. The history which he lays
before the reader comprises, as it were,
the citations occurring in this ext, and it is
only these citations that occur in a manner
legible to all. *To write history thus means to cite
history.* It belongs to the concept of citation,
however, that the historical object in each
case is torn from its context.

Walter Benjamin

If everything is allowed, nothing is possible.

Jean Ricardou[1]

The French translation of the Brazilian poet Haroldo de Campos's 1984 "Concrete" book *Galáxias* contains a preface by Jacques Roubaud called "Sables, syllabes"—itself a kind of prose poem that bears remarkable similarities to de Campos's own work.[2] *Galáxias*, as its author described it in a 1977 essay, "was conceived as an experiment in doing away with limits between poetry and prose, projecting the larger and more suitable concept of *text* (as a *corpus* of words with their textual *potentials*. . . . The *text* is defined as a 'flux of signs,' without punctuation marks or capital letters, flowing uninterruptedly across the page, as a *galactic* expansion. Each page by itself makes a 'concretion,' or autonomously coalescing body, inter-changeable with any other page for reading purposes. There are 'semantic vertebrae' which unify the whole."[3]

The function of the "galaxy" or "constellation" as "limit text" is both verbal and visual: de Campos's strophes (each page contains one long block of "prose" with jagged right margins) are built on what we might call hyper-repetition; they permutate a carefully selected set of syllables, words, and phrases whose "verbivocovisual"[4] echo-structure recalls *Finnegans Wake* as well as such Gertrude Stein compositions as "Regular Regularly in Narrative," in *How to Write*.[5]

"Sables, syllabes," with its rhyming, anagrammatic title—a title that regards each syllable as a unique grain of sand—works in similar ways: Jacques Roubaud's elegiac homage to his friend of many decades has fourteen five- and six-line strophes that begin and end in midsentence: only strophe 1, with its opening "En ce temps-là," recalling Blaise Cendrars's *Prose du Transsibérien*, and strophe 14, with its memory of first reading, some twenty-five years earlier, "the first syllables . . . of GALAXIES," exhibit anything like closure.

The monologue begins with an image from the narrator's past, some twenty years earlier, an early morning street scene. From the window of his room on the rue de la Harpe in the 5th *arrondissement*, Roubaud suddenly sees, directly across the narrow street, in the sunlit window of the Hôtel du Levant at number 18, the unanticipated figure of his friend Haroldo and hails him. *Rue*, *hôtel*, *temps*, *fenêtre*, *lumière*, and especially the punning *levant*— these words, along with precise names, dates, and street numbers, repeat and permutate so as to heighten the sense of presence and produce a further memory, prompted by a photograph of Haroldo taken during a poetry festival in Provence: the bearded Haroldo emerging from the waters of the Mediterranean Sea, rather like Odysseus some twenty-seven centuries earlier found on the shore of the wine-dark sea by the young and innocent princess Nausicaa. Haroldo is remembered rising from the surf, spitting out "des syllabes d'Arnaut Daniel"; indeed, as Roubaud now suggests, shifting in mid-phrase from French to Italian to English, Haroldo is "le forgeron de syllabes" (the blacksmith of syllables), "le fabbro" (the maker), "le poète le plus barbu, le plus écumeux le plus syllabeux le plus idéogrammatique, le plus idéodrammatique le plus pound/poundien . . . pounding upon our ears" ("the most bearded, the most foamy, the most syllabous, the most ideogrammatic, the most ideodrammatic, the most pound/poundian . . . pounding upon our ears"). And "Sables, syllabes" ends with the memory:

je me retrouve parlant avec lui de ce qui nous occupe tous les deux
la po&

sie et dans la po&sie les moments qui sont pour nous les premiers du commencement et du recommencement les moment des cansos des troubadours et les moments de la voix japonaise ancienne qui se rejoignent et se mêlent et également
à des milliers de kilomètres nous frappent nous martèlent nous saisissent nous
persuadent nous émulent enfants de 'l'ère à pound' que nous sommes quand je
revois haroldo après une deux années quand nous parlons ensemble de ce qui
nous occupe nous préoccupe et n'en finit pas de

commencer et recommencer à nous inquièter nous révulser nous enthousiasmer
nous décourager nous stimuler nous replonger dans l'écume indéfinement émi-
etée dans les grains de sable innombrablement énumérés de la lumiére quand
tout cela je me souviens et me ressouviens et retrouve ce moment inoubliable ce
moment de poésie d'il y a vingt-cinq ans où j'ai vue sur la page et commencé le
commencement de lire les premières syllabes les premières lignes immenses et
longues et serrées des GALAXIES

i can see myself talking with him about that which occupies us
both po-&

try and within po-eh-try the moments that are for us the first of the beginning
and rebeginning the moments of the songs of the troubadours and the moments
of the ancient japanese voice that merge and mix equally even thousands of ki-
lometres apart strike us pound us grab us persuade us pronounce us the children
of the pound era that we are when i once again see haroldo after a year or two
when we talk to one another of that which occupies us and preoccupies us and
never ceases to

begin and rebegin to upset us disgust us excite us discourage us stimulate us re-
plunge us into the foam indefinitely dissipating the grains of sand innumerably
enumerated by the light when all this i remember and again remember that un-
forgettable moment that moment of poetry of twenty-five years ago when i saw
on the page and began the beginning of reading the first syllables the first lines
immense and long and taut of the GALAXIES

Note that this passage is designed as a visual as well as verbal composition,
the variants of *commencer* and the prefix *re-* creating a dense graphic field
that alludes to the opening page of the French version of the *Galaxies* itself:

et ici je commence et ici je me lance et ici j'avance ce commencement et je relance
et j'y pense quand on vit sous l'espèce du voyage ce n'est pas le voyage qui compte
mais le commencement du et pour ça je mesure

and here i begin and here i throw myself in and here i advance this beginning and i throw myself in again and i think about it when one sees beneath the sort of voyage it is not the voyage that counts but the beginning of it and for that i count

And there are other visual devices like the line-break that splits up "po&sie," and especially the paragram on "page," which takes us back to "la plage" and its "grains de sable." Indeed, what unites such improbable poets as Haroldo de Campos and himself, Roubaud records, is their derivation from the troubadours on the one hand and Japanese haiku art on the other, the two coming together in the poetry of Ezra Pound.

It is a fascinating *moment de la poésie*, a rapprochement between two seemingly divergent aesthetics: French Oulipo and Brazilian concrete—movements that on the face of it could hardly be more different. In its original formation in the mid-1950s, let's recall, the term *concrete poetry* referred to those poetic texts in which meaning could not be separated from the text's visual form—the distribution of verbal units, whether letters, morphemes, or whole words—on the page. In concrete poetry, as Augusto and Haroldo de Campos and Decio Pignatari put it in their "Pilot Plan" of 1958, "graphic space acts as structural agent."[6] And further: the concrete poem is usually short. "Its most obvious feature," writes Rosmarie Waldrop, "is reduction. . . . Both conventions and sentence are replaced by spatial arrangement."[7] Hence the terms *ideogram* and *constellation*, used by Eugen Gomringer, Oyvind Fahlström, Max Bense, and the Brazilian Noigandres group to describe their poetic texts.

The Oulipo (Ouvroir de Littérature potentielle), which dates from the same period—it started in 1960—said nothing about length: indeed, among the most important Oulipo works is Georges Perec's great novel *La vie mode d'emploi*. Although lyric has always been central to Oulipo concerns—its founders François Le Lionnais and Raymond Queneau invented important poetic constraints—the successes of the movement have largely been in narrative: witness, aside from Perec's own great novels, those of Jacques Roubaud and Harry Mathews. Again, Oulipo differs from concretism in that in the former visual format does not necessarily play a central role. On the contrary, Oulipo is primarily a *literary* movement; its aim, as Roubaud puts it in an introductory essay, "is to invent (or reinvent) restrictions of a formal nature [*contraintes*] and propose them to enthusiasts interested in composing literature." The *potential* of constraints is more important than their actual execution. Most important, "a text written according to a constraint describes the constraint."[8] A classic example, which I cited earlier, is Perec's lipogrammatic novel *La disparition*, where the disappearance of the vowel *e* points to the disappearance of *eux* (them) — those expunged by the Nazis in World War II. But constraints do not always function so thematically; more often they are intensely intertextual, as when Michel Bénabou and Roubaud's sonnet "Les chats" fuses the hemistychs of Baudelaire's "Chats" and Rimbaud's "Bateau ivre" to create "perfect" alexandrines that wittily ironize these great nineteenth-century originals.[9] In their 2009 essay "The Challenge of Constraint" Jan Baetens and Jean-Jacques Poucel give this useful definition:

> A constraint is a self-chosen rule (i.e., different from the rules that are imposed by the use of a natural language or those of convention); it is also a rule that is used systematically throughout the work . . . both as a compositional and a reading device. Constraints are not ornaments: for the writer, they help generate the text; for the reader, they help make sense of it.[10]

Concretism, let's recall, was the product of what Deleuze and Guattari have called a minor literature: it was born after World War II on such peripheries as Brazil and Scotland, Switzerland and Sweden, rather than, as was the case with Oulipo, in Paris, or other movements in any cultural capital. Its affinities were and are with the visual arts as well as with music: Webern's *Klangfarbenmelodie* and Cage's compositions were major models for the Brazilian concretists. Oulipo, by contrast, looks to mathematics for its parameters. Many of its original members, including Roubaud, were mathematicians, and some of its key constraints depend on differential equations. Concretism is related to the senses, Oulipo more to the intellect. Again, concrete poets — Ian Hamilton Finlay, Oyvind Fahlström — often work in isolation, whereas Oulipo is a workshop that depends on admission to membership and regular meetings. Indeed, as Roubaud puts it, "The Oulipo's work is collaborative, and its product — proposed constraints and their illustrations — are attributed to the group, even if certain constraints are invented by individuals."[11]

Yet behind these obvious differences there is a common thread. Take, for starters, the rejection, by both movements, of what Waldrop refers to as the "transparency of the word."[12] In the very first concrete manifesto, Falhström's 1953 "Hipy papy bthuthdththuthda bthuthdy," we read: "It remains . . . to re-endow form with its own set of criteria," the central axiom of poetry being that "like-sounding words belong together." The poet's task is thus to "KNEAD the linguistic material: this is what justifies the label concrete. Don't just manipulate the whole structure; begin rather with the smallest elements — letters, words. Recast the letters as in anagrams. Repeat letters, within words; throw in alien words."[13]

This notion of the nontranslatability and irreducibility of poetic language is echoed by Roubaud: "In modes of speech other than poetry, meaning must be considered public, ideally transmissible; that which is not transmissible is not part of the meaning. In the case of poetry, it's the exact opposite—which is not to say that poems do not contain a transmissible meaning; if there is one, it's there as a surplus."[14]

This emphasis on "words you can't see through" has as its corollary the elimination of ego. "Let's say goodbye," says Fahlström, "to all systematic or spontaneous depiction of private psychological, contemporary cultural or universal problems."[15] Students of Oulipo will recognize this rejection of spontaneous invention and creativity as the central axiom governing the use of constraints: it is the constraint, the Oulipians have argued from the first, that forces the poet to give up an illusory artistic "freedom" in favor of what Roubaud calls "the freedom of the difficulty mastered."[16]

The constraint, we should note, is not necessarily verbal. "In order for there to be an Oulipian constraint," writes the poet Jacques Jouet, "an explicit procedure must be used—a formal axiom whose implications, whose deductive of events—will create the text. The constraint is the problem; the text the solution."[17] One of Jouet's own inventions, for example, is the *poème de métro*, whose constraint is defined in its first exemplar, "Qu'est-ce qu'un poème de métro?"[18]

J'écris, de temps à autre, des poèmes de métro. Ce poème en est un.
Voulez-vous savoir ce qu'est un poème de métro?
Admettons que la réponse soit oui. Voici donc ce qu'est un poème de métro.
Un poème de métro est un poème composé dans le métro, pendant le temps
    d'un parcours.
Un poème de métro compte autant de vers que votre voyage compte de stations
    moins un.
Le premier vers est composé dans votre tête entre les deux premières stations
    de votre voyage (en comptant la station de départ).
Il est transcrit sur le papier quand la rame s'arrête à la station trois. Et ainsi de
    suite.
Il ne faut pas transcrire quand la rame est en marche.
Il ne faut pas composer quand la rame est arrêtée.
Le dernier vers du poème est transcrit sur le quai de votre dernière station.
Si votre voyage impose un ou plusieurs changements de ligne, le poème
    comporte deux strophes ou davantage.
Si par malchance la rame s'arrête entre deux stations, c'est toujours un moment
    délicat de l'écriture d'un poème de métro.

From time to time, I write subway poems. This poem being an example.

Do you want to know what a subway poem consists of? Let's suppose you do.

Here, then, is what a subway poem consists of.

A subway poem is a poem composed during a journey in the subway.

There are as many lines in a subway poem as there are stations in your journey, minus one.

The first line is composed mentally between the first two stations of your journey (counting the station you got on at).

It is then written down when the train stops at the second station.

The second line is composed mentally between the second and the third stations of your journey.

It is then written down when the train stops at the third station. And so on.

You must not write anything down when the train is moving.

You must not compose when the train has stopped.

The poem's last line is written down on the platform of the last station.

If your journey necessitates one or more changes of line, the poem will then have two or more stanzas.

An unscheduled stop between two stations is always an awkward moment in the writing of the subway poem. (translated by Ian Monk)

Such a "poetic" procedure, Jouet claims, has a particular advantage. The metro acts as metronome. "It is a ruled paper. . . . The poem alternates the written (black) line with a blank (white) line. The metro alternates the light of the station stop with the darkness of the tunnel. The poem resembles the space-time of its composition."[19] This tongue-in-cheek account of the metro-poem's form-as-meaning echoes the concretist stress on construction—a construction always threatened, however, by the clinamen inherent in any given system: in this case, how to regard the potential moment when the train gets stuck between stations. Time to compose or time to write down? The metro-poem, in any case, is "a poem struggling against its own marginality—presence in the world, integration of the poem in repetitive everyday life; use of a place reputedly non-poetic."[20] This tongue-in-cheek incorporation of the "everyday" should not be confused, however, with such values as "spontaneity" and directness. As the Flemish poet-critic Jan Baetens puts it in an editorial for his journal *Formules*:

To write with the help of constraints is first of all a procedure that allows us to resist the weight of stereotypes. Literary speech that is not constrained, whether romantic or realist, whether it comes out of the direct expression of self or of the representation of the external world, inevitably runs the risk of falling into the trap of the commonplaces that come to us "spontaneously," especially when we think of writing "about ourselves." Language thinks us and so we must resist its insidious influence so as to rid ourselves of the crushing presence of the *déjà-dit*.[21]

To put it succinctly: *écrire à contraintes entrave le vouloir-dire* (to write using constraints impedes the longing to say something).[22] Thus in *Sables, syllabes*, Roubaud "says" nothing about the book for which he is ostensibly writing his preface, permitting the constraints chosen—the repeated citation of date, time, *arrondissement*, street number—to define the particular mode of composition that is Haroldo's.

Like the concretists, both Oulipo and the related Franco-Belgian Formules group (which has suggested that the decision to write in French—a foreign or at least second language—is itself a valuable constraint)[23] are opposed to such distinctions as the opposition of modernism to postmodernism; there is only, in the present as in the past, the drive to exceed the acceptable limits of discourse.[24] Indeed, in both Oulipo and concretism the recovery of the past—both as source material and as foundational text—is central. Again, given the emphasis in both Oulipo and Concretism on intertextuality, the enemy is not only, as might be expected, the Romantic expressivist lyric but also the poetry of Surrealism. The Surrealists, as Warren Motte notes, "erected the aleatory and the psychological construct based on it, the unconscious as a means to transcendence"[25]—a drive diametrically opposed to Oulipo intentionality and discipline. Augusto de Campos voices exactly the same objection, adding that despite their claim to represent the unconscious, the Surrealists use "normal grammatical phrases, a very conventional structure"; they do not "de-autonomize language structures."[26] Surrealist innovation, in other words, is held to be thematic rather than formal and material: it does not operate at the level of word formation, paragram, or syntax. And so the Oulipians, like the concretists, bypass their Surrealist contemporaries to go back to Duchamp, and beyond Duchamp to Mallarmé. Indeed it is the poetics of *Un coup de dés* that, so to speak, gives permission both to Oulipo and to concrete poetry. And further, the Formules group has positioned itself even closer to concretism in its experiments with hybrid and cross-media works. For whereas Oulipo makes a clear distinction between itself and Oupeinpo (for painters) or Oumupo (for musicians), Baetens, Bernard Schiavetta, Jacques Jouet, and others are now trying to elide these clear lines of demarcation.

Rules, moreover, were always more important to concretists than might appear to be the case when one looks at their early visual inventions like

Gomringer's "silencio." In Oyvind Fahlström's remarkable radio collage called *Birds in Sweden* (1962), with its mix of actual bird calls, invented language, and recyclings of Edgar Allan Poe's "The Raven," the orchestration of sounds is portrayed visually in a series of numerically organized charts. In Ernst Jandl's concrete poems—for example, "der und die," which Charles Bernstein "translates" in *Shadowtime*—grids are often prominent, in this case a grid restricted to common three-letter words, generated by permutation and addition (figure 4.1). And as Inês Oseki-Dépré and David Jackson have shown, de Campos's *Galáxias* is based on elaborate mathematical and musical schemes.[27] Indeed, in Oulipo, as in concretism, the choice of constraint is designed to produce poems in which the semantic is conveyed primarily by the visual and phonic elements. Here form really *is* meaning, in keeping with the early avant-garde doctrines of, say, Velimir Khlebnikov or of the Russian Formalist theorist Roman Jakobson. Then, too, in both Oulipo and concretism intertextuality and appropriation play a major role: in Roubaud's elegy *Quelque chose noir*,[28] for example, the visual format of the strophes is determined by the constraint—the application of the number 9—which relates Roubaud's poetic sequence to its source text, Dante's *Vita Nuova*.

"Oulipian texts," writes Adelaide M. Russo, "are the literature of a belated age, an age in which texts are composed on word processors . . . in which the notion of originality has been replaced by a doctrine of citationality. The very way in which these texts are constituted, often using another text as matrix or point of departure for the Oulipian exercise, reflects an economy based on production through recycling."[29] Our own poets have used recycling to produce complex and intriguing works of unoriginal genius. Language poets from Lyn Hejinian and Steve McCaffery to Joan Retallack and Tina Darragh experimented with constraint-governed citational texts. It was in the next or Conceptual generation, however, that constraint, visual as well as verbal, became central: consider the work of Christian Bök and Caroline Bergvall, Kenneth Goldsmith and Craig Dworkin. Dworkin's "Strand," for example, adapts the Cage mesostic rule to "write through" Wittgenstein's *On Certainty*, using as the key word string the name of the poem's dedicatee, Anh Quynh Bui. And in a more Perecian vein, in her performance piece *Gong*, Bergvall has used constraints to generate a set of "ordinary" declarative sentences that "describe" particular individuals in minute—and ultimately absurd—detail.[30]

The text I want to consider here, however, marks what is perhaps a point of departure in its improbable fusion of Oulipo constraint, concretism, and citationality in its application of a genre seemingly quite alien to such con-

der und die

```
kam der und die kam und die kam vor ihm ins tal und
das war der ort und die sah hin und her und tat das
oft und war müd und bös und wie eis und sah hin und
her bis der kam der ins tal kam und nun los und das
eis weg und der kam und der kam nah und kam ihr nah
und war bei ihr und war nah bei ihr und sah auf ihr
hin und her und die war wie für ihn war für ihn ist
was für ihn ist muß mit und den hut und wie der den
zog und zog aug bei aug auf ihr hin und her und ihr
kam der ist wie ein ist was das ist was das ist für
uns nun los und gib wie das eis weg süß und küß bis
ans end der uhr und tag aus aug und ohr weg nur gut
und naß und süß tau mit rum und nun los bot den arm
und gab ihm den und das ohr und das auf und süd und
ost und zog mit ihr mit ihm mit und das tor war los
und die tür und der tag weg mit eis und müd und wut
und hut und der ihr und die ihm und sog kuß aus kuß
und hob und lud sie auf das ist gut ist für uns und
los und ihn biß und der riß und zog und die ihn und
bot ihm naß und süß tau mit rum und sog was der und
der lag auf ihr und zog und tat und riß und biß und
sog und ihr arm und das auf süd und das ohr die tür
zur see und das amt aus und tot und wer vor mir ist
weg ost weg nur ich auf hin und her hin und hun her
hin her hin her bis rot und süß und wut die see ins
tal riß und goß und den ort naß und müd lag auf uns
```

E. J.

Figure 4.1. Ernst Jandl, "der und die." From *Reft and Light* (2009) © Rosmarie Waldrop.

cerns—namely, what Pound called with reference to his *Cantos*, "a poem including history," or, for that matter, a poem including biography. The highly distinctive text I have in mind is Charles Bernstein's 2005 libretto "about" Walter Benjamin's life and works called *Shadowtime*.

As a cofounder (with Bruce Andrews) of L=A=N=G=U=A=G=E, Bernstein is regularly cited as one of the key theorists of the Language movement, with its resistance to the then dominant notions of authorial presence, "natural" speech, and the ability of language to communicate prior thought and feeling. The thrust of Language poetry, as I have argued in various places,[31] was largely semantic: it concerned itself with how *meaning* is and is not produced, how *reference* works, how, in Bernstein's own words, "there are no thoughts outside of language."[32] In Poundian parlance, language poetry emphasized *logopoeia* rather than *phanopoeia* or *melopopeia*; indeed, this third term was under suspicion in a movement that claimed the "new sentence" as central to an avowed commitment to make poetry from prose, dismissing all established metric and stanzaic structures as inhibiting the forward thrust of the writing.

Yet we should remember that both Susan Howe and Steve McCaffery began their careers under the sign of concrete poetry and that Barrett Watten, Ron Silliman, and Bernstein himself looked to Jackson Mac Low's procedural texts as exemplars: in Silliman's *Tjanting*, for example, the number of words per sentence are generated by the Fibonacci sequence of numbers (1, 2, 3, 5, 8, 13, 21 . . .).[33] In "Hinge Picture" Bernstein himself wrote an homage to George Oppen, generating his stanzas "using an acrostic procedure (G-E-O-R-G-E-O-P-P-E-N), adapted from Mac Low, to select lines, in page sequence from the *Collected Poems*."[34] In *Girly Man* (Chicago, 2006), such list poems as "In Particular" and "Let's Just Say," as well as homophonic poems, ekphrases, and appropriated texts, mark a turn in Bernstein's work from the nonsemantic experiments of the 1980s and '90s to a more intertextual, formally aware, and we might say *literary* lyric. It is a tendency that comes to the fore in this poet's "thought opera" *Shadowtime*, in which appropriation, constraint, and concretist poetics come together in an astonishing ensemble.

A Poem including History

The choice of Walter Benjamin as the subject for the opera *Shadowtime* was made by its composer, Brian Ferneyhough. Benjamin's "understanding of the world largely in terms of allegory and epiphany," observed Ferneyhough in an interview for the *Guardian*, "lay very close to my enduring interest in codes of representation." Accordingly, when the composer approached Bernstein with the idea of an operatic treatment of Benjamin's conceptual domain, he proposed certain parameters:

> I laid out quite stringent numerical constraints—number of lines, number of syllables in a line and so on—for each unit of the text. . . . The most important

precondition, however, was my wish that *the final libretto would also be able to stand as an independently viable poetic work*. This seemed to me essential, if we were to do justice to the key re-representational aspect of the project. All this functioned perfectly—in fact the libretto of *Shadowtime* has just appeared as a book of poetry with Green Integer Press, Los Angeles.[35]

What did this mean in practice? Ferneyhough explains that he gave Bernstein "a series of more or less detailed diagrams from 1998–99 in which the seven-part overall layout, the internal subdivision of each of these parts and their aesthetic-dramatic significance is registered. . . . The work falls into two halves, hinging around the Portal to Hades / Las Vegas nightclub solo piano piece *Opus Contra Naturam*. This was always part of the architecture: any modification of this would seriously disbalance the whole." Accordingly, Bernstein, working with the set of musical constraints and overall musical-dramatic structure provided by the composer, was free to create a verbal text of his own—a text that, as the poet explained it, is "one acoustic element in the overall sonic constellation, a layer, not a foregrounded, articulated voice. Words, and words with meanings even if hidden are veiled, semantically active and allegorical."[36]

Many of us, when we attended the performance of the opera at Lincoln Center in summer 2005, were disappointed that we couldn't "catch" most of the words and certainly not their nuances, double-entendres, puns, anagrams, or paragrams. But if we think of Ferneyhough's opera not as a musical "translation" of the libretto but as a generative device, a series of musical constraints that governed the poetic invention, its function becomes clearer. Here is Bernstein's own account:

> The unintelligibility of the words is a basic condition of most of the opera. At the same time, the words are always there, always being articulated: so you get words that you can hear but not understand, or words that approach the condition of music. But they are still words and the words are bound to the meaning of each scene. . . . In a sense, the opera presents a marked translation of the words, just as the text presents a marked translation of motifs in Benjamin. (e-mail, June 30, 2005)

Now consider how this works. The standard way to write a poetic drama about an important literary figure like Benjamin would have been to proceed biographically, perhaps in the style of Brecht's *Galileo*, in a series of scenes revelatory of the hero's being vis-à-vis historical events and cultural conditions. And indeed, Bernstein's synopsis of scene 1 suggests that a Brechtian drama awaits us:

In September 1940, one step ahead of the Nazi invaders, Walter Benjamin fled France, making an arduous journey, on foot, over the Pyrenees mountains. He died the day after his arrival in Spain. . . .

The primary layer, "War Time," takes center stage. The setting is just over the French border, in the Pyrenees, at the hotel, Fonda de Francis, Portbou, Spain. The time is just before midnight, September 25, 1940. Benjamin has arrived at the hotel with his traveling companion Henny Gurland. The trip has been made more difficult by Benjamin's bad heart: every ten minutes of walking was followed by one minute of stopping. Benjamin's plan was to continue on to Lisbon, and from there to America. But the Innkeeper informs Benjamin and Gurland their transit visas have been voided and that they must return to France. . . . At center stage, the cruel Innkeeper gives the exhausted travelers the bad news, to Gurland's protests and Benjamin's despair. (*Shadowtime*, 18)

It sounds straightforward enough, but even this opening scene is highly stylized, the Innkeeper's simple commands punctuated at every other line by an address, in chiastic form, to the two principals:

I regret to inform you
Herr Benjamin, Frau Gurland
but I must inform you
Frau Gurland, Herr Benjamin
you will understand
Herr Benjamin, Frau Gurland
it is my duty to inform you
Frau Gurland, Herr Benjamin
that your transit visas
Herr Benjamin, Frau Gurland
your transit visas
Frau Gurland, Herr Benjamin
Are not valid (30–31)

And so on for another ten lines; and after the protests of Gurland and Benjamin, the refrain is repeated in a second speech that begins, "We are a nation of laws / Herr Benjamin, Frau Gurland" (35). But this "composition of place" soon collapses, giving way first to flashbacks (Benjamin and his young wife Dora in 1917, Benjamin in dialogue with his close friend the great writer on Jewish mysticism Gershom Scholem, and then with the poet Hölderlin), and soon the entire documentary frame is dissolved, Benjamin's "life" giving way to his own words, which are now "written through," ventriloquized, parodied, anagrammatized, riffed upon, rhymed, translated both literally and homophonically—in short, subjected to linguistic practices that, so to speak, lay bare the devices of Benjamin's own writings.[37]

The disappearance of "character" and "plot" is, of course, appropriate for a theorist for whom memory, as his American editor Peter Demetz noted long ago, "is a remarkable absence of people," whose imagination is spatial rather than historical. And Demetz asks:

> I wonder if it would be possible to listen to Benjamin in a musical rather than a literary way and to concentrate as if his individual writings were fragments of an inclusive score, on the thematic orchestration of his ideas and arguments. Benjamin works with a few intimate leitmotifs that fascinate him throughout his life, regardless of the particular stage of his ideological transformation. The threshold and the city, the *flâneur* and the archeologist of culture—these are a few of his elemental topoi and recurrent figures.[38]

It is this spatial imagination that prompts Bernstein's treatment, the particular irony in his appropriation of Benjamin's words being that this poet-philosopher-critic was himself, as we saw in the discussion of *The Arcades Project*, the ultimate citational writer.[39] What Benjamin wrote of Karl Kraus, for example, applies to his own work:

> To quote a word is to call it by its name. So Kraus's achievement exhausts itself at its highest level by making even the newspaper quotable. He transports it to his own sphere, and the empty phrase is suddenly forced to recognize that even in the deepest dregs of the journals it is not safe from the voice that swoops on the wings of the word to drag it from its darkness. . . . In the quotation that both saves and punishes, language proves the matrix of justice. It summons the word by its name, wrenches it destructively from its context, but precisely thereby calls it back to its origin. It appears, now with rhyme and reason, sonorously, congruously, in the structure of a new text. . . . In citation the two realms—of origin and destruction—justify themselves before language.[40]

Kraus, a great satirist with whom Bernstein might be fruitfully compared, understood, as did the Benjamin of the *Arcades Project* after him, that, in Richard Sieburth's words, one "cites the past not in order to reproduce it, but in order to reveal it, to literalize it, to lay bare its device by the alienating effect of quotation marks" (Sieburth, 31). But in *Shadowtime*, which shows at every turn its author's immersion in and familiarity with Benjamin's manifold writings, citation is complicated by its submission to numerical constraint, rhyming, soundplay, paragram, visual pun, and especially fragmentation, re-location, and the grafting of other German texts—from Heinrich Heine to

Ernst Jandl—onto the language of Benjamin, his name now pronounced with a hard fricative *j* rather than the German *y*-glide, so as to bring him into the American orbit. Ironically, then—and Bernstein's is a deeply ironic take on the Benjamin phenomenon—*Shadowtime*, at one level a libretto, whose performance as opera provides visual and musical complementarity for the verbal text, is, from another angle, a long lyric-dramatic poem that follows Benjamin's own aphorism: to write history is to cite history.

Consider scene 3, "The Doctrine of Similarity," which Bernstein summarizes as follows in the synopsis:

> "The Doctrine of Similarity" consists of thirteen short movements, sung by various groupings of the chorus of the Angels of History. Each of the movements reflects on the nature of history, time, and translation/transformation. The title comes from an essay by Benjamin with a similar name—"Doctrine of the Similar"—in which he considers the ways that the physical sounds of language echo or mimic the primordial structures of the cosmos. In the scene, various numeric patterns create reverberations within and between the text and music. The theme of temporality is explored musically by the use of canon forms throughout the scene. (*Shadowtime*, 20)

In an interview for the British online journal *The Argotist*, Bernstein adds:

> In the libretto, I have the angel of history say the opposite of what Benjamin writes in "The Concept of History." Benjamin writes that "the angel would like to stay, awaken the dead, and make whole what has been smashed." Our angels, in contrast, ask that we imagine no wholes from all that has been smashed. Because for me . . . it's very important not to imagine a totality but rather a multiplicity, the shards, and the sparks around the edges. We don't live in a Messianic moment, the scales have not fallen from our eyes, our seeing is double and triple not unitary. The Benjaminian "now time" (*Jetztzeit*) lets us hear the cathected material moment amidst the multiplicity of omnivalent vectors.[41]

Benjamin's "Doctrine of the Similar" mourns what it takes to be the contemporary "dying out of the mimetic faculty," the faculty of noting the direct similarities between natural and human phenomena, between, say, a human face and a constellation of stars. In our time, Benjamin posits, this "onomatopoeic mode of explanation" has given way to the development of *language* as carrier of the realm of "nonsensuous similarities."[42] "The most recent graphology," for example, "has taught us to recognize, in handwriting, images—or, more precisely, picture puzzles—what the unconscious of the writer conceals in his writing. . . . Script has thus become, like language, an archive of nonsensuous similarities, of nonsensuous correspondences." And further, "the nexus of meaning which resides in the sounds of the sentence is the basis from which something similar can become apparent out of a sound, flashing up in an instant."[43]

Benjamin's meditation on this "magical aspect" of language was completed in the very weeks (February 1933) of the Reichstag fire, which precipitated the final consolidation of Hitler's power and hence Benjamin's flight to Paris in March 1933. Read in this context, "Doctrine of the Similar" could hardly be a more puzzling text, pointing as it does to the persistent gap between Benjamin's private and public worlds, his mental life and the political reality. It is this gap Bernstein seizes upon in the "Amphibolies" of *Shadowtime*'s scene 3: an *amphiboly*, according to the OED, is "a phrase or sentence that can be read in two ways, usually because of the grammatical construction rather than the meaning of the words themselves." A philosophy website gives the following examples from newspaper headlines:

DRUNK GETS NINE MONTHS IN VIOLIN CASE

HIGH SCHOOL DROP OUTS CUT IN HALF

FARMER BILL DIES IN HOUSE

BRITISH LEFT WAFFLES ON FALKLAND ISLANDS

ENRAGED COW INJURES FARMER WITH AXE

STOLEN PAINTING FOUND BY TREE

INCLUDE YOUR CHILDREN WHEN BAKING COOKIES[44]

Bernstein's "amphibolies" are, of course, not just such simple double-entendres. In the first of the canons, as the poet refers to the individual units in keeping with their musical form, we have three poems of thirteen lines each, each line containing only prime numbers of words between 1 and 5. Here is "Amphibolies I (Walk Slowly)":

Walk slowly
and jump quickly
over
the paths into
the
briar. The
pricks are points on a
map
that take
you back behind the stares
where shadows are
thickest at
noon. (62)

This lyric is generally straightforward: it presents a choric representation of the protagonist's fears on the arduous mountain climb, the mind seizing on the similarity between the prickles of the briars and the points on his map. But in the next two lyrics (63–64), both homophonic versions of the first and structurally identical with it, a different "similarity" occurs:

Fault no lease
Add thump whimsy
aver
a sash onto
a
mire. The
sticks are loins on a
gap
not fake
rude facts remind a fear
tear tallow mar
missed case at
loom.

balk sulky
and hum prick fee
clover
an ash insure
at-
tire. The
flicks are joints on a
map
(nutmeg)
glue's knack refines the dare
near fallow bars
quickest latch
gone. (63–64)

Pure nonsense? The language of nonreferentiality carried to an extreme? Not really. For jumbled as these homophonic poems are, their vocabulary—"thump, "mire, "sticks, "gap, "rude facts," "fear, "tear tallow, mar" and "missed case" in 2 "balk sulky," "ant hum prick free," "clover," "nap," "dare," "near fallow bars," "latch," and "gone" in 3—acoustically render the traveler's trials even as they provide a brilliant send-up of Benjamin's "Doctrine of the Similar." If, after all, "the nexus of meaning which resides in the sounds of the sentence is the basis from which something similar can become apparent out of a sound,"[45] then the sound imitation of the homophonic version will convey the very meaning of the original: indeed, "add thump whimsy" and "ant hump prick free" give more graphic images of malaise than does "jump quickly." And the parallelism between the three poems is guaranteed by the numerical constraint of the prime numbers.

There are further variations. "Amphibolies II" (Canon 5), which comes a few pages later and begins "noon / at thickest / are shadows where," is a word-for-word mirror inversion of #1, concluding with "quickly jump and / slowly walk" (68). It yields further appropriate echoes like "take that / map" and the halting phraseology of "the briar / the / the paths into."

"Amphibolies III" (Canon 12), called "Pricks," uses a similar constraint, but now reversing #1 line by line rather than word for word:

Noon
thickest at
where shadows are
you back behind the stares (74)

and concluding with "walk slowly" to make a perfect round. And indeed, Benjamin and his friends do nothing so much as walk in circles.

In the performance itself the words are lost in the "extreme polyphony" produced by layers of musical sound. The libretto, however, adds the dimension of sight: these poems must be seen to be understood, the numerical constraints providing estrangement from the narrative, lines like "that take," "at- / tire," or "tear tallow mar" visually undermining what might otherwise be perceived as continuity. Or again, a rhyming line like "Bulk sulky" enacts the "Doctrine of the Similar" at yet another level, that of visual conjunction. Yet as the verbal reversals and homophonic echoes suggest, this landscape of similarities is in fact a world turned upside down. As was Benjamin's own world in 1933.

Between the three sets of amphibolies, Bernstein gives us some poignant variations. "Dust to Dusk" (64) has eleven words that complement the preceding eleven lines: "The leaves turn dark before the trees are shot with light," with its pun on "shot," suggesting imminent disaster. This poem has its echo in the later "Dusts to Dusks" (74), which reads, "The heavens turn dark before the trees are shot full of light"—a telling variation, for whereas the turning dark of the leaves merely connotes nightfall, the heavens' turning dark, before the lightning flash that follows, suggests cataclysm, doomsday.

There are further ingenious permutations. From the eleven lines of "Walk

Slowly" (63) and eleven words of "Dust to Dusk" (64) , we move in the third poem, "Cannot Cross," to an eleven-stanza ballad, alternating casual individual speech—"Don't want consolation/Just a ticket home" or "Knew a man once/Had no tongue/Walked in fog/Till the fog was gone"—to the more formal first-person plural refrain "It's been so long/Words cannot console us/Where there is sorrow/We cannot cross" (64–65). The $a_4b_3c_4b_3$ ballad stanza is mimed (the Doctrine of the Similar again) by the use of three or four words per line, but that number dwindles to three and then two as gridlock occurs:

> Song is coming
> Find no words
> Cannot cross
> Cannot cross (66)

That gridlock leads directly to one of the key sections of the poem (no. 4), "Indissolubility (Motetus absconditus)," which Bernstein calls in the synopsis a "palimpsestic parody of a late medieval motet from the Montpelier Codex." Here seven prose aphorisms present, in garbled form, variants on Benjaminian statements, for instance from his essay on Kierkegaard (2:703–5), culminating in the sentence "It is never just a matter of recognition as refiguration but redemption through resistance" (*Shadowtime*, 67), the latter phrase epitomizing what Benjamin's lifelong intellectual project is all about. But before we can sentimentalize this notion, Bernstein gives us seven more sentences, this time homophonic versions of the first group, line 14 reading:

> Lit hiss ever just a bladder of recuperation as infantilization gut exemption through insistence. (68)

And that is surely another way of putting it: "exemption through insistence."

Poems 6 and 7 are variants on the prime-number lyrics of the Amphibolies. But number 8 takes a whole new tack. Titled "Anagrammatics," it contains seventeen anagrams on the fourteen letters W-A-L-T-E-R-B-E-N-J-A-M-I-N, the rule being to have the word "Jew" in every line: "Brain metal Jew," "Barn rat linen Jew," "Rat bam Lenin Jew," and so on (72–73).[46] It is the first of the poems in "Doctrine of Similarity" to bring out the Jew in the protagonist's German name, as that name is visualized. And from here it is just a step to the concrete/sound poem (9), "dew and die," a structural/homophonic translation of Ernst Jandl's "der und die" (figure 4.1).[47] The latter has two grids of 13 × 13 (thirteen lines of thirteen words each, each word containing three—and only three letters, with many words, especially the ubiquitous *und* (and) repeated again and again.

Jandl's word grid is a representation of a lovers' rendezvous, reduced to its most basic elements of coming together in a nonspecified setting: there is a valley, ice, a lake, a gateway, a door. The rhyming paratactic units mime the process of sexual coupling and final satisfaction, "he" and "she" gradually turning into a red, wet, and tired "we." But there is also violence in this love-making. "Der" and "die" (note that these words are not personal pronouns but masculine and feminine articles demanding completion by their respective nouns) "riß und biß und zog" (tore and bit and pulled), and near the end, the word *tot* (dead") occurs as the lovers presumably "die" into each other's arms. But the narrative remains unclear; the reader is tempted to move vertically or diagonally as well as horizontally through this precisely laid-out word square.

Bernstein's version (figure 4.2) does not deviate from Jandl's rule—2 × 13 × 13—all the words again having exactly three letters. The only liberty taken with the source is to turn "Der" (he) into "Du," which gives Bernstein the English equivalents "dew and die." In the world of *Shadowtime* there is no sexual union, only the separation of "war mud and bog," of "war tug for kin," of "tic eye and mud and woe" (72). Yet Bernstein's visual poem "dew and die" looks exactly like Jandl's: it even uses some of the same words, although there is no similarity whatsoever between, say, the English *rot* and German *rot* (red) or the English *tot* and German *tot* (dead). Language, it seems, can't quite supply that field of nonsensuous similarities Benjamin hoped to convey.

This argument for irreducibility takes us to number 10, "Schein" (73), three lines of prime numbers followed by a variant. *Schein* is one of Benjamin's key concepts. In an essay fragment on the word as well as in his great essay on Goethe's *Elective Affinities*, Benjamin plays on its connotations, noting that although it may mean mere appearance or even facsimile or simulacrum, the word also designates a shining or showing forth, the glimmer of the numinous, the truth behind the beautiful appearance. "Everything beautiful in art can be ascribed to the realm of beautiful semblance [*Schein*],"[48] writes Benjamin (1:224). The translation isn't quite adequate here because the word *semblance*, used in the Harvard edition, limits the range of meanings of *Schein*; Bernstein knows this and opens up the word's possibilities:

There's no crime like the
shine in the space between
shine and shame.

No shine like the mine between meaning and history. (73)

The aura remains.

And so "Amphibolies III" looks ahead to the poem's "Envoi," with its

9. dew and die

can dew and die can and die can tie his sin tap and
the war dew hoe and die has him and her and tar the
pry and war mud and bog and tug eye and has him and
her bug dew can dew sin tap can and not lie and the
eye wag and the can and the can not and can ire not
and war beg ire and war not beg ire and has out ire
him and her and die war tug for kin war for kin its
was for kin its mob tic and ken hot and tug dew ken
sob and sob hog beg hop for ire him and tug dew ken
can dew its tug art its was the its was the its for
sun not lie and gag tug the eye wag sub and hug but
pun end dew oar and tag irk hog and our wag nor gut
and nab and sub top tic rum and not lie pop ken arm
and gab his ken and the our and the hog and sad and
sit and sob tic ire tic his tic and the rot war lie
and die rut and dew tag wag tic eye and mud and woe
and not and dew ire and die his and sow hug irk hug
and hit and lug tie out the its gut its for sun and
lie and kin bob and dew rib and sob and die kin and
bug his nab and sub top tic rum and sow was dew and
dew lay out ire and sob and tar and rib and bob and
sow and ire arm and the hog sad and the our die rut
zen see and the amp irk and tot and wet for rim its
wag sit wag nor she out him and her him and him her
him her him her big rot and sob and woe die see sin
tap rib and bob and ken orb nab and mud lag out sun

Figure 4.2. Charles Bernstein, "dew and die." From *Shadowtime* © 2005 Charles Bernstein.
Reprinted by permission of the author and Green Integer Books, www.greeninteger.com.

variation on the last line of Mallarmé's "Salut," the famous sonnet placed as
the headpiece to the 1899 edition of *Poésies*.[49] "Salut" is the poet-navigator's
salutation or toast to his fellow poets, exhorting them to make good on "le
blanc souci de notre toile," "the white care of our sail." Here the white sail
or sheet is a metaphor for the blank page of the book, Mallarmé's legacy to

future poets. All the odder, therefore, that in scene III of *Shadowtime*, head-piece becomes coda: the promise of this *salut* (the word also means "salva-tion") remains veiled in ambiguity despite the precise visual symmetry (the constraint is the same as that of "dew and die") of its three lines:

> The blank sail of our soil [toil]
> The blank toil of our sail [veil]
> The blank soul of our toil [soil]— (75)

The stage is thus set for Benjamin's descent into the underworld, which occurs in the next scene (IV) of the opera.

How Oulipo Is It?

Strictly speaking, *Shadowtime* is not an Oulipo work. There is no master constraint governing or generating the whole; indeed, the articulation of its parts is eclectic and unpredictable. Yet the Oulipo axiom, "A text written according to a constraint describes the constraint," could hardly be more ap-plicable than it is here. Whether combining lines made of prime numbers, in-venting homophonic translations, devising word squares based on the work of the concrete poet Ernst Jandl, or adapting Mallarmé's "Salut" to the word count (3-5-4-2-3-4-[4]) of each line of his coda, Bernstein is dramatizing the obsession with order in what is a curiously disordered life. For Benjamin, thought and action exist on separate planes. Bernstein's "poem including history" thus takes the measure of the Benjaminian ethos not by biographi-cal narrative or thematic exposition but spatially, in keeping with Benjamin's own spatialization of history in "A Berlin Chronicle" or the *Arcades Project*. Hence the resort to concrete poems like "dew and die" and "Salut," hence the mirror imaging of the "Amphibolies" to chart Benjamin's trajectory and the failure of his escape.

Again, Bernstein uses citation to measure, evaluate, and critique the all-consuming citationality of his protagonist. Here, the libretto implies, is a great critic who believes in the reality behind the *Schein* or "semblance" but cannot avoid those pricks that are "points on a / briar" as well as "points on a / map." Bernstein's source texts—Benjamin's own writings, the poetry of Jandl and Mallarmé, Hölderlin and Scholem, Heine's *Lorelei* and Goethe's *Faust*—function, as does the language of de Campos's *Galáxias*, to produce a particular constellation, densely layered and verbivocovisual.[50]

In comparison to earlier Language poems, including Bernstein's own, *Shadowtime* signals the return of the repressed, which is to say, the desire to write a poem of semantic density even though here, as in such earlier poems as "Lives of the Toll Takers" or "Let's Just Say," there can be no closure, no covering statement, no center or set presence. The *Stillstand* of *constellation* is only momentary: its inevitable dissolution leads to another and yet another amphibole or paradox. Bernstein's "transcreation," to use Haroldo de Campos's word,[51] of Walter Benjamin's textual world is at once homage and elegy, lyric and critical essay, an "ideogrammatic" language game in which the unexpected is always around the corner. But why should that surprise us? As the poet puts it in a later scene called "One and a Half Truths" (106):

Just a-
round the corner is another corner

5

"The Rattle of Statistical Traffic": Documentary and Found Text in Susan Howe's *The Midnight*

We lack confidence in our authenticity.
Henri David Thoreau

In citation the two realms—of origin and destruction—justify themselves before language. And conversely, only when they interpenetrate—in citation—is language consummated.
Walter Benjamin

To quote is to adduce words as facts, as exhibits, documents, to lift them out of context, to isolate them, to make them self-evident.
Richard Sieburth[1]

"Vagabond Quotations"

Halfway through Susan Howe's complex book-length poem *The Midnight*[2]— a poetic text that embeds varieties of prose as well as treated photographs, reproduced paintings, maps, catalogs, facsimiles of tissue interleaves, and enigmatic captions in what is a tripartite sequence of short, highly formal-

Figure 5.1. Susan Howe, page 72 from *The Midnight*. Copyright © 2003 Susan Howe. Reprinted by permission of New Directions Publishing Corp.

ized lyrics—we find an item titled "ALB," followed by the image of a postage stamp from EIRE (Ireland), portraying the poet's maternal great-aunt Louie Bennett (figure 5.1). Underneath the stamp, Howe places the following paragraph:

> The first of a series of Irish suffrage societies began in 1908 when Hanna Sheehy Skeffington and Margaret Cousins founded the Irish Women's Franchise League (IWFL). Aunt Louie Bennett's name was on the subscription list for the Irish Women's Suffrage and Local Government Association (IWSLGA) in 1909 and 1910; in 1911 she was appointed an honorary secretary. After WWI she was intensely involved in the Irish labor movement and served as General Secretary of the Irish Women Workers' Union (IWWU). In 1932 she became the first woman President of the Irish Trade Union Congress (ITUC), a position she held until 1955. She died in 1956. Recently her face appeared on a 32p Irish stamp, and there is a bench dedicated to her memory in Stephen's Green.[3]

What place does such a dry, factual paragraph have in a text ostensibly classified as *poetry*? How do those dates (seven in all), names, and acronyms function in what purports to be imaginative writing? Is the paragraph an encyclopedia entry? Not quite, given its reference to *Aunt* Louie Bennett (the ALB of the caption), but otherwise it does read like one.

Found text, and especially documentary, has always been important to Susan Howe. Her long lyrical montage-essay "Sorting Facts; or, Nineteen Ways of Looking at [Chris] Marker" (1996) begins with an epigraph from the great Soviet film director Dziga Vertov:

the FACTORY OF FACTS.
Filming facts, sorting facts. Disseminating facts. Agitating with
facts. Propaganda with Facts. Fists made of facts. . . .
Hurricanes of facts.
And individual little factlets.
Against film-sorcery.
Against film-mystification. (1926)[4]

Vertov's and Marker's lyric-documentary films provide a model for what Howe calls poetry as "factual telepathy": " I work," she declares, "in the poetic documentary form."[5]

A *document* (from the Latin *documentum*, meaning lesson, proof, instance, specimen, charter) is defined by the OED (no. 4, 1751) as "something written, inscribed, etc., which furnishes evidence or information upon any subject, as a manuscript, title-deed, tomb-stone, coin, picture, etc." But the term *documentary* was not used until 1926, and then with reference to film; the *Oxford American Dictionary* defines the adjective as follows: "Of a movie, a television or radio program, or photography) using pictures or interviews with people involved in real events to provide a factual record or report." As such, Tyrus Miller reminds us, the documentary *has* generally been taken as the antithesis of the modernist artwork with its obliquity, difficulty, and heightened self-consciousness: "Documentary, in contrast, seem[s] to draw its energy and inspiration from the antithetical realm of the everyday, the popular world upon which modernist art and writing had demonstratively turned its back. . . . Honesty, accuracy, and openness to the contingent details of the empirical world were premium values in the documentary aesthetic, and objectively existing 'reality' its formal touchstone."[6]

The fabled "accuracy" of contemporary docudrama and reality TV is, of course, an elaborate simulacrum, the irony being that the easier it becomes to alter photographs or to introduce hidden changes into existing text, the more reassuring may be the presence of an actual date or surname. "Constatation of fact," Ezra Pound called it, and the sense of the real provided by archival documentation stands at the heart of Pound's *Cantos* as of Walter Benjamin's *Arcades*. Indeed, in our own information age the lyric self is increasingly created by a complex process of negotiation between private feeling and public evidence. I am not only what my subconscious tells me but a link — an unwitting one, perhaps — in a cultural matrix. Here names and dates play a central role: the most important event in recent memory, after all, is known by its date — 9/11.

Consider that biosketch of Louie Bennett, Susan Howe's maternal great-aunt. In an earlier section, titled "Pandora," we read, "The relational space is the thing that's alive with something from somewhere else" (*M* 58). In this case, that something else is an odd inscription: "My great-aunt Louie Bennett has written the following admonition on the flyleaf of her copy of *The Irish Song Book with Original Irish Airs*, edited with an Introduction and Notes by Alfred Percival Graves (1895): '*To all who read*. This book has a value for Louie Bennett that it cannot have for any other human being. Therefore let no other human being keep it in his possession.'" This admonition is presented as a caption underneath a reproduction of the flyleaf itself, inscribed in a large scrawl. But the admonition obviously wasn't honored: not only did this *Irish Song Book* pass out of Louie Bennett's possession, but someone marked it up: on the facing page, partly covered by tape, is a stick figure, presumably drawn by a child (figure 5.2). Below the illustration we read:

> Graves's collection, part of a larger New Irish Library series edited by Sir Charles Gavan Duffy, holds lullabies, ballads, laments, songs of occupation, dust of political conflict. How can the same volume contain so many different incompatible intrinsic relations? . . . Names are only a map we use for navigating. Disobeying Aunt Louie's predatory withdrawal, or preservative denial, I recently secured the spine of her Irish Song Book with duct tape. Damage control—its cover was broken. So your edict flashes daggers—so what. (*M* 59)

Here—and this is characteristic of Howe's writing—what begins as a matter-of-fact description of an object, in this case a book, quickly turns oblique. "Names," we are told aphoristically, "are only a map we use for navigating," and the reference to "damage control" now leads from the literal (duct tape) to the need to place Aunt Louie's admonition in context:

> some anonymous American preschooler has sketched a stick figure on the facing flyleaf—a merry unintegrated familiar—more diagram than imp—from oral tradition—from wilds and mountains—running sideways—toward the gutter—indifferent as twilight—maybe superior to you—maybe the source of your power[7]

This is how booklore is disseminated. The anonymous preschooler—evidently one of Howe's own children[8]—puts his or her own stamp on what is after all a book containing lullabies and songs to be read to children. And the child is now presented as free spirit, running toward the gutter, which is here also the street gutter where "imps" play. The "you" refers to Aunt Louie but also to the poet herself, whose "power" comes from tapping into her Irish family history. Here is the passage below the verso:

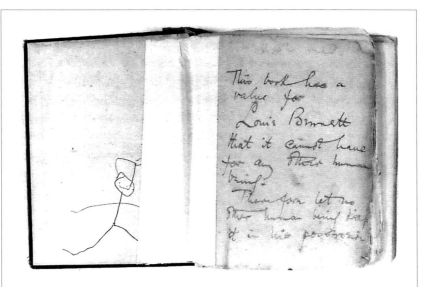

To all who read. This book has a value for Louie Bennett that it cannot have for any other human being. Therefore let no other human being keep it in his possession.

Figure 5.2. Susan Howe, page 59 from *The Midnight*. Copyright © 2003 Susan Howe. Reprinted by permission of New Directions Publishing Corp.

Why shouldn't I? In all transactions of life we have to take a leap. My mother's close relations treated their books as transitional objects (judging by a few survivors in my possession) to be held, loved, carried around, meddled with, abandoned, sometimes mutilated. They contain dedications, private messages, marginal annotations, hints, snapshots, press cuttings, warnings—scissor work. Some volumes have been shared as scripts for family theatricals. When something in the world is cross-identified, it just is. *They* have made this relation by gathering— airs, reveries, threads, mythologies, nets, oilskins, briars and branches, wishes and needs, intact—into a sort of tent. This is a space children used to play in. The country where they once belonged. A foreign audience will always be foreign. (*M* 60)

The Midnight itself is just such an instance of "scissor work." But how does the poet's meditation on the dislocated "space children used to play in" relate to the factual entry on Louie Bennett's contribution to Irish politics, placed under the heading "ALB"? Is the dignified general secretary of the Irish Women Workers' Union, depicted on the postage stamp, the same person who declares with tongue-in-cheek bravado that no one else may have her *Irish Song Book*? How sort out such different aspects of what the poet ruefully calls her "maternal Anglo-Irish disinheritance" (*M* 66)? And what about Howe's mother, Mary Manning—Irish actress, dramatist, novelist, critic, friend of fellow Anglo-Irish Protestant Samuel Beckett, wife of Boston Brahmin, Harvard law professor, and biographer Mark DeWolfe Howe—Mary Manning, whose death at the age of ninety-four in 1999, the "midnight" of the twentieth century, was the catalyst for Howe's book?

"A true account of the actual," Thoreau quipped in a passage Howe likes to cite, "is the rarest poetry."[9] How to recast the elegiac memoir—a memoir, in this case, of Howe's mother as well as of her other maternal relations—this became the challenge, a challenge made difficult by the surplus of information available to readers in the age of the Internet. Traditionally, elegists have assumed the right—indeed the necessity—to make judgments. Yeats, for example, writing his great elegy for Robert Gregory in 1916, could mythologize his not-so-heroic subject, celebrating Lady Gregory's son, tragically shot down in World War I, as "soldier, scholar, horseman," indeed "our Sidney and our perfect man." W. H. Auden's 1939 elegy "In Memory of W. B. Yeats" makes an eloquent case for Yeats's brilliance as a poet despite the necessary recognition of his shortcomings: "You were silly like us. / Your gift survived it all." Twenty years later, Robert Lowell's family elegies in *Life Studies* are distinguished by their pointed, if loving, critique of his once-notable Beacon Hill blueblood family.[10]

But today, as the conflicting information found in obituaries testifies, generally acceptable statements about the dead are much harder to make. Increasingly, the information, but not its assessment, is at our fingertips. Search for "Louie Bennett" on Google and you find more than ten sites, beginning with the following from the Princess Grace (Monaco) Library (EIRE):

LIFE 1870–1956; b. and brought up at Temple Hill, N. Dublin; ed. Dublin, London and Bonn, where she studied singing; became journalist; helped establish the Irishwoman's Suffrage Federation, 1911, closely involved in 1913 Lock-Out Strike; elected 1st woman President of Irish Trades Union Conference, and elected to executive of Labour Party, 1927; resisted Labour Party support for Fianna Fáil, also 1927; issued novels incl. *Prisoner of His Word* (1908), on Thomas Russell; founder Irish Women Workers' Union; close friend and colleague of Helen Chenevix; latterly resisted proliferation of nuclear energy and advocated establishment of joint council with Northern Ireland to deal with these and other problems; d. 25 Nov, at her home, St. Brigid's, Killiney.

[TOP]

WORKS *The Proving of Priscilla* (London: Harper 1902); *A Prisoner of His Word : A Tale of Real Happenings* (Dublin: Maunsel 1908), 240pp.; *Prisoner of His Word*

(Dublin: Maunsel; rep. 1914), 240pp.; *Ireland And A People's Peace: Paper Read by Miss Louie Bennett at a Joint Meeting of the Irishwomen's International League and the Irish Section of the Union of Democratic Control, Feb. 27, 1918* (Dublin/London: Maunsel and Co. 1918), 16pp.

[TOP]

CRITICISM R. M. Fox, *Louis Bennett: Her Life and Times* (Dublin: Talbot Press 1958), 123pp. [INFRA]; Diane Tolomeo, 'Modern Fiction,' in *Recent Research on Anglo-Irish Writers*, ed. James F. Kilroy (MLA 1983), [q.p.]; Margaret Ward, 'Nationalism, Pacificism, Internationalism: Louie Bennett, Hanna-Sheehy Skeffington and the Problems of "Defining Feminism",' in Anthony Bradley and Maryann Gialanella Valiulis, ed., *Gender and Sexuality in Modern Ireland* (Massachusetts UP 1997) [q.p.]; Rosemary Cullen Owens, *Louie Bennett* [Radical Irish Lives Ser.] (Cork UP 2001). See also Christina Murphy, *The Women's Suffrage Movement and Irish Society in the Early Twentieth Century* (Brighton: Harvester Wheatsheaf 1987).

BIBLIOGRAPHICAL DETAILS R. M. Fox, *Louis Bennett: Her Life and Times* (Dublin: Talbot Press 1958), 123pp., ded. to Helen Chenevix; CONTENTS, Author's Note [7]; Early Years [9]; Keynote [19]; Going Forward [33]; Suffrage, Peace — and Connolly [40]; Baptism of Fire [52]; Shouldering the Burden [64]; Impact of War [74]; Peace Offensive [83]; Leadership [96]; Work and Vision [113] .[11]

Howe's own "factual" account represents literally a fraction of the above. It does not refer to Louie Bennett's youthful singing lessons in Germany, or to her novel, enticingly called *A Prisoner of His Word*, or to Aunt Louie's mysterious relationship with Helen Chevenix. My curiosity piqued, I quickly glanced at the other Bennett items and learned (from Rosemary Fox's 1958 biography, a Google book) that Louie Bennett was evidently a member of an important lesbian circle of suffragettes and Irish nationalists. I also discovered that Louie Bennett was an acquaintance of the Countess Constance (Gore-Booth) Markiewicz, the "political prisoner" of Yeats's poem by that name ("On a Political Prisoner") and one of the key figures of "terrible beauty" in "Easter 1916"; together with her sister, the countess was also the subject of one of Yeats's great elegies, "In Memory of Eva Gore-Booth and Con Markiewicz." Lissadell, the Gore-Booth home, was one of the great country houses of the Sligo region, mythologized a number of times by the poet as an emblem of the Anglo-Irish Ascendancy. Indeed, to start with the Bennett thread in *The Midnight* and to proceed along the route made possible by the EIRE entry above is to come first to the "woman question," so important to Yeats, who castigated those of his female friends, beginning with Maud Gonne, whose voices had grown "shrill" from what he took to be their "unwomanly" absorption in politics and public life, and then to the role of Yeats's poetry in the life of Mary Manning Howe and her children. Just as Pound's *Cantos* catapult the reader into the world of Malatesta, Cavalcanti, Confucius, Eleusis, the Church of San Zeno in Verona, and the Sienese bank Monte de Paschi, so Howe's documentary "evidence," juxtaposed to her lyric and visual images, takes us into the complex world of the Anglo-Irish middle class in the period *entre deux guerres*.

Indeed, as in the case of "the Possum" (Eliot) or Fordie (Ford Madox Ford) in *The Cantos*, a given reference in *The Midnight* points both *outside* the text to the countless memoirs, biographies, and gossip about this or that Irish writer, actor, or relative who had anything to do with the poet's maternal background, and *inside* its covers to the diverse and contradictory clues that are woven together to create the book's "factual telepathy"—its layered double portrait of mother and daughter, Mary Manning and Susan Howe. In the poet's own words (*M* 58): "The relational space is the thing that's alive with something from somewhere else."

Four Ducks on a Pond

The Midnight opens with a reproduction of the title page of *The Master of Ballantrae: A Winter's Tale* by Robert Louis Stevenson, covered by a tissue interleaf—or more accurately, the facsimile of one.[12] On the page that follows, we read:

> There was a time when bookbinders placed a tissue interleaf between frontispiece and title page in order to prevent illustration and text from rubbing together. Although a sign is understood to be consubstantial with the thing or being it represents, word and picture are essentially rivals. The transitional space between image and scripture is often a zone of contention. Here we must separate. Even printers and binders drift apart. Tissue paper for wrapping or folding can be used for tracing. Mist-like transience. Listen, quick rustling. If a piece of sentence left unfinished can act as witness to a question proposed by a suspected ending, the other side is what will happen. Stage snow. Pantomime.
>   "Give me a sheet."

Characteristically, Howe's prose shifts seamlessly from documentation (the first sentence) to a statement of poetics (on the rivalry of word and image), to the insertion of personal expression—"Here we must separate"—that may well refer to a "separation" very different from that of word and image or page and interleaf. The paragraph obliquely introduces the central concerns of *The Midnight*: the contradiction between image and verbal caption, the transparency of tissue paper as analogue for the "bed hangings" and curtains to come—the "spectral scrap" that divides one thing from another or provides it with cover, a punning "stage snow" (show) or "pantomime."

Dividing lines, margins, borders: the role of these and their various crossings in Howe's poetry has frequently been discussed. Stephen Collis, for example, comments on *Bed Hangings I*, the opening section of *The Midnight*:

> Beginning with the discovery of a copy of *Bed Hangings: A Treatise on Fabrics and Styles in the Curtaining of Beds, 1650–1850* in the gift shop of Hartford's Wadsworth Athenaeum, Howe proceeds to explore the relationship between the history of "opus scissum," the "cutwork" that was "Queen Elizabeth's favorite form of lace" and the literary "cutwork" of the poet-assembler who "cut[s] these two extracts from *The Muses ELIZIUM* by Michael Drayton." Text and textile rub against each other in typically paratactic proximity: "versification a counterpane," "a cot cover, an ode, a couplet, a line," in the mention of those who "Could wave and read at once . . ."[13]

The resulting assemblage alludes to many literary and historic figures familiar to readers of *Thorow*, *Pierce Arrow*, and *Frame Structures*, from Jonathan Edwards to Charles Peirce and Emily Dickinson. "Bed Hangings" itself, as Susan Bee's parodically "genteel" images for the Granary Press edition suggest,[14] remains dedicated to Howe's New England roots. But the prose sections of *The Midnight*, as well as the final lyric sequence "Kidnapped," turns from the world of the American father, the Harvard jurist-professor Mark DeWolfe Howe, to the "matter of Ireland"—the "Ireland" transmitted to Anglo-Irish children in the wake of World War II.

But why the opening spotlight on Robert Louis Stevenson's *Master of Ballantree*? The popular Scottish novelist of the late nineteenth century would seem at first to be a writer quite alien to Susan Howe. Those popular late nineteenth-century boys' adventure stories—*Treasure Island*, *Kidnapped*, *The Master of Ballantrae*—even the classic tale of the split personality, *Dr. Jekyll and Mr. Hyde*—hardly seem the stuff of Howe's aurally and visually charged imagination. Yet *The Midnight* not only begins with the Stevenson title page but concludes with a section called "Kidnapped." And throughout its pages, there are references to Uncle John (Manning's) marked-up copy of Stevenson's *Master of Ballantrae*, with special reference to 1745, the year of the last Jacobite rebellion, which ended all hope for the restoration of the Stuart monarchy (see *M* 73). At least five of *The Midnight*'s illustrations, moreover, present drawings and engravings of dramatic Stevenson episodes, these

Figure 5.3. Susan Howe, page 56 from *The Midnight*. Copyright © 2003 Susan Howe. Reprinted by permission of New Directions Publishing Corp.

complemented by the cropped postcard facsimile of Girolamo Nerli's well-known portrait of the novelist (*M* 56):

> What if what we actually see is mistakenly dubbed appearance? Uncle John has pasted a postcard with a reproduction of Count Girolamo Nerli's half-length portrait of the author, seated in a slouching or lounging posture, just inside the front cover of *Ballantrae*. Nerli visited the Stevensons during 1892, at Vailima, their newly built wooden two-story house ("an Irish castle of 1820 minus the dirt"—Anonymous) in Samoa.

The Nerli portrait is juxtaposed to another fragment Uncle John Manning pasted inside the cover of *Ballantrae*—the photograph of a naval officer in full uniform, his back turned to what looks like an explosion. No doubt the two pictures (figure 5.3) represent the contrast between Manning's prosaic life as a civil engineer, working for the Electricity Supply Board, and his literary, more exotic aspirations. Uncle John's last years in a meager managed-care facility called New Lodge on Morehampton Roadin Dublin (*M* 54) prefigure the fate of his sister Mary Manning. On the last page (verso) of "Square Quotes II," facing a recto photograph of little Mary (age seven) with her jump rope and ribbons in her hair, we read the following biographical account:

> I have one of the last photographs taken of Mary Manning Howe Adams pinned to the wall over my desk. She is sitting on her La-Z-Boy chair with an old lap robe woven in Connemara, in her two-room apartment at The Cambridge Homes near Harvard Square on Mount Auburn Street. She appears to be astonished, slightly submissive but sweetly welcoming nevertheless. I can tell she is acting for the camera. The Cambridge Home is "an assisted living residence that fosters independence, camaraderie, and well-being." They still send us promotional literature although she has been dead since 1999. Their most recent annual development report is titled "Growing Older in Community: Mastering the Challenges of Aging." When she was a resident she had a blunter way of putting it: "We're already in the coffin, Dear—but the lid isn't closed yet." (*M* 146)

The photograph described so carefully here is pointedly *not* among Howe's illustrations for *The Midnight*; a picture, in this instance, would limit the suggestibility of the poet's ekphrasis. Howe's account provides a number of "hard facts"—the "La-Z-Boy" chair, Connemara "lap robe," and "two-room apartment" on Mount Auburn Street. But note that, with the possible exception of the chair, these facts are not deducible from the picture at all: the viewer cannot know where the lap robe in question was made, much less where the room where Mary sits is found. Fact, even hard fact, is always subject to elaboration or interpretation. Then, too, the sharp old lady's bon mot about the coffin (however accurate or not) is framed by the narrator's somewhat catty remark "I can tell she is acting for the camera"—a remark that undercuts the image of Mary's "slightly submissive but sweetly welcoming" appearance. But of course Mary Manning *was* first and foremost an actress, so why wouldn't she be acting here? Or is her daughter imposing her own ironic judgment on the absent photo?

Both Mary and John Manning, as presented in *The Midnight*, are drawn to Robert Louis Stevenson by their own self-exile; both can relate to his *dépaysement*: the chronicler of his native Scotland who had to seek warm climates for his health, settling finally in his "Irish castle minus the dirt" in Samoa, where exotic foreign dialects became his passion:

> Accent is the link that connects syllables together and forms them into a note or a tone of voice. In his recently completed novella *The Beach of Falesà* R L S had hoped to picture the modern world of the Pacific—phonetically. "You will know more about the South Seas after you have read my little tale, than if you

had read a library. . . . There is always the exotic question; and everything, the life, the place, the dialects—traders' talk, which is a strange conglomerate of literary expression . . ." (*M* 57)

To picture the world phonetically: this would become Howe's own pursuit. But the deeper link to Stevenson—the hidden figure beneath the "filmy fabric" of the tissue paper flyleaf—is the familiar (perhaps too familiar) poetry book every middle-class English-speaking child owned until at least the mid-twentieth century: Stevenson's *A Child's Garden of Verses*. Neglected for decades as naive, simple, and singsongy, erased from all the university anthologies (Norton, Oxford), this popular collection of children's poems is surely due for reassessment:

> When I was down beside the sea
> A wooden spade they gave to me
> To dig the sandy shore.
> My holes were empty like a cup,
> In every hole the sea came up,
> Till it could come no more.[15]

Stevenson's ballad stanza (*aabccb*), with its alternate tetrameter and trimeter lines, suspends its meaning till the last word: no more sea because there is no longer a hole to receive it: the rhyme *cup/ up* says it all. It is the same sense of loss we find in Mary Manning's "favorite of all poems," William Allingham's "Four Ducks on a Pond"

> Four Ducks on a pond,
> A grass-bank beyond,
> A blue-sky of spring
> White clouds on the wing:
> What a little thing
> To remember for years—
> To remember with tears. (*M* 79)

"Four Ducks on a Pond" was Howe's original title for *The Midnight*. Perhaps, the poet suggests, this late Victorian Anglo-Irish poem reminded Mary Manning "of the beautiful landscape around Dublin in comparison to the hideous (or so she felt) landscape in the Cambridge/Boston area. I always wondered that *something so simple could be so loaded with emotion for her*, but I suppose it represented the essence of nostalgia for her lost youth in another country and to this day it keeps playing in my head any time I sit in a park looking at ducks. Aunt Louie's garden in Killiney (where we stayed the summer of 47) was to me the most beautiful place I had ever experienced. Just up the road from the sea, past a druid circle in a dark grove of trees."[16]

Gardens, groves, druid circles: the "white clouds on the wing" of Allingham's little poem may well refer to swans, and one remembers that Yeats's "wild swans at Coole" were also counted—there were "nine-and-fifty." "Analogies," as Howe remarks after quoting "Four Ducks on a Pond," "pass like lightning" (*M* 80). Indeed, the poem "served as an audible symbol of desire and remorse. . . . Allingham's unreal reality points to the cold mystery of windows lit in strange houses as opposed to your own house when you are outside looking in" (80).

This conclusion is odd, given that there are no windows mentioned in "Four Ducks on a Pond." But Howe has provided the missing link most ingeniously, pasting into the paragraph just cited an image of a double-page spread, with the final page of Yeats's romantic play *Baile and Aillin* on the left and the title page of his 1904 volume *In the Seven Woods* on the right, the two nearly hidden by Mary Manning's own tipped-in bookmarks (figure 5.4). The Seven Woods was Lady Gregory's estate, of which Coole Park was a part; the opening line of Yeats's "Coole Park and Ballylee, 1931" is "Under my

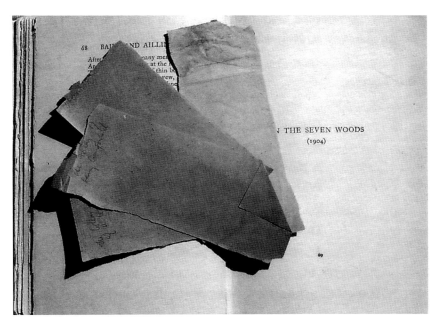

Figure 5.4. Susan Howe, page 80 from *The Midnight*. Copyright © 2003 Susan Howe. Reprinted by permission of New Directions Publishing Corp.

window-ledge the water race," and the beautiful "ancestral house" Lissadell is characterized by its "great windows opening to the south."[17] In "writing through" her mother's copy of Yeats's *Later Poems* (see *M* 177, note), Howe thus juxtaposes Mary Manning's acting career at the Abbey, where *Baile and Aillin* was performed, as well as her love of the Irish balladry represented by "Four Ducks," to a poetry more sophisticated than Stevenson's or Allingham's but partaking of the same Irish sources—namely, the poetry of Yeats:[18]

> Maybe one reason I am so obsessed with spirits who inhabit these books is because my mother brought me up on Yeats as if he were Mother Goose. Even before I could read, "Down by the Salley Gardens" was a lullaby, and a framed broadside "He wishes for the Cloths of Heaven" printed at the Cuala Press hung over my bed. I hope her homesickness, leaving Dublin for Boston in 1935, then moving on to Buffalo where we lived between 1938 and 1941, then back to Cambridge, Massachusetts, was partially assuaged by the Yeats brothers. She hung Jack's illustrations and prints on the wall of any house or apartment we moved to as if they were windows. Broadsides were an escape route. Points of departure. They marked another sequestered "self" where she would go home to her thought. She clung to William's words by speaking them aloud. So there were always three dimensions, visual, textual, and auditory. Waves of sound connected us by associational syllabic magic to an original but imaginary place existing somewhere across the ocean between the emphasis of sound and the emphasis of sense. I loved listening to her voice. I felt my own vocabulary as something hopelessly mixed and at the same time hardened into glass. (*M* 74–75)

Here again Howe produces a "paragraph" (prose poem?) that moves from flat statement ("my mother brought me up on Yeats") to the documentary assurance of place-names and dates, to lyric fantasy. The broadsides as windows look ahead to those windows of mysterious houses mentioned in connection with "Four Ducks on a Pond." The "waves of sound" connect not only to Mary Manning's past and future but to the worlds of mother and daughter: the "three dimensions, visual, textual, and auditory" are the dimensions of *The Midnight* itself.

This passage, then, dramatizes more fully than could any summarizing statement or recounting of childhood incident the bond between mother and daughter. Yeats's *Later Poems*, inscribed by six Irish actresses who were Mary's friends (see *M* 75), contains four narrow brown paper markers with the faded titles of Yeats poems. "Sometimes I arrange the four snippets as if they were a hand of cards, or inexpressible love liable to moods. I like to let them touch down randomly as if I were casting dice or reading tea leaves.

'The Collar-bone of a Hare' has just fallen on 'The Cap and Bells.' She loved to embroider facts" (*M* 76).

Here two aesthetics diverge. For the actress Mary Manning, "poetry" is the verbal magic that takes us to realm of the imaginary. For Susan Howe, such "magic"—lovely but not quite grounded, as in Stevenson or Allingham—must give way to the knottier, tenser language that is Yeats's. Whereas Mary Manning "loved to embroider facts," her daughter, following Yeats's example, learned to cast off the Romantic "Coat," "Covered with embroideries / Out of old mythologies" (*Poems*, 127). Indeed, Yeats's locutions now become grist for Howe's own "articulations of sound form in time," her very particular language games." Thus,

> Now "The Folly of Being Comforted" tip-in has fallen so it covers "The Heart of Woman" in such a way I can only see
>
> O
>
>   N
>
> T   rest;
>
> He
>
> An
>
> O
>
> T
>
>   m;
>
>   s,
>
>   h.

Here is Howe's source poem, "The Heart of a Woman":

> O what to me the little room
> That was brimmed up with prayer and rest;
> He bade me out into the gloom,
> And my breast lies upon his breast.
>
> O what to me my mother's care,
> The house where I was safe and warm;
> The shadowy blossom of my hair
> Will hide us from the bitter storm.
>
> O hiding hair and dewy eyes,
> I am no more with life and death,
> My heart upon his warm heart lies,
> My breath is mixed into his breath. (Yeats, *Poems*, 60–61)

This is Yeats at his most fin-de-siècle: in *Autobiographies*, he disavows the "overcharged colour inherited from the romantic movement." "I deliberately reshaped my style," he recalls, "deliberately sought out an impression as of cold light and tumbling clouds." "The Folly of Being Comforted"[19] was one of the first poems to exhibit what Yeats referred to repeatedly as "an emotion I described to myself as cold."[20]

How appropriate, then, that the "Folly" bookmark should fall on "The Heart of Woman." Howe's "writing through" retains only a skeleton of letters, rather in the vein of Ian Hamilton Finlay's concrete poems—a key influence on Howe's poems of the 1970s.[21] Like Finlay's "Homage to Malevich," whose print block "Black Square" arrangement of words and letters Howe discussed in an early essay,[22] her version of Yeats's "Folly" creates complex lettristic play. The *O* is the first letter of line 1, but the *N*, not quite in line with "O," is the last letter of the capitalized title. *O* is the first letter of both poems, and here it anagrammatically gives us "ON" or the first two letters of Yeats's first word, "One." Then, reading down, we have "The" and "An" with the suggestion of "An OT[her]"—appropriate because for both speakers there can be no *other*. And the skeletal poem concludes with a "sh" for silence but also, perhaps, for **S**usan **H**owe.

Self-Portrait in a Citational Mirror

Howe's "writing-through" of "The Folly of Being Comforted" implies that however "cold" the emotion of Yeats's 1903 poem, a century later its rhetoric inevitably demands revision: love poetry can no longer be so direct and passionate. Then, too, the poet's erasure prepares us for the elaborate verbal play and fragmentation of the lyrics in "Kidnapped" that follow. For example:

> Book I am sorry fair
> Covering have fallen
> Silent O Moyle fair
> maiden by cloudlight
> Book I am sorry yet
> say we recollect it
> in *Tenant* (M 165)

What links the "prose" of *The Midnight* to the "Kidnapped" lyrics is the marked citationality of the latter. In this particular poem, for example, Howe pastes in another popular Irish ballad, Thomas Moore's "Song of Fionnula," which begins, "Silent, oh Moyle, be the roar of thy water." Such signature phrases as "fair/maiden" and "by cloudlight" carry on the Irish folk thread. The lyric breaks off in midtitle, Anne Brontë's *Tenant of Wildfell Hall* (the Brontës figure repeatedly in *The Midnight*), another Romantic favorite that Mary Manning passed on to her children. No doubt Susan Howe thinks of herself as a "tenant" to those master poets who are here memorialized.

"Irish oral history" and "Fisherman seaweed seven"—this latter a reference to Finlay's "Fisherman's Cross," a poem carved on stone, juxtaposing the words *seas* and *ease*—are brought together in the next poem (166), and on the facing page, Yeats's poetics are related to the Gate Theatre Company, of which Mary Manning was a member:

> Reader of poetry this book
> contains all poetry THOOR
> BALLYLEE seven notes for
> stage representation May
> countryside you reader of
> poetry that I am forgotten
> Long notes seem necessary
> Unworthy players ask for
> legend familiar in legend
> the arrow king and no king (*M* 167)

Here the allusions to the two early Yeats poems "The Arrow" and "King and No King," as well as to the poet's celebrated tower "Thoor Ballylee," are seen in the context of Mary Manning's "seven notes for/stage representation" as well as the "May/countryside": May, one suspects, refers not only to the season but to May Beckett, the mother of Mary's great friend Sam Beckett, who during their idyll in the summer of 1936 worked closely with Mary in the theatre.

Yet *The Midnight* is hardly an Irish nostalgia trip containing sweet memories of "Four Ducks on a Pond," Thomas Moore balladry, or even Thoor Ballylee. "Unworthy players," we read in line 8 above, "ask for legend." Worthy ones, presumably, demand a certain "constatation of fact." Early on in *The Midnight*, we find the following passage about Mary Manning:

> In May 1944 the actor and director Micheál Mac Liammóir published an excerpt from his unpublished memoirs called "Some Talented Women" in Sean O'Faoláin's magazine *The Bell*. It included a description of my mother:
>
> > Rehearsals were in progress for a new play, "*Youth's the Season*" by a new authoress—a Dublin girl called Mary Manning whose brain, nimble and obser-

vant as I was, could not yet keep pace with a tongue so caustic that even her native city . . . was a little in awe of her, and one all but looked for a feathered heel under her crisp and spirited skirts. "Did you hear what Mary Manning said about so-and-so?" was a favorite phrase; and her handsome, rather prominent eyes, deeply blue, and dangerously smiling, danced all over the room in search of prey. Copy was what she probably called it, but one knew that by the time it appeared in a play or newspaper column as a delicately barbed anecdote, it would be very well-worn copy indeed; much more like badly mauled prey than copy.

Like many pullers from pedestals Mary Had A Heart and as Mr. Henry Wood might have said, that was not only "in the right place" but in perfect working order. An impulsive sympathy was fundamental in her nature; what people called her cattery was simply a medium through which she expressed her social ego. Her ruling passion was ambition. She worshipped success. It was the most natural reaction of a temperament set in the major key against the country in which she had lived all her life and where everything had failed; and it was inevitable that she should later have married an American and gone to live in Boston. (*M* 49–51)

Why would Howe cite this particularly unflattering, indeed cruel assessment of her mother in her own memoir? How do we reconcile Mac Liammóir's portrait of the malicious girl whose "ruling passion was ambition" and who "worshipped success" with the warm, imaginative Mary Manning who tirelessly conveyed her love of poetry to her daughter?

The plot thickens. In "Scare Quotes II," Howe presents an extract from an unnamed biography, beginning with the sentence "Born Alfred Willmore in 1890, Micheál Mac Liammóir started life in Kensal Green, London."[23] "Straight" documentation, these facts immediately call Mac Liammóir's own account into question: the Abbey Theatre insider, it seems, was no Irishman at all but an impostor of sorts from lower-class London. And further, Howe's own version of Mac Liammóir's career mentions neither the plays he wrote for the Abbey nor his later one-man show about Wilde, *The Importance of Being Oscar*; rather, her biographical sketch recounts such petty details as his "earliest stage appearance in *The Goldfish* (1911), written and produced by Miss Lila Field, with music composed by a person whose name appears on the program as Mr. Eyre O'Naut," with its play on Eire, naught, and aeronaut (*M* 118). We next learn that Mac Liammóir, aka Willmore, "doubled as Macduff's son and the Second Apparition of a Bleeding Child (for no additional fee) in Sir Herbert Beerbohm Tree's production of *Macbeth*" (*M* 118). Hardly the stuff of star biography! And the seemingly informational account

concludes with an anecdote about Mac Líammoir's meeting with Sarah Bern-
hardt, whose "indescribable brilliance and seductiveness" he gushes about
even as he wickedly exposes the "uncanny stillness of the brown lace fring-
ing her wrists" as a fraud, whispering to a fellow actor that the lace was
"Gummed to her hands, dear'" (*M* 118).

Given these particulars, is Mac Liammóir's description of Mary to be
taken seriously? Where does gossip end and truth begin? On the facing page
(*M* 119; see figure 5.5 below), Howe takes another stab at characterizing her
mother, this time focusing on her "survival tactics during a time of war, revolution, counter-revolution" (*M* 119). But it is the two photographs that frame
the emigration story that are most telling. The upper one is annotated in the
list of illustrations at the back of the book as "Photograph of Mary Manning,
circa 1913. Caption reads, 'Watching an aeroplane / Mary Manning'" (*M* 177).
Nothing in the rather muzzy photograph of a young girl holding her hat in-
dicates that she is watching an airplane. But the unseen caption does relate to
the photograph at the bottom of the page, which depicts, not as one might
expect, Mary as an old lady as compared to Mary the young girl, but rather
the first page of her last address book, composed not long before her death
at age ninety-four. *A* is evidently for Aer Lingus (800-223-6537) and also for
Audio-Ears, 484-8700; the entry above "Aer Lingus," ending 8729, is hidden.
Mary, one might say, is still "watching" for planes, no doubt to take her back
to her beloved Ireland. Aer Lingus: the name of the Irish airline suggests
both song (air) and language (lingus, lingua), whereas Audio-Ears, the name
of a well-known hearing-aid service, brings the realm of sound into the picture. Then, too, "Ear" is an anagram on "Aer." Song, language, sound: these
are Mary Manning's domain, at least as her notepad is reconstructed by her
daughter. The most ordinary references, the poet suggests, are charged with
meaning, if we know how to read them. And even the cross-outs are significant: the first number contains something behind the 6, and there is what
looks like an 8 crossed out after "Audio-." It is the shaky error-prone penman-
ship of an old person.[24]

Names, numbers, citations, lists, photographs: such "constatations of
fact" constitute what is paradoxically Howe's ambiguous evidence. Even
the lyrics of "Kidnapped" rely on "winnowing each slip for re- / appearance"
(*M* 171), the references to the Noh Theatre once more recalling Yeats, whose
"Sailing to Byzantium" is alluded to in the line "Tattered coat our journey
out" (*M* 171) and who supplies the "memory cradle" (172) for the entire book.
Most startlingly, the title *The Midnight* recalls two major Yeats poems that are
never mentioned by name in the book: "Byzantium" and "All Souls' Night."

Mary Manning had crossed the Irish Sea several times, though never the English Channel, and had crossed the Atlantic Ocean both ways twice (third class). Economic survival tactics during a time of war, revolution, counter-revolution, and the traumatic birth of a nation, meant setting out as a poor relation. So, after being an actress, a theatre critic, a magazine editor, the author of two plays and a novel, she arrived in Cambridge, Massachusetts in 1934 at the home of her Aunt Muriel where she met my father and became a faculty wife and a mother.

Even into her nineties she kept leaving in order to arrive one place or another as the first step in a never ending process somewhere else.

Figure 5.5. Susan Howe, page 119 from *The Midnight*. Copyright © 2003 Susan Howe. Reprinted by permission of New Directions Publishing Corp.

Midnight is the hour of sudden illumination, the epiphanic moment, whose emblems in "Byzantium" are the "great cathedral gong" striking the hour, as well the "starlit or moonlit dome" of Hagia Sophia—a dome that "disdains / All that man is, / All mere complexities, / The fury and the mire of human veins." Stanza 4 reads:

> At midnight on the Emperor's pavement flit
> Flames that no faggot feeds, nor steel has lit,
> Nor storm disturbs, flames begotten of flame,
> Where blood-begotten spirits come
> And all complexities of fury leave,
> Dying into a dance,
> An agony of trance,
> An agony of flame that cannot singe a sleeve. (*Poems*, 248)

And "All Souls' Night" begins with the stanza:

> Midnight has come and the Great Christ Church bell
> And many a lesser bell sound through the room;
> And it is All Souls' Night.
> And two long glasses brimmed with muscatel
> Bubble upon the table. A ghost may come:
> For it is a ghost's right,
> His element is so fine
> Being sharpened by his death,
> To drink from the wine-breath
> While our gross palates drink from the whole wine. (227)

In a nice irony, Susan Howe's own "All Souls' Night" takes place not in some mysterious, otherworldly realm but in the Houghton Library at Harvard, where she, a degreeless would-be scholar, has come to study the manuscripts, under lock and key, of Emily Dickinson. Again, the emphasis is on realistic documentation: the Houghton vestibule, we learn, is "10 feet wide and 5–6 feet deep," with "plate glass" double doors looming ahead:

> Passing through this first vestibule I find myself in an oval reception anti-chamber about 35 feet wide and 20 feet deep under what appears to be a ceiling with a dome at its apex. I think I see sunlight but closer inspection reveals a ceiling with a dome at its apex reveals electric light concealed under a slightly dropped form, also oval, illuminating the ceiling above. This first false skylight resembles a human eye and the central oval disc its "pupil." Maybe ghosts exist as spatiotemporal coordinates, even if they themselves do not occupy space. (*M* 120)

This description, at once precise and surreal, recalls the Beckett of *The Lost Ones* or *Imagination Dead Imagine*: can a scholarly library really be so threatening? The narrative continues in this vein as the poet makes her way through coatroom and gift shop, through the Edison and Newman rooms, till finally she enters the Reading Room or Houghton Library proper. The library mix-up that follows (the poet's credentials are called into question because her ID cards bear her married name, Susan von Schlegell) is perceived, irrationally but graphically, as Howe's ultimate humiliation: "I feel the acne rosacea on the Irish half of my nose getting worse. I am blushing, defensive, desperate, and this is only the public sector" (*M* 122).

But then something strange happens. As the waiting reader glances around, she notices the bookcases bearing engraved titles in gold, arranged in groups of threes: "One, taller than the rest, has a blood-red leather binding with gold lettering: Presented to Charles I at Little Gidding" (*M* 123). In an epiphany, the reference to Nicholas Ferrar's 1633 book brings to mind "'Little Gidding,' Eliot's fourth Quartet [which] has served me as a beacon for what poetry might achieve." And so her mind turns, via Emily Dickinson, to the Concordance Room at Little Gidding in England, the Gospels of the Four Evangelists, the design of the leather volumes, and the response to them by King Charles in 1642—a circuit, incidentally, that can clearly include *The Master of Ballantrae*. Entering the world of the books themselves, the poet begins to rally. But her "ordeal" is not yet over. Finally assigned locker number 26 and admitted to the Reading Room, the novice meets new obstacles. She doesn't know how the buzz-in system works; she feels mocked by the inquisitive eyes of the seasoned scholars—and then, to top it all, "the material I requested isn't there. They whisper among themselves, glance at me now and then, and politely but firmly say they don't have it. They ask to see the Curator's letter. I don't have it" (126).

The deflation and despair are palpable. "I have waited weeks for this moment," remarks the narrator melodramatically. "I think of the disarming of the Antinomians in 1637, coinciding with the founding of Harvard College in Cambridge, a provincial village of mainly British immigrants" (*M* 126). However absurd at the literal level, such analogies are the very fabric of Howe's writing. "In a chiastic universe," as she puts it, "only relations exist" (*M* 127). The narrative is suspended—fragments about Frederick Olmsted intervene—and only two pages later does the Houghton Library motif come back, this time as the subject of an annotated background sketch, perhaps from the Harvard brochure:

The Houghton Library built in 1942 (the year "Little Gidding" was published) is named in honor of Arthur A. Houghton (Harvard '29), chief executive of Steuben Glassworks at Corning, New York. Under his management, Steuben's use of independent designers brought out a new discipline to glassmaking. The *American National Biography* tells us that Houghton showed he was serious about producing a quality product by smashing every piece of glass (over 20,000 pieces valued at one million dollars) in the Steuben warehouse about one month after he assumed control. "From ash can to museum in half a generation" became the company's slogan. (*M* 130)

These facts could hardly be more deflationary. The august library on the most august campus: is a career of smashing glass really the road to book collecting and connoisseurship? Yet this Jamesian plutocrat really did collect treasures: "Emily Dickinson's heavily marked copy of Emerson's *Poems* is in the Emily Dickinson Room on the second floor in a book-case behind locked glass" (130). And this transferred epithet (it is the bookcase, not the glass, that is locked) is followed by the caption "Never-Never Land" and a cropped portrait of Nicholas Ferrar. But the final deflation is yet to come, in the following notice, "To Whom It May Concern" (131):

> The books in the Emily Dickinson room have been repeatedly studied and examined with the hope of finding annotations of the handwriting of Emily Dickinson. After years of study, no one has found a single mark that could be positively assigned to her.
>
> In the process of this fruitful examination the books have suffered, and many of them have been transferred to the repair shelf. In order to avoid more useless wear and the shattering of 19th century publishers' cloth cases, we have closed the Emily Dickinson Room Library for further examination.
>
> Yours Sincerely,
> Roger E. Stoddard
> Curator of Rare Books

Below this letter, Howe has placed a page from John Manning's copy of *Alice in Wonderland*: the sequence "In a Little Bill" depicting a humiliated giant Alice bursting the seams of her Lilliputian room.

Here the found text and illustration measure the absurdity of Howe's situation more fully than could any direct narrative account. She who knows that the Dickinson fascicles do indeed bear crucial marks revealing the poet's intent is not permitted to examine them. The regime of power, of "library control," that Howe has feared from the outset has won out — at least temporarily.

Documentary, in other words, is in Susan Howe's poetic lexicon both threat and necessity. Roger E. Stoddard's "To Whom It May Concern" represents the oppressive letter of the law, constraining the poet even as similar documents once challenged her mother and her Aunt Louie. Yet only by adopting the language of the library and the database—the language of facts, dates, historical ledger, map, dictionary, biographical entry, literary quotation—can the contemporary poet create what is paradoxically a new poetic sphere. Howe's lyric "bed hangings," originally published separately, are themselves tissues of citation, to be covered and yet laid bare by bookmarks, paper tip-ins, photographs. In the assemblage that is *The Midnight*, everything is at once separate and interwoven. The postage stamp bearing Aunt Louie's picture is pasted beside Mary Manning's tipped-in bookmarks, these and many other scraps of paper and old snapshots defining what Howe wryly calls her "Anglo-Irish disinheritance."

The prose portion of *The Midnight* concludes on an elegiac note as Howe pays tribute to a facet of that inheritance not usually talked about—her own irreducible Irish accent. In British English, *either* is pronounced "eye-ther," never "eether" (*M* 145). Such laws are not to be violated. But in imperatives begin new possibilities. *Either* may well be pronounced *eye-ther*, but one can transpose the two middle letters of *Eire*, right above it in the dictionary, and derive *Erie*, "the most southerly of the Great Lakes" (*M* 145), on whose shores in Buffalo Howe spent her early childhood years.

From *Eire* to *Erie*: it is Mary's—and also Susan's—trajectory. "Each phoneme has an indeterminate nanosecond kink, each vowel its evocative vocalic value." At this juncture, prose gives way to the lyric of the coda, which concludes with the "sound twist" of the lines:

> Style in one stray sitting I
> approach sometime in plain
> handmade rag wove costume
> awry what I long for array

When *documentary* reaches a certain density, it morphs into its opposite—the hyperreal of "factual telepathy." As in Perec's *La Vie mode d'emploi*, the more "individual little factlets" the text generates, the less the reader knows what they mean. In Howe's memoir, the allusive is finally the elusive: the handmade *array* of the *stray* gone *awry*.

6

Language in Migration: Multilingualism and Exophonic Writing in the New Poetics

The limit: music needs no translation. Lyric poetry: closest to music — and posing the greatest difficulties for translation.

Walter Benjamin[1]

With the Warsaw Express, I arrived at the "Berlin Zoologischer Garten" [Zoo] and discovered a "B" in "Berlin," a "C" in "Zoologischen" and an "A" in "Garten." The alphabet always reminds me of the Middle East. Vilém Flusser wrote, "The A still shows the horns of the Syrian steer, the B still the cupolas of the Semitic house, the C (G) still the hump of the camel in the Near Eastern desert."

Yoko Tawada[2]

In the citation above from *Sprachpolizei und Spielpolygotte* (Speech police and polyglottal play), Yoko Tawada recalls her first view of Berlin — the view of a writer born and raised in Japan who, at age twenty-two, came on a visit to Germany and never went back. For Tawada, a native speaker of a language whose grammar makes no distinctions of gender, case, definite and indefinite articles, or singular and plural, indeed that uses no prepositions, each German (more accurately, each Western) word, phrase, or idiom becomes a conundrum. The alphabet itself poses a special challenge: Tawada cannot resist the

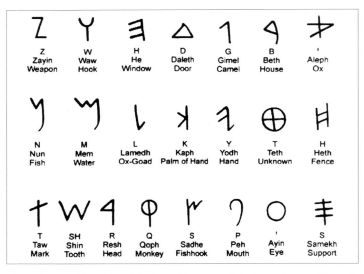

Figure 6.1. The Phoenician alphabet, with names of the letters inserted (http://www.phoenician.org/alphabet.htm). Image by Sanford Holst in *Phoenicians: Lebanon's Epic Heritage* (Cambridge and Boston Press, 2005). Used by permission.

tendency to "ideogrammize" the individual letters of the modern alphabet, whose Near Eastern roots provide a link to her own Far Eastern world (see figure 6.1). Aleph, Beth, Gimel: in their derivations, the names of these letters seem fitting, given that our Western numbers are, of course, Arabic numbers.

The introduction of foreign-language citations into a given piece of writing is hardly new: from the references to Latin texts in Thomas Browne's *Religio Medici* to the transcription of the French conversation of the upper classes in Tolstoy's *War and Peace* to the network of foreign allusions in Eliot's *The Waste Land*, we are accustomed to a poetry or fiction that exceeds its monolingual borders. But there is a significant difference between the function of the "foreign" citations in *The Waste Land* and their role a century later in the global context of shifting national identities, large-scale migration from one language community to another, and especially the heteroglossia of the Internet. The writing of poetry under these circumstances calls for a new set of language games.

The Language Vortex: Eliot and Pound

For Eliot, the role of foreign-language citations (in his case almost exclusively Latin, Greek, Italian, French, and German) is to heighten the authenticity, as well as the exoticism, of the allusion in question. When, for example, Eliot cites, near the end of *The Waste Land*,[3] Gerard de Nerval's sonnet "El desdichado," "Le Prince d'Aquitaine à la tour abolie" (The prince of Aquitaine at his broken tower), as an analogue to the poet's own sense of dispossession, the French original is designed to give the reference a mysterious aura as well as a certain distance, as if to say, my immediate feelings can best be expressed in the words of this remarkable and enigmatic nineteenth-century French poet. And the Nerval reference is, in its turn, collaged into a sequence of allusions ranging from English nursery rhyme ("London Bridge is falling down . . .") to Dante's *Purgatorio*, to the late Latin of the *Pervigilium Veneris*, and finally the Sanskrit of the Upanishads. "Aurally," Craig Raine remarks, "the range of registers here introduces us to the auditory equivalent of the Silk Road and the spice trail. The exotic is in our mouths and in our ears."[4]

Such self-conscious and learned linguistic display has its own curious limits. Note, for example, that when Eliot refers to the Old Testament, as in the citations he himself identifies as stemming from Ezekiel or Ecclesiastes or Isaiah, his source is hardly the original Hebrew or Aramaic but rather the King James Bible. Partly this is a matter of historical and cultural circumstance: Eliot knew no Hebrew and neither did his classically educated audience. But it is also a telling omission: whereas a Wagner citation (*Frisch weht der Wind* . . .) evidently required the original German, the Hebrew prophets had long since turned into native English speakers. Indeed, the foreign-language citations in *The Waste Land*, culminating in the esoteric transliteration of "Datta, dayadhvam, damyata" (Give, sympathize, control) and "Shantih shantih shantih" (Eliot's note tells us pretentiously, "'The Peace which passeth understanding' is our equivalent to this word"), are more epideictic than integral to the poem's meaning. If, in other words, the momentary note of transcendence introduced into "The Fire Sermon" in the citation from Verlaine's "Parsifal" — "*Et O ces voix d'enfants, chantant dans la coupole*" (l. 202) — had been rendered in English (And oh those children's voices, singing in the dome), the tenor of the passage in question would be unchanged, but its "foreign" aura, enhanced by the assonance of open O's in O/coup*ole* and the rhyme of en*fants*/chant*ant*, would be lost.

The Waste Land depends on such effects, the language shifts inevitably slowing down the reader's absorption of the text and countering the speed of the collage cuts. But Eliot himself seems to have felt that the polyglossia of *The Waste Land* had its limits for the self-consciously *English* poet he had become; by the time he wrote *The Four Quartets*, the collage mode with its tissue of literary allusions — the Italian of Dante, the Latin of Ovid, the French of Baudelaire—has all but vanished in favor of the authoritative and largely "pure" English of the poet's maturity:

> Here is a place of disaffection
> Time before and time after
> In a dim light: neither daylight
> Investing form with lucid stillness
> With slow rotation suggesting permanence
> Nor darkness to purify the soul
> Emptying the sensual with deprivation
> Cleansing affection from the temporal.[5]

"Burnt Norton," the first of the *Quartets*, has two Greek epigraphs from Heracleitus;[6] subsequently, although there are plenty of buried allusions to earlier poems, there is only a single foreign citation in the entire sequence: "Twenty years largely wasted, the years of *entre deux guerres*" in *East Coker*, part 5.[7] And this French phrase was hardly esoteric in British parlance of the time.

The multilingualism of Ezra Pound's *Cantos* is of a very different order. If Eliot carefully embeds the foreign, usually literary allusion inside what is of course an English poem, Pound produces a multiform text whose language layers intersect so as to create the meaning of a given passage. The Malatesta Cantos (8–11) are an early case in point. Their astonishing blend of English, Italian, Latin, and up-to-date American dialect and slang along with Business English creates a wholly distinctive verbal texture, especially since the "translations" of florid Renaissance letters are rendered in a hyperformal English that functions parodically in the context. Here is the conclusion of Canto 9:

> That's what they found in the post-bag
> And some more of it to the effect that
>   he "lived and ruled"
>
> "*et amava perdutamente Isotta delgi Atti*"
> e "*ne fu degna*"
>   "*constans in proposito*"
> "*Placuit oculis principis*"
> "*pulchra aspectu*"
> "*populo grata   (Italiaeque decus)*"
> "and built a temple so full of pagan works"
>   i.e. Sigismund
> and in the style "Past ruin'd Latium"

The filigree hiding the gothic,
      with a touch of rhetoric in the whole
And the old sarcophagi,
      such as lie, smothered in grass, by San Vitale[8]

"He 'lived and ruled'": the short phrase, cut, it seems, from a longer sentence in the chronicle that was Pound's source, is intentionally flat. Of course Sigismundo Malatesta, the lord of Rimini, "lived and ruled" but what and how? The casual "to the effect that . . ." is now punctuated by a dramatic passage in Italian from Pius II's *Commentaries*: "*Et amava perdutamente Isotta degli Atti* "(And he loved to distraction Isotta degli Atti), "e *ne fu degna*" (and she was worthy of him).[9] Here the shift to Italian heightens the immediacy of the chronicle: the ability to love so *perdutamente* is presented as compensating for Sigismundo's earlier crimes, especially since Isotta is pronounced by the pope himself to be deserving of such love.

In the next line, Pius's Italian account shifts abruptly into Latin. *Constans in proposito* (constant in purpose) refers to Horace, *Odes* 3.3:

> *Iustum et tenacem propositi virum*
> *non civium ardor prava iubentium,*
> *non vultus instantis tyranni . . .*

> (The man tenacious of his purpose in a righteous case is not shaken from his firm resolve by the frenzy of his fellow-citizens bidding what is wrong, not by the face of the threatening tyrant . . .)[10]

The phrase is one Pound also used at the conclusion of Canto 34 to praise John Quincy Adams: *Constans proposito / Justum et Tenacem*" (C 171). The reference is to an ivory cane with a gold ring around it that was presented to Adams in 1844; engraved on the ring were the words "To John Quincy Adams *Justum et Tenacem Proposito Virum*" (*Companion*, 138–39). In Canto 34, the epithet *Constans proposito*, placed underneath Pound's visual image of the pyramid-shaped marker (written in English and Hebrew) found by Adams near Buffalo, is accompanied by the Chinese ideogram for "integrity" (figure 6.2).

In seamlessly linking the authoritative Horatian reference to Pius's praise of Isotta degli Atti's legendary beauty ("*pulchra aspectu*") and charisma—she is *populo grata (Italiaeque decus)* (pleasing to the people [and an ornament to Italy])—the poem presents Sigismundo's beloved as a lady of great constancy and righteous resolve. Indeed, a few lines later with the quotation "Past ruin'd Latium" (a paraphrase of Walter Savage Landor's Victorian poem "Past ruin'd Ilion"), she becomes another Helen of Troy.

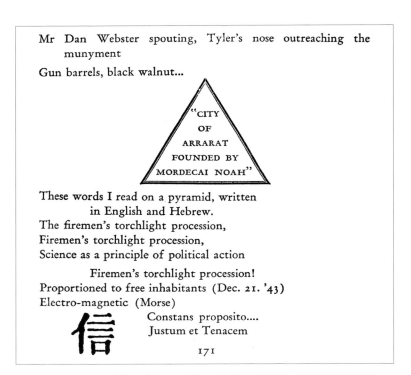

Mr Dan Webster spouting, Tyler's nose outreaching the
munyment
Gun barrels, black walnut...

"CITY
OF
ARRARAT
FOUNDED BY
MORDECAI NOAH"

These words I read on a pyramid, written
in English and Hebrew.
The firemen's torchlight procession,
Firemen's torchlight procession,
Science as a principle of political action
Firemen's torchlight procession!
Proportioned to free inhabitants (Dec. 21. '43)
Electro-magnetic (Morse)
Constans proposito....
Justum et Tenacem
171

Figure 6.2. Ezra Pound, from "Canto 34." From THE CANTOS OF EZRA POUND,
copyright © 1934 by Ezra Pound. Reprinted by permission of New Directions Publishing Corp.

It is the shift in language registers throughout this passage that produces
the equivocal image of Malatesta's Renaissance Italy. Rome, Byzantium,
fifteenth-century Rimini, and twentieth-century America are juxtaposed on
a single plane, even as Pound's protohypertextual poem can relate Malatesta
to John Quincy Adams, can link the free verse of Canto 9 to the pyramidal
frame of Canto 34, papal commentary to Chinese ideogram, the acoustic to
the visual. The method, as the poem itself tells us, depends upon "the filigree
hiding the gothic, / with a touch of rhetoric in the whole." Pound's language
reenacts the role of the delicate tracery on the stone carvings of the Tempio,
making strange the seemingly familiar Gothic church.

Contemporary multilingual poetics owes much to Pound, especially to
his anticipation of digital linkage in the creation of narrative assemblage.
Still, however many language registers Pound introduces into *The Cantos*,
there is never any doubt but that the voice that orchestrates these ingenious
variations is a well-versed and expert English speaker, a speaker whose voice

moves easily from the imperative of "Lie quiet Divus" (C 1) and "Hang it all, Robert Browning" (C 2) to the personal narrative of "I sat on the Dogana's steps" (C 3) or the parenthetical "I wonder what Tsu Tsze's calligraphy looked like" (C 80). It is this voice that playfully reminds us of the name of the famed Oxford college — "Magdalen (rhyming dawdlin')" — and imitates the president of that "*kawledg*," conversing about "a moddddun opohem he had read" (C 74, p. 465).

Such comic spellings testify, of course, to the power of both poet and reader to distinguish between proper English and mispronunciation, between "correct" speech and comic accent. Linguistic idiosyncrasies, in languages ranging from Chinese to Greek to contemporary French *argot* and American Western twang, are, in other words, measurable against a norm: we can laugh at the reference to Clemenceau as "frogbassador" (C 464) because we know that *frog* is a slang epithet for French and that the reference is thus to the French ambassador. Or again, Pound's imitation Spanish accent when he recalls that back in 1906, a certain Padre José Elizondo told him, "Hay aquí mucho catolicismo — (sounded catoli*th*ismo) / y muy poco reliHion" (C 537), strikes a resonant note because the poet *knows* all about the distinction between spelling and pronunciation in Peninsular Spanish. Again, when we come to the fragment "Le Paradis n'est pas artificiel," we understand that the statement is made in French because it alludes to Baudelaire's well-known book on haschish, *Les paradis artificiels* (see C 458); the possibility for paradise persists, but it is — now shifting to Italian appropriate for Pound's location in the detention camp at Pisa — "spezzato [broken] apparently." And in the next line, the now authoritative voice of the poet remarks wistfully, "It exists only in fragments" (458).

Questions of Travel: Caroline Bergvall's *Say: 'Parsley'*

But what happens when there is no more commanding voice to assess those "fragments"? In a world of relentless global communication, poetry has begun to concern itself with the processing and absorption of the "foreign" itself, given the vagaries of travel and migration, whether of persons or of speech samples and forms of writing. Consider the work of the French-Norwegian poet and conceptual artist Caroline Bergvall, who moved to the United Kingdom in 1989, when she was twenty-seven. A graduate of the Sorbonne, Bergvall received an MPhil from Warwick and has made her main home in London ever since. In her 2005 collection for Salt Press called *Fig*, there are three important multilingual poems: the English-French "About Face," the arrangement of Dante translations called "Via," and the text of the installation piece *Say Parsley*, first commissioned for the Spacex Gallery in Exeter in 2001.[11]

"Via," which I have discussed elsewhere,[12] is a constraint-based text, entirely composed of citations—specifically the forty-seven English translations of the first tercet of Canto 1 of Dante's *Inferno*:

> Nel mezzo del cammin di nostra vita
> mi ritrovai per una selva oscura
> che la diritta via era smarrita

By arranging the translations alphabetically (by the first letter of the first line, beginning with "Along the journey of our life halfway"), regardless of chronology, and placing the last name of the author and date in parentheses following the citation, Bergvall has produced an astonishing text that demonstrates just how impossible—and yet how inevitable—translation is. Dante's *selva oscura* is alternately dark, sunless, darkling, gloomy, great, obscure, shadowy, and darksome; his *via diritta* may be the nearest way or the right one, the direct road or the proper path; that road is *smarrita*—lost, blocked, strayed from, not to be found. The cited translators range from famous nineteenth-century poets like Longfellow (1867) to contemporaries like Robert Pinsky (1994) and include established translators from Henry Francis Cary (1805) to Allen Mandelbaum (1980), and such obscure figures as James Innis Minchin (1885) or Geoffrey L. Bickersteth (1955). Equalized by the alphabet game and deindividualized by the omission of the translator's first name, these cited tercets (some rhymed *aba* as in the terza rima, some in free verse or prose) convey the brilliance of the original, whose every word resonates with possible meanings even as they produce an independent poem written in a curious "midway" doggerel, repeatedly rhyming variants *midway/astray* and beginning lines with "amid," "in the middle of" and "halfway," so that sound chiming produces a kind of chant, offset every fourth line by the discordant sound and image of an ordinary proper noun and date.

During the writing process—"some two years in all," Bergvall recalls in her headnote for *Fig*—"it was as if the many systematic acts of counting and collating were carrying with them a motive interior as much as ulterior to the work being generated. The minutiae of writing, of copying out, of shadowing the translators' voicing of the medieval text, favored an eerie intimacy as much as a welcome distance. . . . Increasingly the project was about keeping count and making sure. . . . Making copy explicitly as an act of copy. Understanding translation in its erratic seriality" (*Fig*, 65).

Say: 'Parsley' begins at the opposite end. If "Via" collates and assembles translations of Dante's Italian text, *Say: 'Parsley'* takes a finite body of English words so as to understand their potential for *translation*, whether into the various idiolects and dialects circulating in the United Kingdom or in the warring speech registers of Belgium, specifically Flemish-speaking Antwerp, where English has replaced French as the second language of choice. In this "differential" text—we have the print version, a series of installations (Exeter 2001, Liverpool 2004, and Antwerp 2008), and a digital sound/screen version on the Internet—translation and translatability are viewed in political as well as poetic terms.[13]

Bergvall's headnotes, like Susan Howe's, move easily from documentary fact to poetic play. In exploring "speaking patterns. Slips of the tongue or of the culture" (*Fig*, 50), Bergvall takes as her point of departure the shibboleth. The Hebrew word *shibboleth* (שׁבוֹלת) literally means the part of a plant containing grains, such as an ear of corn or a stalk of grain, or, in different contexts, "stream, torrent." It was used in Judges 12:4–6 by Jephthah "as a test word by which to distinguish the fleeing Ephraimites (who could not pronounce the *sh* of *shibboleth*) from his own men the Gileadites" (OED no. 1). As such, it came to mean (OED no. 2) "a word or sound which a person is unable to pronounce correctly; a word used as a test for detecting foreigners, or persons from another district, by their pronunciation." Here is Bergvall's own commentary on *shibboleth*.

> Speaking is a give-away. My tongue marks me out. It also trips me up, creates social stuttering, mishearing, ambiguities. Say what. The shibboleth provides an extreme case of speech as gatekeeper. The massacre of tens of thousands of Creole Haitians on the soil of the Dominican Republic during the dictatorship of Trujillo in 1937 is still perhaps the most recent documented example of such a shibboleth at work. For failing to roll the /r/ of "*perejil*" (parsley). This familiar anodyne word makes the horror all the more disturbing.[14]

In Creole, the language of the Haitian peasant, *r* is pronounced like *w* and there is no Spanish *j*, which is pronounced hard against the back of the throat to give us "perrehíl."

One language's shibboleth is another's everyday speech. In English the word *parsley* is readily articulated, even as the parsley plant is one of the most common. Bergvall, herself an exophonic poet, writing as she does in a second, or at least secondary, language, is keenly aware of subliminal shibboleths: "In the culturally pluralistic, yet divided, and markedly monolingual society of contemporary Britain, variations in accent and deviations from a broad English pronunciation still frequently entail degrees of harassment and verbal, sometimes physical, abuse, all according to ethnic and linguistic background" (*Fig*, 51). For the Exeter version, Bergvall and her collaborator Ciarán Maher made recordings of speech overheard in London cafés and shops, choosing words on the "parsley" model "for their tricksy difficulty yet familiar (i.e. English) association. Say, 'rolling hills.' The thick English 'l' and liquid 'r' are especially prone to pronunciation variations" (*Fig*, 51).[15]

The reference here is to the fact that the Japanese language (as well as other East Asian languages heard increasingly in the UK) does not have separate sounds for the /r/ and /l/ phonemes. In Japanese, the /r/ sound is pronounced as an alveolar lateral flap /ɾ)/, articulated with the tongue flapped against the hard palate behind the front teeth, so that it sounds like a Spanish soft /r/. Because the Japanese language does not have a separate equivalent for the English /l/, Japanese speakers not fluent in English are often unable to distinguish between the /r/ and /l/ sounds.[16] Thus they often mispronounce English words containing either sound, leading to endless ethnic jokes: "election" is confused with "erection," "clap," with "crap"; flight attendants tell passengers to have a good "fright," while serving their customers "flied lice."

Say: 'Parsley' was designed as one response this particular form of discrimination:

> We . . . worked out pairings of words which were likely to yield the most variations on hearing. Pairs with dissimilar speech resonances: Proper/English, Nothing/Certain, Speak/Freely. The way the loudspeakers were placed, on two walls in the farthest room each carrying only one word per channel, spoken an octave apart, was a classic psychoacoustic set-up. Listeners were caught in their own ears, created their own sense of what they heard, moved around the room, piecing together the pairings only to discover more words in the recesses of their hearing, their memory ear. Some thought they heard Italian words, others Hungarian. Hidden or disused first languages resurfaced in this physical and social comprehension game. A grid of plumb-lines, pendular, pong-ping, punctuated the upper floor [see figure 6.3].[17]

The accompanying poem, reproduced in *Fig*, defamiliarizes "ordinary" speech by means of rhyme, pun, paragram, misspelling, typo, and fragmentation:[18]

Say this language heels
language keals
over
S wallow in i
F hollow hollow fall low
S peak s low ly lie low

Say this feels c loose
the big mous the chokes
has a bong st r uck
in the throat
Spooks lulls angage language
Pulls teeth out
for the dogs
Keep watch r at s the gate
of the law
Say: "pig"
Say this
enflamed
gorge d

Figure 6.3. Stills from *Say: 'Parsley'* (2008), a data piece conceived for the siting of Caroline Bergvall's installation at MuHKA, Museum of Contemporary Arts (Antwerp, May 28 to August 17, 2008), as presented on Bergvall's website (http://www.caroline bergvall.com). Reproduced by permission of Caroline Bergvall.

And now follows the imperative "Say 'pig'" followed by thirty-one other one- and two-syllable words, most of them quite common and many rhyming or varying by a single phoneme (e.g., "crumple," "crumble") or rhyming, culminating in the line "Say: 'parsley.'" A subtle difficulty is built into the catalog, of which more in a moment, with pairs such as "gurgle"/"turgle," where the first word is a common, onomatopoeic noun or verb, while the second is urban slang for sneaking up behind someone and grabbing their backpack and shaking it," as in "John *turgled* the guy in the bathroom vigorously."[19]

The print version does not record the polyglot phonetic transcription of the words in question, but the recent presentation of *Say: 'Parsley'*, installed at the Museum of Contemporary Arts in Antwerp in summer 2008, provides an astonishing turn of the screw. In this Belgian city, where Flemish and Dutch vie with the English that is the lingua franca of the non-natives, Bergvall's vocal rendering of the spoken English list prompts a set of "translations" that reveal a great deal about the way we process language. Here is the video of that double-entendre, as reproduced on Bergvall's website.[20] The chart below provides the spoken list on the left, and the translations from "pig" to "parsley" and back again in the second and third:

	↓	↑
PIG	pig	pig
FIG	figue	fig
FAG	vague	fag
FOG	vogue	fog
FROG	frock	frog
FRIG	fric	fric
TRIG	truk	truk
TRIM	drum	drum
TRAM	tram	tram
TRAMP	trap	trap
TRUMP	trom	trom
TRUMPET	trompet	trompet
CRUMPET	kroket	kroket
CRUMPLE	kromte	kromte
CRUMBLE	kronkel	kronkel
RUMPLE	rimpel	rimpel
RUMBLE	rommel	rommel
RUBBLE	roddel	roddel
BUBBLE	bobbel	bobbel
PUDDLE	buidel*	pummel*
CUDDLE	kuiter	kuiter

CURDLE	keuter	keuter
GIRDLE	keutel	keutel
GURGLE	keuvel	keuvel
TURGLE	teugel	teugel
TURTLE	treuzel	treuzel
MYRTLE	meute	meute
MORTAL	mortel	mortel
PORTAL	portaal*	borstel*
PORTLY	portie*	porsie*
PARTLY	paartje*	paartche*
PARSLEY	parsley	parsley

The listener/reader first assumes that the pop-up menu in column 2 (from pig to parsley), which then reverses (from parsley to pig in col. 3), provides phonetic translations into Flemish of the spoken English words. But the transcriptions generated seem to follow no perceivable rules. Sometimes the translated word looks very similar, as in the case of "trompet" and "mortel." But most of the transcriptions cannot be anticipated: why, for example, is "girdle" (rhymes with "curdle" but spelled with an *i* rather than a *u*) heard as "keuvel" or "trig" as "truk"? Indeed, the more one listens, the less the transcription in question makes sense. Why, for example, should "tramp" become "trap" whereas "trumpet" is understood as "trompet"?

More important: I found that I could not copy the spoken list, no matter how hard I tried, until I turned off the sound and just looked at the writing on the wall. So ingrained in my mind are the English words that I could not follow the "foreign" transcription while hearing the familiar sound. And further: it was only after listening dozens of times that I realized that the list of words, read continuously by Bergvall both forward and backward, does not stay the same. Thus "portal" can be "portaal" or "borstel"; "puddle" can be "pummel" or "buidel," and so on (see asterisked words). Sometimes a change occurs when the list is reversed. Then, too, in the reverse list the last five words (first five in the sequence) — "frog," "fog," "fag," "fig," "pig," — revert to the correct English. Why is that? Has the audience caught on? Is the recorder broken? Or are these monosyllabic words, with their short vowel sounds ending on the voiced stop /g/, easier to repeat?

Say: "parsley." *Parsley* gives us the structural key here, for after the first four monosyllabic words, the *r*'s kick in — they are present in the next twenty-eight words, whereas *l*'s occur in nineteen of them. The alliance of *r* and *l* as in "partly" (*paartje, paartche*) creates special problems for the listener/reader. But even here no rule applies, because *parsley* comes out perfectly.

This version of *Say: 'Parsley'* thus calls into question some deep-seated language assumptions.

First, Bergvall questions the notion that the division between "Flemish" and "French" speakers in Belgium is, as many now think, inevitable, that the nation can (or should) be divided along language lines. The transcriptions on our list above are equivocal: Are they Flemish ("kronkel")? French ("vague")? Or perhaps, like "paartche" ("for partly"), spoken by African immigrants? Can the word itself identify the "true" Belgian? On the evidence of "Say Parsley," phonetic transcription—and, by extension, "real" translation—seems, on the contrary, to be impossible. Every time one recites a rhyming, echoing list, there are slight variations. As in Gertrude Stein's "Arthur a Grammar" or "Stanzas in Meditation," time makes the difference. Repetition is never precise reproduction. One cannot, so to speak, "say parsley." And yet in our culture such words can become shibboleths, used to discriminate against those perceived as "outsiders." Language as conduit thus becomes language as object—a *fig* to contemplate. That "object, " however, remains curiously opaque. To *hear* the English word makes it all but impossible to *see* its "foreign" visual equivalent. In this Cagean poetic construct—a construct itself a kind of chant that haunts the eye/ear—*sound*, far from underscoring *sight*, almost always undercuts it.[21]

Traces of Cultural Collision:
The Language Games of Yoko Tawada

Trumpet: trompet: Bergvall's Antwerp audience could get at least some of her spoken words right. But what happens when the poet's adopted language has no common elements with her mother tongue? This is the case with Yoko Tawada, the Japanese poet and fiction writer who took the Trans-Siberian train from Tokyo to Hamburg in 1982 (when she was twenty-two) and stayed in Germany, now writing in her second language. Tawada's poems and short stories, as well as her remarkable critical poem-essays, have as their great subject the role of what she herself has called in a Japanese book by that title (not yet translated) *exophony*. Here is an extract, translated by Keijiro Suga:

> To write literature is at the opposite end from repeating and recombining arbitrarily the words that you hear on a daily basis. It is an attempt to face and confront the possibility of the language in which you write. By consciously doing so, the traces of your memory are highly activated and your mother tongue, your older linguistic stratum, intervenes to transform the actual language you use for creation.

When I write and read aloud sentences in German by searching [for] the correct rhythm, my sentences come out differently from the usual, natural sounding German. People say my sentences in German are very clear and easy to hear, but still they are "not ordinary" and deviant in some ways. No wonder, because they are the results of the sound that I as an individual body have absorbed and accumulated by living through this multilingual world. It is of no use if I tried to delete my accents or remove my habits in utterance. Today a human subject is a place where different languages coexist by mutually transforming each other and it is meaningless to cancel their cohabitation and suppress the resulting distortion. Rather, to pursue one's accents and what they bring about may begin to matter for one's literary creation.[22]

In Tawada's case, the situation is further complicated by the fact that hers is a Asian language—a language most Westerners even today feel no obligation to learn. Perhaps, she argues, this can be turned to an advantage: "When a writer whose mother tongue is a minor language begins to create in a major language such as English, a certain change occurs in the *target* language. The change is not limited solely to the linguistic level. A particular take on history, or a new sensorium to grasp the magical, come into literary language."[23] The smallest, simplest word takes on special importance. As Tawada explains it to Bettina Brandt:

The German word for to translate [*übersetzen*] can also mean "to steer a boat from one shore to the other." In Japan we use *honyaku* for "to translate," which is a Sino-Japanese word, a word of Chinese origin. . . . The first ideogram of his word suggests a slightly dramatic and romantic gesture, which means "to turn over," or "to flip over," not simply turning a page. In performances I like to read my work in several languages—including in the available English translations—and I hope to visualize the act of translation through this gesture.[24]

In keeping with this gestural poetics, Tawada's 2007 *Sprachpolizei und Spielpolygotte* (Speech police and polyglot play) begins with a poem, "Slavia in Berlin," in which ordinary German street conversation is viewed from the angle of the foreign visitor, who processes simple directions and bits of information according to the place-names they contain:

"Hier Ägypten es aber kein Prag."
"Ich were sie schon Finnland"[25]

where "Ägypten" (Egypt) sounds like "gibt es" (there is) and "Finnland" like "finden," in the sentence: "Here there is no Prague." / "I'll find it. Or again, "San" as in "San Francisco" and "San Diego" is understood as the first syllable of the German "San-atorium." It is a playful introduction, but the next piece,

"An der Spree" (On the Spree; the reference is to the river that divides central Berlin) is both darker and disorienting. Here is the opening:

> I am in Europe, I don't know where I am. One thing is sure: the Near East is quite near from here. The place from which the Near East is quite near, is called Europe. When I was still living in the Far East, the Near East was quite far.
>
> But this too was a mistake. The Near East was not so far from the Far East, as was thought in the Far East. The Silk Road rapidly connected one point to another. So the old imperial city Kyoto was built by the Persians who migrated beyond China to Japan. Kyoto is thus a Persian city. The Near East is the place that is near everywhere. Europe lies there where the Silk Road ends.[26]

Tawada's seemingly "simple" prose is a variant on the Wittgensteinian language game. Consider the following passage in the *Philosophical Investigations*:

> Someone coming into a strange country will sometimes learn the language of the inhabitants from ostensive definitions that they give him; and he will often have to *guess* the meaning of these definitions; and will guess sometimes right, sometimes wrong.
>
> And now, I think, we can say: Augustine describes the learning of human language as if the child came into a strange country and did not understand the language of the country; that is, as if it already had a language, only not this one.[27]

Tawada's narrator poses precisely as such an innocent—one who has not yet learned what the term *Near East* refers to. But of course she knows quite well, just as she now knows that the name of the downtown railway terminal, Berlin Zooologischer Garten, refers to the Berlin Zoo and not to an image of camels, as figured in the *G*s and *C*s of the printed name (see epigraph). In juxtaposing the Augustinian equation of word and thing to the Wittgensteinian axiom that "the meaning of a word is its use in the language" (no. 43), the poet is able to confront the fissure—or call it collision—between her own two worlds.

"An der Spree" begins with a meditation on numbers—the Chinese numbers of her childhood that have no zero, the straight and diagonal lines that make up Roman numerals (and are used sequentially to designate train tracks in the station), and the more "advanced" Arabic ones that identify the different trains: "The Indian numbers wandered toward the West. In the West, the Arabs took over these numbers and spread them around Europe. Since then those in Europe can do arithmetic quickly. You can see right away who has more and what is better" (*Spiel*, 14).

What, then, is this thing called Europe? In the course of Tawada's prose poem, it emerges as the Arabic zero, missing in the poet's mother tongue. Its "Siamese twin," the Near East, haunts it everywhere; witness the Dragon of the fabled Ishtar Gate in the Pergamon Museum, right in the middle of the Spree: "It had the eyes of a fish and the body of a cat. The forelegs reminded me of a lion, the hind those of an eagle. A horn and two crooked ears graced the head. His tongue was split three ways; he was thus multilingual. From here, his place of birth is not far away. He came to Berlin from the Near East and was named the striding dragon" (15). As soon as the summer sun comes out, the Spree turns bright blue, reminding the narrator that its waters eventually run into the Nile. Everything is connected, and yet the division between East and West Berlin, still experienced by the narrator as she rides on the U-Bahn, spells out the lack of real connection. Contemplating her impending visit to America, where she has an East German (Sorb) friend, who refers to Kleist's "Marquise of O" as the "Marquise of Zero," she anticipates the view of the Pacific, "her" ocean and yet entirely different from the one she knew as a child. Besides, "the water doesn't remain where it is now. Another water flows into it. It moves as the clouds above it move." And yet in a bookshop where she buys two postcards—one of the Brandenburg Gate, the other the former building site on the Potsdamer Platz—she reads about a Berlin artist who has tried to produce his own clouds in a studio. Evidently it's easy:

> I. Fill a glass case with dusty air. II. Spray it with water. III. Stir the mass of water and air. IV. Let sit for a while. V. Carefully take the mass out of the case. VI. Set it into the open air or, even better, right away on a mountain so that the cloud doesn't have far to rise. A newborn cloud doesn't have much strength. The artist painted the clouds the color of the national flags because he thought even the clouds had an ideology and a history. The clouds put on trousers when they fly to Russia.

This last sentence, an allusion to Mayakovsky's great poem "The Cloud in Trousers," brings the narrator back to her Berlin reality. On the U2, she goes to Pankow and checks into a pension on the Mayakovsky Ring. Again a circle, again zero. At her desk in her rented room, she writes a postcard. "I will stay here. But I don't know where I am." She writes a second card: "I am coming to you. But where are you actually?" (22). And now we read:

> If there is a zero, one knows that there is an empty place. If there is no zero, one is overlooking a free place. That's why one cannot, without zero, orient oneself nor do arithmetic well. I drew a zero on a piece of stationery and wrote next to it,

"Look, the zero is India. The Far East is exactly as far from point zero as is Europe. The zero in the middle, on the left the Near East with its Europe, on the right the Far East: this is a symmetrical picture. Now I know where I am." (22)

No wonder, the poet concludes, that in the Far West (California), a third of the computer scientists are from India. "They operate between zero and one." Whereas, "I sit east of the East Coast on the Spree and have still not understood what zero is" (22). The abacus, after all, knows no zero. You push a stone from bottom to top to designate 1, when you get to 5, you push from top to bottom: "There is no stone that designates zero. A stone is never less than a stone. But is zero less than one? Zero [*null*] swallows the phrase, whether something is less or more" (23).

Like numbers, *words* have meaning only within a given system, only relationally. "East," "West," "Far East," "Far West": it all depends on your perspective. The Museum "Island" on the Spree in Berlin, the recently divided city (its Mayakovsky Ring, now Yoko's "home," was once the seat of the East German government), can be viewed as the great crossroads or as an empty circle, zero itself. Or again, Berlin is the site of sinister collision: even the clouds, after all, wear trousers.

Tawada's poetic language is not like that of many of her Asian American contemporaries (Theresa Hak Kyung Cha, Myung Mi Kim), a mongrel language: it is entirely "German"—but a German whose ordinary words, especially proper names, are everywhere measured against their absent Japanese equivalents. In a stunning lyrical essay called "Metamorphosen des Heidenrösleins," the poet deconstructs Goethe's famous ballad "Heidenröslein," a poem set to music by Schubert that every German schoolchild once knew by heart and still a well-known song around the world—witness the thirty-plus versions, spoken and sung, now available on YouTube, including a Japanese video sung by Herman Weng. Here the key word is *Heiden*: Goethe's is a wild rose, one that grows on the open heath or meadow: "Röslein auf den Heiden" appears twice in each stanza as a refrain:

Sah ein Knab' ein Röslein stehn,
Röslein auf den Heiden,
War so jung und morgenschön
Lief er schnell, es nah zu shen,
Sah's mit vielen Freuden.
Röslein, Röslein, Röslein rot,
Röslein auf der Heiden.

Knabe sprach: Ich breche dich,
Röslein auf der Heiden!
Röslein sprach: Ich steche dich,
Daß du ewig denkst an mich,
Und ich will's nicht leiden.
Röslein, Röslein, Röslein rot,
Röslein auf der Heiden

Und der wilde Knabe brach
's Röslein auf der Heiden;
Röslein wehrte sich und stach,
Half ihm doch kein Weh und Ach,
Mußt' es eben leiden
Röslein, Röslein, Röslein rot,
Röslein auf der Heiden.[28]

Tawada tells us she learned this song in Japan, where the first two lines become "warabe wa mitari / nonaka no bara."[29] The three-syllable word *warabe* means "Knabe"—boy—but Japanese uses no article and omits the verb *sah* (saw); then, too, the word for "Röslein" is not repeated. The music, Tawada notes, forces an unnatural accent on the third syllable of *warabé*, as later on other syllables, so that the Japanese words lose their separate identity and the sense of Goethe's poem more or less evaporates. Such loss of identity, Tawada suggests, has its value, for the reader/listener begins to notice things that may well escape the poem's Western audience.

Goethe's ballad, based on a medieval folk song, has invariably been read as a love poem: like so many rose poems in our tradition, the rose is the beautiful and desired young girl who blossoms, ripens, is "plucked" by the amorous male, and "dies," whether literally or figuratively. Goethe's biographers usually read "Heidenröslein" in the light of the poet's youthful affair with Friederike Brion, the innocent young daughter of the village pastor at Sesenheim. Critics who speak of the poem (or Schubert's song) declare that its subject is not a flower but "deflowering"—indeed rape.[30]

Tawada's own reading of "Heidenröslein" has to do with her understanding of the term *Die Heiden*, the plural noun derived from the *Heide*, wild meadow or heath, meaning "heathens, pagans." When, in the sixteenth century, Catholic missionaries came to Japan, she remarks, perhaps they thought that the heathens had to be converted to Christianity before they would stop plundering the earth of its fruits. *Heiden*, she posits, relating "Heidenröslein" to other Goethe lyrics as well as to the novels *The Sorrows of Young Werther* and *Elective Affinities*, is regularly related to conversion. Our current slogans such as "Save the forests" and "Save the children of the Third World" always imply that those to be converted are "heathens" or at least those Others who have not yet seen the light.

In this scheme of things, it is important that the word *Röslein*, is grammatically neuter. Tawada knows very well that in German, grammar and gender don't always match—the sun, for example, is feminine (*Die Sonne*), the moon (*Der Mond*) masculine. But the neuter case of the diminutive *Röslein* provides a case for the flower's bisexuality. Then, too, this little wild rose is no shrinking violet. In stanza 2, Röslein warns the boy that, if plucked, it will prick him and that furthermore, "Ich will's nicht leiden" (I won't tolerate it). In stanza 3, the wild rose fulfills this threat, and in the enigmatic lines 18–19 we read that no moaning and groaning ("Kein Weh und "Ach") helped him, that he "mußt es eben leiden": he had to put up with the pain. The will to violate the flower, in other words, does not go unpunished.

Goethe, as Tawada knows, was no sort of Christian: his concept of redemption involves recycling rather than removal. Thus at the climax of Faust II, *Heiden* (pagans) in the form of fauns, witches, giants, and figures from Greek mythology cast a spell that brings the rose petals strewn on Gretchen's grave back to life. It is in this sense that Gretchen is *gerettet* (saved). The revenge of nature is real: as the *Heidenröslein* warns its destroyer, he will have something to remember it by.

It is an ingenious argument for an ecological reading of a poem or song usually understood as the generic lament for the transience of beauty and love. But it is not the persuasiveness of Tawada's argument qua argument that is at issue here but rather the role such creative reading plays in Tawada's own exophonic poetics. The point about *Heiden* would not be—indeed has not been—noticed by the native German reader; it is only in "making it strange" that the exophonic writer raises the deeper issues of both reading and writing poetry. Indeed, so careless are our usual reading habits that in actual transcriptions of "Heidenröslein" found on the Internet, the pronoun *ihm* (him) in line 18—"Half *ihm* doch kein Weh und Ach"—is falsely transcribed as *ihr* (her), transforming the entire meaning of the ballad: "Half *ihr* doch kein Weh und Ach": "No oh's and ah's could help *her*."

What a difference a phoneme makes! The title piece of Tawada's *Sprachpolizei und Spielpolyglotte* was originally written as an homage to the great Austrian experimental poet Ernst Jandl, whose "der und die" is riffed upon by Charles Bernstein in *Shadowtime* (see chapter 4), and whose collections of poems, bearing titles like *lechts und rinks* (reft and light) and *Laut und Luise* (loud and Louise, the pun being on *leise*, soft) provide Tawada with a set of generative citations in the essay itself.[31]

Sprachpolizei opens with a series of questions, presumably those the poet herself is regularly asked by well-meaning friends and colleagues:

> Does the Japanese language have a grammar too, or do people speak without any rules?
>
> How do you mean?
>
> Is there gender? No? Are there plural and singular? No? Is there declension? No? Are there prepositions? No? Definite and indefinite articles? No?
>
> "Is there botany in Japan or do plants grow without rules?" (25)

So alien is a language without those Western oppositions—masculine-feminine, singular-plural, definite-indefinite article—and without prepositions, that Japanese evidently strikes Germans (indeed any European or American) as having no grammar at all: hence the absurd question about botany. In return, Tawada cannot understand why nouns *should* be masculine or feminine—"do words have wombs?"—especially since gender is so often arbitrary: "Is *der Rock* [skirt] masculine, while *die Hose* [pair of trousers] is feminine?"

But it is not just a question of a foreign grammar to be mastered. The words themselves, as we saw in the case of *ihm* and *ihr* in *Heidenröslein*, give way to paragrammatic possibilities not apparent to the native German speaker. Suppose, the poet wonders, you were to separate the two words in the compound *Radfahren* (to ride a bike). Would the break suggest that there are two bikes in use?

> When you prefer to write the two words together, we are riding a tandem. Here comes a policeman who says it is against the law to ride a tandem on the new street in the Inner City. Why? We've always used a tandem before. We can't divide the bicycle in half. (*Spiel*, 26)

The stubborn literalism of Tawada's logic (one thinks of Rimbaud's "j'ai voulu dire ça littéralement et dans tous les sens")—a literalism that makes it impossible to read *through* the words in question—raises the stakes of poetic possibility. The compound noun *Mundharmonika*, divided differently, becomes *Mundhar* (mouthhair) plus *Monika*. "But what is a mouthhair? A hair that grows in the mouth?" (*Spiel*, 27). Evidently Ernst Jandl, whose poems Tawada cites throughout, uses the phrase in his "straßenelend in westberlin"—literally, "street misery in West Berlin," which has five words instead of the German three. In Tawada's new lexicon, this would suggest—wouldn't it?—an increase in poverty.

How, in any case, to deduce the meaning of a foreign word from its physical appearance? "What happens if one writes 'Anna' with two small *a*'s and two small *n*'s? Then Anna becomes as small as Alice in Wonderland." Or again, "Some think the length of a word can be measured by the number of its letters. *Leben* [life] has five letters, whereas *Krankenversicherung* [health insurance] has nineteen." What is the relationship between the two? And how does one learn what a given suffix might mean? "Many adjectives end with 'ant,' for example: significant, redundant, elegant, or arrogant. All the same, everyone knows that an elephant can never be an adjective" (*Spiel*, 30). This last example complicates the issue even further because "everyone" must refer to native speakers for whom "the meaning of a word is its use in the language" (Wittgenstein). For the exophonic poet, such commonsensical notions as that one cannot call someone "my elephant friend," or observe that "she gave an elephant speech," take some time to learn, and when the distinctions become clear, these may be precisely the locutions the poet wishes to use, as when the narrator of Beckett's *How It Is* refers to a "llama emergency dream" or an "asparagus burst abscess."

Having invented language games for the adjectives and adverbs, the small qualifiers like *nur* ("only," "just"), and the homonyms and antonyms, Tawada concludes her meditation with a *lettriste* passage:

> A sentence is a form of power. A word is a riddle. A letter is a traveler. He can leave the sentence. In his stead comes another. A *G* is replaced by a *P*, so *Gott* becomes *Pott*. A P is exchanged with a G, so your record [*Platte*] becomes a smooth disc [*Glatte Scheibe*]. . . . You cross the border between *l* and *r*, between a long and short vowel, between *ö* and *e*. The Lord [*der Herr*] is no hell [*Hölle*]. And he doesn't go there. But the Lord [*der Herr*] hears what has happened in Hell [*der Hölle*]. I suddenly remember the Japanese word *Jigokumimi*, which translates literally as "the hearing of hell" [*das Hören der Hölle*]. It means someone who is hard of hearing, who can hear well only when someone speaks badly of him. So clear hearing [*Hellhörikeit*] also takes you to hell. The punishment occurs because of the confusion between *Hölle* and *Hell*. Catholic grammar waits eagerly for the punishment and deliberately plays the wicked child. (35–36)

Hölle, hören, Herr, hell (hell, hear, Lord, light): substitute these words for one another or place them side by side and remarkable things happen. *Hölle*, it turns out, needn't be hell.

"Last year's words," we read in Eliot's "Little Gidding," "belong to last year's language." This is an important admission on Eliot's part. And in *ABC of Reading*, Pound insists that "good writers are those who keep the language efficient. That is, keep it accurate, keep it clear."[32] For these great modernists, efficiency and renewal went hand in hand with a cleaning-up operation, the poet's aim being, in Eliot's words, "to purify the language of the tribe." But in the twenty-first century, *purity* can hardly be the norm, given the polyglot speech of our "tribe" of citizens. On the contrary, if poetry is, in Pound's words, "the most concentrated form of verbal expression," if it is "language charged with meaning to the utmost possible degree" (*ABC*, 36, 28), the "charge" must include continuous infiltration and translation—a watchful steering of one's boat "from one shore to another." Say parsley.

7

Conceptual Bridges / Digital Tunnels: Kenneth Goldsmith's *Traffic*

Again the traffic lights that skim thy swift
Unfractioned idiom, immaculate sigh of stars,
Beading thy path — condense eternity:
And we have seen night lifted in thine arms.
Hart Crane, "To Brooklyn Bridge," 1930[1]

Right now you've also got jam-ups on the
Brooklyn Bridge, bumper-to-bumper to
Brooklyn but the lower roadway is wide
open. The Brooklyn Bridge is swamped.
Kenneth Goldsmith, Traffic[2]

The Brooklyn Bridge, whose elegant "curveship" Hart Crane and other Modernists celebrated as the emblem of a new visionary engineering, is now just another of the many clogged arteries — bridges and tunnels — connecting the island of Manhattan to the surrounding landmasses — Brooklyn and Queens to the east, the Bronx to the north, New Jersey to the west. Those headlights, once seen from the city's skyscrapers as constituting a "swift unfractioned idiom, immaculate sigh of stars," have become the glare of the giant gridlock of the New York nightscape. Bridge, tunnel, highway traffic — or even passage through one-way city streets, whether in New York or London, Athens or Beijing — has become a fact of life that we accept with a sigh or shrug as we navigate our way through it, ears tuned to those radio "sigalerts," as we call them in Los Angeles, that tell us which freeway to avoid, which tunnel is undergoing roadwork, and which bridge is blocked by an overturned vehicle.

Traffic is the second volume of Kenneth Goldsmith's *Trilogy*. The first, *Weather* (2005), transcribes a year's worth of daily weather reports for the tri-state area (New York, New Jersey, Connecticut) from the New York radio station WINS (1010 AM); *Traffic* (2007) records a twenty-four-hour period of WINS's "Panasonic Jam Cam [Camera]" New York traffic reports at ten-minute intervals on the first day of a holiday weekend; the third, *Sports* (2008), contains a broadcast transcription of an entire (five-hour) baseball game between the New York Yankees and the Boston Red Sox in August 2006, as reported by the well-known Yankees commentators John Sterling and Suzyn Waldman.

Transcribing weather forecasts, traffic reports, play-by-play Yankee Stadium broadcasts: what could be more pointless than such neo-Dada games? Goldsmith himself has added fuel to the critical fire by insisting that his "conceptual" pieces are "boring," "unreadable," and "uncreative." In a widely disseminated manifesto published on the website of the august Poetry Foundation of America, for example, he declares:

> Conceptual writing or uncreative writing is a poetics of the moment, fusing the avant-garde impulses of the last century with the technologies of the present, one that proposes an expanded field for 21st century poetry. . . . Conceptual writing obstinately makes no claims on originality. On the contrary, it employs intentionally self and ego effacing tactics using uncreativity, unoriginality, illegibility, appropriation, plagiarism, fraud, theft, and falsification as its precepts; information management, word processing, databasing, and extreme process as its methodologies; and boredom . . . as its ethos. Language as junk, language as detritus. . . . *entartete sprache*, everyday speech, illegibility, unreadability, machinistic repetition. Obsessive archiving & cataloging, the debased language of media & advertising; language more concerned with quantity than quality. . . . With the rise of appropriation-based literary practices, the familiar or quotidian is made unfamiliar or strange when left semantically intact. No need to blast apart syntax. Conceptual writing is more interested in a *thinkership* rather than a readership. Readability is the last thing on this poetry's mind. Conceptual writing is good only when the idea is good; often, the idea is much more interesting than the resultant texts.[3]

And in the related "Paragraphs on Conceptual Writing" Goldsmith adds, "In conceptual writing the idea or concept is the most important aspect of the work. When an author uses a conceptual form of writing, it means that all of the planning and decisions are made beforehand and the execution is a perfunctory affair. The idea becomes a machine that makes the text."[4]

If this last passage sounds familiar, it's because "Paragraphs on Conceptual Writing" is an almost verbatim recycling of Sol LeWitt's foundational statement on Conceptual art, first published in *Artforum* in 1967 and widely disseminated.[5] In the sentences above, substitute "author" for "artist," and "text" or "writing" for "art," and the two are identical. Was Goldsmith, then, too lazy to make up his own theoretical statement? Is he just pulling our leg? Or is his "plagiarism" in fact a sly way of reinforcing his argument that aesthetic concepts formulated in the art world half a century ago, and now so widely accepted that they are no longer subject to debate, are treated as suspect in a literary world that has not yet caught up with the visual arts?

How do we account for the time lag? Unlike the visual arts or music, architecture or dance, photography or video—art forms that turn to the verbal to convey the "idea or concept" at issue—literature is, by definition, always already made of language: indeed, it *is* language, no doubt defamiliarized and reconstructed but the language we all use nevertheless. Accordingly, the prominence of language in the visual field of the artwork—a situation central to Duchamp's *Readymades* and, by the 1960s, to the work of Joseph Kosuth and Yoko Ono, Yves Klein and Lawrence Weiner, as well as to the dance pieces of Yvonne Rainer—has no real parallel in poetry. Duchamp could take an ordinary dog comb and make it count as "art" by giving it the caption "Classify combs by the number of their teeth." Or again, he endowed a nondescript French window (not so nondescript since its panes were made not of glass but green leather and hence opaque) with the ambiguous title *French Widow*. To make a comparable move in poetry, one would have to eliminate or at least decompose all the words and phrases. Concrete poetry comes close to this goal, breaking down larger coherent phrasal units into assemblages of morphemes and letters to be looked at. Sound poetry is even more radical: at its best, as in the work of Henri Chopin or Steve McCaffery, "translation" into coherent semantic units is quite impossible, although the suggestibility quotient of the enunciated sounds may be quite high.

Goldsmith's own poetry began under the sign of concrete poetry (see the elegant word/number constellations in his early artist's book *73 Poems*), and his recorded "singings" of the "big" theorists—Derrida and Baudrillard, Adorno and Benjamin—may be classified as "sound poems," in their move to undermine meaning in favor of pitch and rhythmic structure.[6] But the so-called Conceptual works, beginning with *Soliloquy* (2001)—the transcription of every word Goldsmith spoke for a one-week period in New York City (but not those of the many people he spoke to)—are designed to look like normal "books," one block of print following another in what we might call "referential" prose. In Conceptual writing, as opposed to Conceptual art, Goldsmith implies, positioning himself against the Sol LeWitt he "plagiarizes," the issue is less to bring together diverse media (e.g., word and image) than it is to relate the stated conceptual germ ("this book reproduces a year's worth of daily weather forecasts") to the text itself. But because both concept and resultant text draw on the same linguistic base, most readers have taken Goldsmith at face value when he declares, "I am the most boring writer that has ever lived," or again, "You really don't need to read my books to get the idea of what they're like; you just need to know the general concept," and so on.[7] Indeed, Goldsmith's provocative equation of poetry with "word processing" or "information management" has met with strong resistance from the poetry community—not just from the Establishment but, perhaps surprisingly, from such well-known experimentalists as Ron Silliman.

"What does it mean for a work of art to be eminently likeable and almost completely unreadable?" Silliman wonders in a long entry (2006) on his influential poetry blog. "This is the ultimate trick at the heart of the project of Kenny Goldsmith's self-announced uncreative writing." Since the poet's "projects, by design, never stand on their own," Silliman argues, the reader invariably turns to "the cult of the artist as his own work of art." And egotism is not the only problem: another is the refusal of history. For in merely recycling the words of others—whether from the New York Times as in Day or from radio as in Weather—Goldsmith denies the very possibility of the poet's ability to have perspective on the cultural moment, much less to critique it. A valueless synchronicity becomes all: indeed, "Kenny Goldsmith's actual art project is the projection of Kenny Goldsmith."[8]

This argument sounds reasonable if we assume that what Goldsmith says about a given work is equivalent to what it is. For Silliman and similar critics of the books in question, there is evidently never a question but that Day (2003) is a mechanical transcription of a single day's copy of the New York Times, that the earlier Fidget documents every move Goldsmith's body made for a twenty-four-hour period, or that Soliloquy records every word Goldsmith uttered for a week in 2000.[9] It is the poet, after all, who insists that it is only the "concept" of these books that counts, that indeed it is impossible to "read" Day or Fidget or Soliloquy.

"Never trust what writers say about their own work," observes Walter Benjamin, himself a master of appropriation, in a note for his Arcades

Project.[10] In the case of Conceptual art, this warning makes little sense, given that, by definition, what the Conceptual artist *says* about the work is often equivalent to the work itself, as in the case of Robert Rauschenberg's famous "telegram"—"This is a portrait of Iris Clert if I say so"—sent to the Iris Clert Gallery in Paris in response to its request for a Rauschenberg painting. But "Conceptual" poetics works somewhat differently: in Goldsmith's own case, the appropriated text is often submitted to a particular Oulipo-like constraint that complicates the process, even as the materiality of the text—its visual dimension—plays a central role.

Consider the place of D. H. Lawrence's short story "The Rocking-Horse Winner" in Goldsmith's six-hundred-page volume *No. 111. 2.7.93—10.20.96,* published in 1997. In an interview, I asked Goldsmith if he had ever read Lawrence's brilliant modern parable, which he includes without title or acknowledgment in what he calls his "useless encyclopedic reference book."[11] *No. 111* is an assemblage of all the phrases collected by the poet between the two dates listed in the title that end in the ubiquitous phoneme *schwa* ("er" as in "fath*er*"); the phrases are organized alphabetically by syllable count, beginning with one-syllable entries for chapter 1 ("A, a, aar, aas, aer, agh, ah, air . . ."), two for chapter 2 ("A door, à la, a pear, a peer, a rear, a ware"), and ending with chapter VMMCCMMVIII, the 7,228-syllable "Rocking-Horse Winn*er*."[12] In response to my question, Goldsmith insisted he had never read Lawrence's story, except insofar as he had counted its syllables:

> I only chose that story because the last syllable of the last word in the story, *"win-ner,"* ended in an "er." Because the story had more syllables than any other entry in the book, it was used as the last chapter. So theoretically, I felt that I could have included any short story or even full-length novel into *111* and would have been justified in doing so. It was just a matter of nerve or finding the courage to do so. . . . I know it sounds prudish or puritanical, but for me to read "The Rocking Horse Winner" as is—within the context of *No. 111*—would destroy some crucial conceptual part of my book.[13]

But is the selection of "The Rocking-Horse Winner" really just a matter of chance? Would any short story—there must be hundreds whose title ends on *er*, for example, "The Secret Sharer"—do? In an essay for *Open Letter*, Molly Schwartzburg notes:

> The story brilliantly describes the ultimate "one-trick pony": a toy horse—and a boy—that can only do one thing over and over again. Just as the boy helps his uncle win massive purses at the racetrack, Goldsmith produces massive books. And like the Goldsmith of *Day,* Lawrence's unnamed boy is utterly uncreative. . . .

The name of the winning horse is merely a fact that he knows before anyone else. . . . . Goldsmith and the boy are doubles of a sort: like the boy, Goldsmith rides his hobbyhorse, and yet at the same time, seems to be undertaking a deeply serious project.[14]

And one could posit further connections. Like the John Cage who regularly insisted he had never bothered to read Joyce's *Finnegans Wake*, a text he "wrote through" quite frequently, Goldsmith wants us to believe that Lawrence's story is mere grist for the conceptual mill. But then the description of the constraint used throughout *No. 111* is itself dubious: Goldsmith claims to be arranging, by syllable count, all the phrases collected between February 7, 1993, and October 20, 1996, that end in *schwa* (er), but how were these in fact assembled? In chapter 6, for example, there are six six-syllable units ending in *er* that begin with the letters *b-o*: "Bob The Anal Fissure," "Bolshevick Behavior, bootblack wickerwhacker, bored to a bellwether, both knew how to shower, Boy what a bagbiter." From what sources could these disparate and fantastic items have been "collected"? And why these and no others like "born to be wealthier"? We are given the ostensible rules of the game, but what is the game?

Nothing but an actual reading of the text can clarify the questions of choice and chance that arise here and elsewhere. This is as true of the *Trilogy*, with its ostensibly simple transcriptions of weather, traffic, and sports reports, as of *No. 111*, *Soliloquy*, and *Day*. Suppose, then, that we put aside, for the moment, Goldsmith's insistence that his books are "unreadable" and read *Traffic* as a book about traffic.[15]

Midnight Gridlock

Traffic is the second installment of what should properly be called *The New York Trilogy*.[16] All the speech recorded in these books, from the WINS daily weather reports to the twenty-four-hour traffic alerts to the commentary on the Yankees game, is entirely New York material. Indeed, a stranger would not recognize many of the names included: such commonly used abbreviations as BQE (Brooklyn-Queens Expressway) and LIE (Long Island Expressway) may be unfamiliar even to those, like myself, who grew up in New York. More important than names: the ballpark is New York's iconic Yankee Stadium, the weather is New York weather—which is to say extreme and unpredictable, ranging from scorching summers to glacial winters—and the traffic flow is determined by the basic fact that Manhattan is an island: a very crowded island. Los Angeles traffic may be just as heavy and the distances to be traveled even greater than in New York, but it doesn't quite have the grid-lock produced by the dependency on bridges and tunnels. And San Fran-cisco, which also depends on its bridges, offers fewer options, so that there is less scrambling for the hot tips offered by WINS's Jam Cam. Then, too, the dramatic seasonal contrasts that characterize New York are absent from San Francisco and Los Angeles; in the latter, according to a common quip, there are only two seasons—day and night. The rhythm of the different cir-culation systems is thus quite variable.

The twenty-four-hour WINS traffic reports (numbered American-style, 12 to 12, rather than from 0 to 24, but with the designations a.m. and p.m. missing) take place, we learn in the very first sentence, on a "big holiday weekend." But which holiday is it? For all the seeming precision and doc-umentary veracity of Goldsmith's book, one can't tell. There are no refer-ences to ice or snow, so it does not seem to be Christmas or New Year's or even Presidents' Day; there is no turkey talk, so it doesn't sound much like Thanksgiving, which is, in any case, more than just a weekend. Memorial Day? The Fourth of July? Labor Day? There are no identifying tags—a situa-tion that makes the reader wonder how Goldsmith managed to erase any and all references to specific holiday paraphernalia such as Fourth of July fire-works or Memorial Day gravestones. Indeed, we don't even know whether the legal holiday is a Friday or a Monday and thus whether the twenty-four-hour cycle transcribed in *Traffic* is that of Thursday midnight through Friday midnight or later in the weekend. Then, too, by the end of the narrative, the traffic has eased up enough to suggest that we have reached the end of the holiday: if alternate side-of–the-street parking rules will be in effect "tomor-row," the next day must be a workday. But how can this be the case—how do we get from beginning to end of the holiday weekend in twenty-four hours, whichever the legal holiday?

There is, in other words, something surreal about this seemingly ordi-nary sequence of traffic reports. Not only do the particular weekend and day of the week remain elusive, but consider the cover (figure 7.1). It cannot be a photograph of New York—as the larger source photograph (figure 7.2) makes even clearer, given the predominance of small old cars on the road, the obviously foreign buses, and taxis, the sign "Mudanzas" (Spanish for "Mov-ers") on the big rig in the center lane, and the foreign license plate (971 BSK) on the second car in front. Then, too, New York drivers are unlikely to get out of their cars to inspect the scene as the men (no women visible) do here, but the urge to step outside the car may also have to do with the weather—

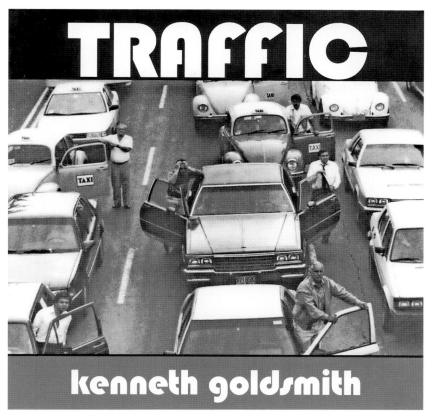

Figure 7.1. Front cover of Kenneth Goldsmith's *Traffic* (Los Angeles: Make Now, 2007).

it seems to be a very hot day—or with the sighting of an accident up ahead. The many long-sleeved white shirts suggest, moreover, that this photograph dates from an earlier time—say, the 1970s. The six-lane highway (with dangerous access lanes) may well be in Mexico City, the sly implication being that New York circulation in the twenty-first century can be channeled through the images of gridlock in the smog-ridden chaotic thoroughfares of the Mexican metropolis of thirty or forty years ago.

But our climate is also very different. In WINS-speak, accidents are viewed as something to avoid by taking another route: "On the Garden State Parkway north near the Bergen tolls, an accident has two right lanes closed off" (W 33), or "They're clearing that accident over by the Brooklyn-Queens Expressway, all lanes are being reopened" (W 70). The personal element—represented by the anonymous men on the cover—has been erased. Indeed, in its focus on traffic tips rather than travelers, *Traffic* positions itself as a cu-

Figure 7.2. Anon., photograph used for the cover of *Traffic*.

rious antidote—or at least response—to such searing critiques of postmodern automobile traffic as Jean-Luc Godard's *Weekend* (1967).[17]

Godard's famous *nouvelle vague* film follows a bourgeois Parisian couple as they leave for a weekend trip across the French countryside to collect (by murder, if need be) what they consider to be their rightful inheritance from the wife's parents. After a breakdown on the road, the couple gets involved in scenes of violence, killing, and even cannibalism: the film is designed to present traffic as the emblem of the brutal consumerism of the capitalist class. Thus the film's most famous scene is an eight-minute tracking shot of a traffic jam on the country road outside Paris (figure 7.3). It is a shot almost unbearable to watch and listen to: bombarded by a soundtrack of incessant honking of horns, we see cars, trailers, and trucks wiggling through the traffic, stuck in the roadside ditches, overturned, going backward, and crashing

Figure 7.3. Still from Jean-Luc Godard, *Weekend* (1967).

into one another. Bleeding corpses line the roadside, even as passengers in some of the stalled vehicles play cards or car-to-car volleyball, embrace, sunbathe, have picnics, and flag down each other's cars. Only at the very end of this seemingly interminable sequence does the couple's black convertible pass the police barrier and make a right turn into the "open" countryside, the sound of screeching horns giving way to pop music. And of course, their newfound mobility doesn't last long.

Weekend presents a terrifying image of traffic as an embodiment of the evils of consumerism in a heartless society. Technology is seen as the enemy of the human spirit: the automobile pollutes and ultimately destroys the natural world. Godard's is the antithesis of F. T. Marinetti's Futurist dream in which "combustion engines and rubber tires are divine. Gasoline is divine."[18] But the spirit of 1968 with its Maoist fervor and taste for violence has not lasted: in the new century, Godard's indictment of contemporary consumer culture is as anachronistic as is Marinetti's celebration, in the 1909 manifesto, of his beautiful black shark of a motor car overturned in a ditch. Indeed, in our own moment the weekend traffic crunch is nothing if not normative, quite simply the condition of everyday life. And here Goldsmith's *Traffic* is apposite.

Unlike *Weekend*, or, for that matter, unlike J. G. Ballard's great science-fiction novel *Crash* (1972), where, in the novelist's own words, "the car crash, a sinister portent of a nightmare marriage between sex and technology," is used "not only as a sexual image, but as a total metaphor for man's life in today' society,"[19] *Traffic*, written as it was at the beginning of the new century, takes the minute-by-minute traffic incidents it records very much in its—forgive the pedestrian term—stride. Submitting his chosen Jam Cam reports to the Aristotelian unities of time, place, and action, Goldsmith has produced a vivid representation of contemporary urban life in all its ritual, boredom, nervousness, frustration, fear, apathy—and also its pleasure. Goldsmith's book casts no blame, finds no first cause, and attributes no venality to anyone, nor does it assume that traffic has brought out the worst in us. Rather, traffic is that which *is*—messy, unbearable, infuriating, debilitating, but also challenging, invigorating, and unpredictable. Traffic is both an existential and a linguistic challenge: the anonymous Jam Cam voice tries to liven things up by using colorful phrases like "what a doozy," "snail's pace," "absolutely crawling," "stacked up," "getting clobbered," "the makings of a rough ride."[20] And yet the real action of this twenty-four-hour period can be conveyed only by the anchors' description of what is happening, one moment at a time.

Among the great ironies of radio traffic reports, as they are transcribed here, is that they tell us so little and that their predictions are so often wrong. At 12:31 (in the opening chapter), "midnight gridlock" has taken over both bridges and tunnels: "there is a stalled bus inside the Lincoln Tunnel that is refusing to move, blocking all access to New Jersey" (T 2). But by 1:21, less than an hour later, the reporter is telling us that the "Lincoln Tunnel [is] still your best way across the Hudson River" (T 6), and at 1:51, "the good news" is that "the Lincoln Tunnel, that's still the best way across the Hudson" (T 7). Then again, tunnels and bridges, all of them, are the greatest gamble, for once the driver has opted for the George Washington Bridge or the Midtown Tunnel, there is no turning back and no alternative. Elevated highways like the Major Deegan, running through the East Bronx, are more user-friendly; clogged as they are, they might just reopen. Here is the entry for 11:21 on the getaway morning:

> Whoa! What a backup lining up to the tolls here at the Holland and Lincoln Tunnels. We now have probably close to a twenty minute wait lining up for the tolls at the Holland Tunnel from all approaches, and twenty-five to thirty minutes coming down into the Lincoln Tunnel. Still pretty good along the GW Bridge. And we had an accident and construction on the Tappan Zee Bridge in Westchester, but not a bad looking ride overall. The Brooklyn Bridge has gotten very slow coming back into Manhattan and the delay coming into the Midtown Tunnel has ballooned. There's gotta be over a thirty-minute backup, it goes back up to before the BQE [Brooklyn-Queens Expressway]. As I look in live here on the Panasonic Jam Cam, you do have delays along the Whitestone and Triboro

Bridge too. And if you're in Manhattan coming downtown, it has improved a bit on the West Side Highway and the FDR Drive, especially the FDR Drive in the 90s. But what has gotten worse is Broadway. Don't get involved in Broadway at all. (T 53)

This radio bulletin, as Goldsmith transcribes it, makes for theater of the absurd. There is an accident on the Tappan Zee Bridge, yet the report maintains that the bridge crossing is "not a bad looking ride overall." The Whitestone and Triboro bridges, connecting the Bronx and Queens to Manhattan, are jammed, but they feed into the FDR Drive, which is "OK," whereas Broadway is inexplicably jammed. The Jam Cam reports suggest no solution, no corrective; they merely offer practical alternatives for specific problems. Here's a tip: take the Holland Tunnel rather than the George Washington Bridge. Given the existential situation—too much available money, too many cars, too many places to go, even on weekends and even through bumper-to-bumper traffic—there is little that can be done to change things. But problems also produce solutions; one must be flexible and *inventive* so as to find another road—an alternative. Driving, in this scheme of things, becomes a mental challenge—how to get there—rather than a preplanned move toward one's destination. Getting there, ironically, really does become half the fun!

John Cage often cited the Zen koan "If something is boring after two minutes, try it for four. If still boring, try it for eight, sixteen, thirty-two, and so on. Eventually one discovers that it's not boring at all but very interesting."[21] It is in this sense that Goldsmith's "uncreative" and "boring" narrative becomes increasingly absorbing. The more traffic bulletins one reads, the more questions occur. Where, for starters, are all these people going and why? If it is common knowledge that "big holiday" weekend traffic is unbearable, why subject yourself to it? What percentage of New Yorkers stay home? And what is the difference between those who come *into* the city and those who *go out*? Between the natives, who have a shared vocabulary as to the LIE Expressway, Tappan Zee Bridge, FDR Drive, and so on, and the strangers who try to take the straightest path recommended by MapQuest, only to find themselves stuck in the Holland Tunnel for hours?

And what about the traffic anchors themselves, those invisible voices that deliver the reports at ten-minute intervals? From the perspective of a Godard—or, say, a Guy Debord[22]—to be an anchor would be, no doubt, to be confined to one of the lowest circles of hell, aiding and abetting what should in any decent society be banned as a menace. But when, out of curiosity, I googled the radio station 1010 WINS, the first item that appeared was a bio-graphical sketch of one such job-holder:

> Pete Tauriello has been 1010 WINS morning traffic anchor for 18 Years. Pete began his radio career 29 years ago at Seton Hall University as a disc jockey on WSOU. . . .
>
> "The last thing I ever expected to be was a traffic reporter," he says. "I sort of fell into this job and then fell in love with it, so here I am 18 years later and lucky enough to be on the biggest radio station in the world!"
>
> Pete has a BA in communications, and has been married to his college sweet-heart, Maureen, for 25 years. His 3 children, Sean 22, Kim 19 and Mark 14, keep him as busy off the air as he is during the morning rush hour!
>
> Ask him what his favorite jam cam is and he'll tell you, "It has to be our East River camera. I'm a bridge freak and I get to look at these beautiful works or archi-tecture all day at the touch of a button. I really can enjoy both of my passions . . . radio and beautiful bridges . . . and they pay me too. I ask you, does it get better than that?"
>
> As far as his favorite traffic story goes, "One day we had this gigantic water main break and the subway stations looked like waterfalls. I was called upon to do this story for our sister station in Chicago, WMAQ." His biggest fear? "That all the traffic jams will one day be solved and I'll be out of a job."
>
> Pete, don't worry about it.[23]

Twin passions: "radio and beautiful bridges." What makes this little vignette so amusing is its element of genuine surprise—a surprise too often absent in the pages of so-called original writing. The Canadian Coach House Press has recently published a book of poems by the experimental feminist poet Sina Queyras called *Expressway*, a book that, according to the book jacket, "ex-poses the paradox of modern mobility: the more roads and connections we build, the more separate we feel." And the poems, with their strong indict-ment of the "corporations and commerce" that have allowed expressways to dominate our lives, includes lines like the following:

> Car Crashes into Petrol Station Making a left-hand.
> His car was broadsided.
> Fatal car crash in Al Ghusais. Police investigate.
> Survivor remembers. Impact. Crash.
> Plane crash-landed on a major expressway.
> "Honeybee" dies in Two-car accident.
> Near Mustang Road.
> Does this scene look familiar?[24]

Perhaps too familiar. The "real" action, when we turn to the minute-by-minute transcriptions in *Traffic,* is much more variable and surprising. Escaping the city on a holiday weekend—or, conversely, coming into the city on the holiday weekend—is seen as a challenge to be overcome by the alert driver. Paradoxes—nothing as abstract or general as "modern mobility," but such paradoxes as that, on the eve of a holiday weekend, midnight turns out to be the worst time to travel because it is the hour when "holiday" road repair is scheduled—haunt the scenario. Despite such "setbacks," the narrative moves from pain to progress, from the "Hudson River horror show" of 12:01 (T 1) and the "absolute nightmare" of 1:11 (T 5) to the moment at 11:01 the following evening when the report begins with the words "It's been a long day here but there is an end in sight on the East Side as we are actually beginning to see movement on the southbound FDR for the first time in hours now that that accident's been cleared by the 59th Street Bridge" (T 111). By 11:21, our anchor person is exclaiming, "And a happy holiday to you too" (112). The tunnels to New Jersey are "looking swell," the GW Bridge "still moving nicely," and "no delays at the Verrazano [Bridge]." There is always, of course, a collision somewhere—right before midnight on Highway 134 in Yorktown. But the final entry (12:00) of the book reads as follows:

> We're over the hump and into the official holiday weekend. I want to wish everybody out there a safe and happy holiday, especially when traveling on the road this weekend. If you're trying to get out of town now, you're in for an easy time of it. No reported delays around the metropolitan area as I see it live on the Panasonic Jam Cam. Let's head over to the East River where we've got no reported delays running the length of the river from the Battery on up to the Triboro. FDR is moving nicely as well. No reported incidents on the West Side Highway which, if you recall, oh, say about six hours ago was simply not moving at all with delays up to three hours. Now it's deserted. And here's what you need to know about the bridges and tunnels: all the East River crossings moving well. No reported incidents at the Triboro, 59th Street Bridge, Queens-Midtown Tunnel. Looking down to the Williamsburg, Manhattan and Brooklyn Bridges, it's one big green light. And over in Jersey, it's never been better with traffic flowing smoothly across the Hudson at both the Lincoln and Holland Tunnels. Even the GW Bridge which has been choked for what seems like the last twenty-four hours is now flowing like water. Remember, alternate side of the street parking rules are in effect for tomorrow. (T 115)

"One big green light"—can life really be so beautiful? From east to west, north to south, traffic is "flowing like water." A triumphant conclusion, worth waiting and struggling for! But of course as the last line—the refrain throughout the piece—suggests, however peaceful that midnight moment is, the cycle never stops: by tomorrow the streets, tunnels, and bridges will once more be clogged.

"Remember, alternate side of the street parking rules are in effect tomorrow." This admonition, which is repeated with minor changes at set intervals throughout *Traffic*—a kind of reality check on the chaotic traffic flow, heralding, as it does, the end of the holiday weekend—gives the book its very particular rhythm. As in minimalist music, a single chord, like the name "GW Bridge," is introduced, repeated in different contexts, and then diminished while a second motif comes to the fore. The melodic phrase "bridges and tunnels" is repeated again and again, with only the slightest variation.

The "alternate parking" refrain, which will appear more than sixty times in the "every ten minutes on the 'ones'" traffic sequence, makes its first appearance at 4.31 a.m.:

> Don't forget the alternate side of the street parking rules, if you do manage to drive into the city, will be suspended for the duration of the holiday, but you'll still have to pay the meters. (T 18)

The warning continues to appear, in shortened form and slightly altered wording, every ten minutes or so until, shortly before 8 a.m., traffic is so choked up that the focus shifts from the Manhattan streets themselves to the movements of the trains, buses, and ferries that serve as traffic alternatives— the Long Island Railroad, Jersey Transit's commuter rail, the Staten Island Ferry, Westchester County Bee Line Buses. Only by 10:41 are cars themselves moving adequately enough for the "alternate side" rule to be mentioned. Jams become worse in the course of the day, and when alternate side parking is mentioned again. it is to say (5:21) that "tomorrow, alternate side parking back in effect citywide in all Five Boroughs" (T 83). From here on out, the refrain is steady: by 11:51 we hear, "Alternate side of the street parking rules are back in effect" (T 113).

But wait a minute: what happened to the holiday? If the alternate side rules were suspended in its honor, how long were they actually in effect? Goldsmith's "factual" narrative, plotted so carefully and divided into neat block-paragraph segments, turns out to be wholly implausible, indicating as it does that this holiday weekend is over before it has even begun. For before anyone can take advantage of the open parking situation, the alternate side rule is back in effect. Time's linear progress, in other words, is illusory: it cannot encompass the events supposed to occur at particular moments on the scale; indeed, time collapses into space. If the final section (12:00), defined as being "over the hump and into the official holiday weekend," is terminated by the resumption of normal traffic rules "tomorrow," then the weekend has all but never happened.

Goldsmith's "transcription" is thus hardly passive recycling. The design of the book emphasizes the hour in question, that hour (e.g., 3:00) printed in boldface on an otherwise blank page, thus calling special attention to the new "chapter." But the chapter separation is illusory, as "events" merely continue. Moreover, these numeric titles are left undesignated (a.m. versus p.m.), and the individual entries, so specifically referring to the exact time of day (e.g., 5:11), never tell us which day this is. In skipping from one day to the next, or starting in midweekend, Goldsmith's book thus transforms the intersection of time and space into a wholly surreal situation. The weekend, far from extended as it is in Godard's film, is here telescoped to fit into twenty-four hours. But in the digital age, a marked segment does not signal any particular chronological frame, even as "place" can be multiple and "action" simultaneous. At the same time, the "plot" ironically turns out to be a perfect Aristotelian one with beginning, middle, and end, as the image of the nightmare city gives way to a momentary vision of the open road—"one big green light" pointing us into the future.

Inevitably, too, this green light recalls the one at the end of Daisy's dock in F. Scott Fitzgerald's *Great Gatsby*. Consider that novel's famous final paragraphs:

> And as I sat there brooding on the old, unknown world, I thought of Gatsby's wonder when he first picked out the green light at the end of Daisy's dock. He had come a long way to this blue lawn, and his dream must have seemed so close that he could hardly fail to grasp it. He did not know that it was already behind him, somewhere back in that vast obscurity, beyond the city, where the dark fields of the republic rolled on under the night.
>
> Gatsby believed in the green light, the orgiastic future that year by year recedes before us. It eluded us then, but that's no matter—tomorrow we will run faster, stretch out our arms farther. . . . And one fine morning—
>
> So we beat on, boats against the current, borne back ceaselessly into the past.[25]

Traffic gives these memorable images of desire an interesting spin. The cars skimming the Long Island Expressway "against the current," headed toward the waters of Long Island Sound, "beat on" into an unknowable future that, as we have already seen with respect to the narrative's time course, is already past. Like Gatsby, *Traffic*'s drivers long to reach "that vast obscurity beyond the city" where all those tunnels and bridges lead, to the streets beyond—streets never mentioned in the radio bulletins. And unattainable as those mysterious "dark fields of the Republic" are, "tomorrow we will run faster" to get there.[26] "Over in Jersey it's never been better with traffic flowing smoothly across the Hudson."

"The Madness of the Unexpected"

The July/August 2009 issue of *Poetry* features a little anthology of "Flarf and Conceptual Writing," edited by Goldsmith. In the introduction, he declares:

> Start making sense. Disjunction is dead. The fragment, which ruled poetry for the past one hundred years, has left the building. Subjectivity, emotion, the body, and desire, as expressed in whole units of plain English with normative syntax, has returned. But not in ways you would imagine. This new poetry wears its sincerity on its sleeve . . . yet no one means a word of it. Come to think of it, no one's really written a word of it. It's been grabbed, cut, pasted, processed, machined, honed, flattened, repurposed, regurgitated, and reframed from the great mass of free-floating language out there just begging to be turned into poetry.[27]

This, like Goldsmith's earlier provocations, has prompted strong objections from fellow poets: Ron Silliman, for example, has again risen to the bait, declaring that no, no, disjunction is not dead at all, and that indeed Goldsmith's own transcriptions (e.g., of the *New York Times* in *Day*) are full of disjunctive words and phrases. As for the claims made for appropriation: "the use of found language being folded, spindled & mutilated in a variety of fashions" is hardly news; consider "Jackson Mac Low's use of insurance texts in *Stanzas for Iris Lezak*, or Kathy Acker's appropriation of the work of Harold Robbins in the 1970s."[28]

Such accusations recall nothing so much as the uproar over Duchamp's ready-mades (from the time of their inception in the 1910s well into the 1960s)—an uproar that the artist himself aided and abetted by insisting that "the choice of readymades is always based on visual indifference and, at the same time, on the total absence of good or bad taste." "I don't believe," Duchamp famously told Pierre Cabanne, "in the creative function of the artist." "He's a man like any other. . . . Now everyone makes something, and those who make things on canvas, with a frame, they're called artists. Formerly, they were called craftsmen, a term I prefer."[29] Such statements must, of course, be understood in context. Duchamp took his "art" very seriously indeed, his objection being not to art as such but specifically to what he took to be the excessive importance given by the artists of his own day to "retinal" art:

> Since Courbet, it's been believed that painting is addressed to the retina. That was everyone's error. The retinal shudder! Before, painting had other functions: it could be religious, philosophical, moral. . . . Our whole century is completely retinal, except for the Surrealists, who tried to go outside it somewhat. And still they didn't go very far! In spite of the fact that Breton says he believes in judging from a Surrealist point of view, down deep he's still really interested in painting in the retinal sense. It's absolutely ridiculous. It has to change.[30]

It has to change. These hardly sound like the words of an artist who doesn't care. "I tried constantly," said Duchamp, "to find something which would not recall what had happened before." And by "what happened before," he meant before in his own work as well as that of others, prompting him to turn to the reproduction in miniature of his earlier work in the boxes and *boîtes en valise* rather than the making of new ready-mades or paintings. "Everything," he tells Cabanne, "was becoming conceptual."[31]

Everything, one might add, including Duchamp's own statements on art, which must be read carefully and contextually in order to understand the artist's actual conception of art making. The same is true for Goldsmith. When, in the *Poetry* feature, he outlines the relation of Conceptual poetry to Flarf and presents specific poets from each category for our consideration, he is, I would argue, producing what is itself a conceptual piece, designed to produce debate as to the *value* of particular movements—movements from which, in fact, Goldsmith has kept his distance, even as Duchamp never quite allowed Dada to claim him as one of its own, citing instead such influences as that of the Cranach paintings he saw in Munich in 1912 and the use of the mathematical perspective of machine drawings he studied at the Bibliothèque Sainte-Geneviève in Paris.[32]

But why the need for so much displacement, so much ironic self-invention? Why call oneself boring or indifferent or uncreative when one obviously has a passionate desire to *create* something new? For Goldsmith, as for such of his precursors as Andy Warhol, John Cage, and especially Duchamp, art defines itself by its struggle with its immediate past. For Duchamp, this meant the retinal art of the Post-Impressionists and Cubists. Since he wouldn't (or couldn't) emulate the painting skills of Picasso or Matisse, Braque, or Gris, he decided at a critical moment to "do something else."[33] But this emphatically did not mean that anything goes or that anyone can be an artist. On the contrary, the enemy was a particular kind of painting, then dominant in Europe as in America.

Goldsmith, educated at the Rhode Island School of Design, was trained to be a visual artist—a painter and sculptor. But since his coming of age coincided with a general acceptance of Conceptual, Minimalist, and Language art, he could move elsewhere only by shifting to the verbal/musical realm, rethinking art issues from the outside: his now celebrated and unique website Ubuweb gives special prominence to avant-garde musical composition, sound poetry, and film. And indeed, only from the outside could it become clear to Goldsmith that the art discoveries of the later twentieth century could function to renew the poetry world. At the same time, from his vantage point the Language school, with its emphasis on nonreferentiality and the dissolution of the first-person lyric mode, was itself still rooted in aesthetic issues no longer fully relevant. Whereas poetry anthologies and blogs continue to this day to debate the relationship of experimental to traditional, raw to cooked, "post-avant" to the "school of quietude" (Silliman's terms),[34] it must have seemed to Goldsmith, as to such other Conceptualists as Caroline Bergvall and Christian Bök, Craig Dworkin and Jan Baetens,[35] that as in Duchamp's case, the time had come to do something else.

Ergo, poetry that doesn't look like any poetry we've seen, presented as "unreadable" so as to challenge us to read it. Its premise, Goldsmith has suggested, is that in a digital environment, language, once "locked onto a page," has become "completely fluid; it's lifted off the page and therefore able to be poured into so many different forms and take so many different shapes and really be molded and sculpted in a way that wasn't possible before."[36] The WINS traffic reports, for example, seemingly identifiable by precise time, can be taken from different calendar dates and spliced to produce a new construct. A similar realignment takes place in *The Weather* or, in a different form, in *Fidget*, where despite the ostensibly "full" record of the body's every movement in the course of a twelve-hour time period, there are curious omissions. The protagonist, for starters, never dresses: as Rubén Gallo notes, "The body wakes and walks about, showers, drinks, and masturbates, but never once does he put on an item of clothing. . . . The nudity of *Fidget* extends beyond the body. The book is . . . a nude text in which language has been stripped down to its most basic elements. . . . The movements included in the book are completely detached from emotions or other affective responses. . . . *Fidget*'s body is thus naked, abject, and machine-like."[37]

Fidget could not have been produced without a tape recorder: Goldsmith taped a small microphone to his body and went about his day describing each of his movements as fully and accurately as possible. But what *is* accuracy in this context? Having completed his experiment, Goldsmith turned from recording to transcription—a process by no means "natural"; on the contrary, in his role as "word processor" Goldsmith has drastically edited the tape so as represent the movements of a hypermechanical body, a body twitching, pressing, stretching, grinding—in short, so "fidgety" it could never sit still long enough to write what is transmitted to us as a piece of *writing*.[38] It is this paradox that animates *Fidget* throughout. *Traffic* similarly "freezes" the speech flow of the radio anchors, creating, in the final analysis, a long minimalist poem, whose Oulipo constraints, visualization of repeated proper names, and mutating signs create textual "bridges and tunnels" that challenge our reading habits.

Indeed, a reading of the *New York Trilogy* takes us back to Benjamin's *Passagen-Werk*, the site of those intricately appropriated and defamiliarized texts that reimagine the ethos of the Second Empire from the vantage point of a soon-to-be Nazi-occupied Paris of the 1930s. Who knows how the "holiday weekend" circulation system detailed so exhaustively (and yet so ambiguously) in *Traffic* will play itself out in the decades to come? Will Manhattan still be accessible by means of the same bridges and tunnels? Will city parking, alternate-side or otherwise, have been eliminated completely? Or will the streets empty out as digital communication replaces "real" transport? And how will poets conceptualize that unimaginable future?

Afterword

Craig Dworkin and Kenneth Goldsmith's new *Anthology of Conceptual Writing*[1] features many texts that have anticipated or taken up the challenge posed by what Goldsmith has called "uncreative writing." Vanessa Place's *Statement of Fact*, for example, is composed of actual court records and police reports, detailing such cases as that of sixty-plus counts against a particularly indefensible rapist, followed by his fruitless appeal—a record that become more and more ambiguous, puzzling, and contradictory as the detailed facts are laid out and the felon's victims' own complicated stories unfold.[2] The more doggedly factual and informational the set of documents presented, the more it manifests a surreal edge.

A similar process occurs in Craig Dworkin's own *Parse*.[3] As the endnote tells us, *Parse* is a "translation" of a widely used 1874 grammar book by the Reverend Edwin A. Abbott called *How to Parse: An Attempt to Apply the Principles of Scholarship to English Grammar*. Abbott's treatise, available to this day and currently a Google book, tries to rationalize every possible grammatical slot, beginning with the definition in chapter 1, "Subject and Object": "The Subject of a Verb in a stating sentence is the word or collection of words answering to the question asked by putting 'Who?' or 'What?' before the Verb." In Abbott's system, this definition is followed by "Caution I. If the Verb is accompanied by an Adverb, as 'He *seldom* sleeps' . . . the Adverb should be repeated in the question: 'Who *seldom* sleeps?' Answer: 'He,' Subject." But as Wittgenstein shows so fully in the *Philosophical Investigations*, not every word in the language can be thus defined. Dworkin's own parsing provides literal renditions of every single punctuation mark or word in Abbott's how-to book, creating a composition with a surreal edge, as in the following:

> parenthesis cardinal Arabic numerical parenthesis marks of quotation *Definite Article subject preposition of the infinitive active present tense transitive verb infinitive mood definite article direct object* past tense verb period marks of quotation (*Parse*, 18)

The more complete the description of the units in a given sentence, the less we know. Indeed, the hyperrationalism of Dworkin's codified grammar recalls Beckett's *Watt* in its mania to communicate what is finally incommuni-

: 167

cable. What, the Duchampian author seems to be asking, *is* grammar anyway? And could we return to origins, "translating" Dworkin's sentences back into the sentences they purport to describe?

In his earlier *Dure*, Dworkin's intertext is an unsigned 1519 self-portrait by Albrecht Dürer that bears the inscription "Do der gelb fleck ist and mit dem finger darauff deut do ist mir weh," which Dworkin translates, "Where the yellow spot is and where I am pointing with my finger, that is where it hurts."[4] The title *Dure*, from *durus* (Latin for "hard"), refers both to the enigmatic art of Dürer as well as to the English derivatives of *durus* like *duration*, *durable*, and *endure*. And Dworkin's intricate citational mosaic-poem examines the poet's own ability to *endure* a particularly painful but very obliquely treated love affair.[5]

In a related vein, the Belgian poet Jan Baetens, whose work has close ties with Oulipo, has produced a witty and moving "novelization" of Jean-Luc Godard's classic 1962 film *Vivre sa vie* by transposing the film's twelve "chapters" into fifteen highly formal love poems—pantoums, hepta-syllabics, reduced sonnets, rhopalic verses—that bear witness to the power of lyric to distance the banality of everyday life and to ironize the film's didactic approach to that life via homage to its visual images, the very images the lyric sequence can render only verbally.[6] As in the case of Dworkin's *Dure*, Baetens's experiment allows for the revival of love poetry by other means.

Meanwhile, Goldsmith is working on a new book to be called *Capital*, modeled on Benjamin's *Arcades Project* and set in New York in the century leading up to the turning point of 9/11/2001. For the past five years, Goldsmith explains, he has been scanning and digitizing every book he could find "about" about New York and then electronically cutting and pasting their "best parts," throwing away the remainder "like empty husks." Thus although the book, which will be finished when it is the exact length of *Arcades*, is made entirely of appropriated text, the passages in question, sorted into folders with alphabetically arranged titles (ranging from "Abstraction," "Advertising Signage," "Alcohol, Bar, Drugs," and "Amnesia" to "World's Fair 39," "World's Fair 64," and "Writing") and cross-referenced without attribution (except in the bibliography at the end), the actual composition of *Capital* will depend on the artist's particular choices. "In the end," says Goldsmith, "I want this to be neither reference book nor history book. It should not have any function whatsoever except to give a completely poetic and subjective view of the way one person might find his way through the mass of literature written about the capital of the twentieth century, New York."[7]

The selection process, rule-bound as it is, with Benjamin's *Arcades Project* providing the parameters, is ultimately carried out *according to taste*, as John Cage put it some twenty years ago in characterizing his own "writings-through," ostensibly generated by chance operations.[8] *According to taste*: it is important to remember that the citational or appropriative text, however unoriginal its actual words and phrases, is always the product of choice—and hence of individual taste. Let me cite once more Antoine Compagnon's *La seconde main*:

> When I cite, I excise, I mutilate, I extract. There is a primary object, placed before me, a text I have read, that I am reading, and the course of my reading is interrupted by a phrase. I return to the beginning; I reread. The phrase reread becomes a formula, isolated from the text. The rereading separates it from that which precedes and that which follows. The chosen fragment converts itself into a text no longer a bit of a text, a part of a sentence or a discourse, but a chosen bit, an amputated limb, not yet a transplant, but already an organ, cut off and placed in reserve.[9]

In the twenty-first century, it is those "reserve" organs, no longer mere fragments but often the texts themselves, that people the poetic landscape. Sometimes the graft works, sometimes it doesn't. But the difference, in Gertrude Stein's words, is spreading.

Notes

CHAPTER ONE

1. Walter Benjamin, "The Author as Producer" (1934), in *Selected Writings*, vol. 2, *1927–1934*, ed. Michael W. Jennings, Howard Eiland, and Gary Smith, trans. Rodney Livingstone (Cambridge, MA: Belknap Press / Harvard University Press, 1999), 771; Charles Bernstein, "Manifest Aversions, Conceptual Conundrums, & Implausibly Deniable Links," *Poetry*, February 2009, http://www.poetryfoundation.org/journal/feature.html?id=182837.

2. *Times Literary Supplement*, September 20, 1923. This review was reprinted in the *TLS*'s "Then and Now" series, June 4, 2009, http://entertainment.timesonline.co.uk/tol/arts_and_entertainment/the_tls/article6430746.ece. Edgell Rickword's review is also reprinted in Jewel Spears Brooker, ed., *T. S. Eliot: The Contemporary Reviews* (Cambridge: Cambridge University Press, 2004), 110–12. Brooker's invaluable book includes the whole gamut of responses to *The Waste Land*, from Edmund Wilson's praise to the newspaper critiques: see 75–120.

3. Poems by Rickword (1898–1922) appeared in the *Oxford Poetry* 1921 anthology, alongside those of Edmund Blunden, Robert Graves, Richard Hughes, and others. He studied French at Oxford, adored Baudelaire, and published *Rimbaud: The Boy and the Poet* in 1924. In 1934 he joined the Communist Party and edited the *Left Review*. See Charles Hobday, *Edgell Rickword: A Poet at War* (London: Carcanet, 1989); Rickword, "A Conversation with Edgell Rickword," interview by Alan Young and Michael Schmidt, *PN Review* 1 (1973): 73–89.

4. "Then and Now," *Times Literary Supplement*, June 4, 2009. In fact, Eliot uses six different foreign languages in *The Waste Land*: French, Italian, German, Latin, Greek, and Sanskrit. I discuss this issue more fully in chapter 6.

5. For a useful discussion of the sources and use of these and the other direct quotations in *The Waste Land*, see Elizabeth Gregory, *Quotation and Modern American Poetry* (Houston: Rice University Press, 1996), 25–72.

6. The magic lantern is a central symbol in the opening chapter of Proust's *Du Côté de chez Swann*, published in 1913; the entire novel, *A la recherché du temps perdu*, was published in 1922, the same year as *The Waste Land*.

7. Antoine Compagnon, *La seconde main ou le travail de la citation* (Paris: Éditions du Seuil, 1979), 29. My translation.

8. Walter Benjamin, "Karl Kraus" (1931), in *Selected Writings*, vol. 2, *1927–1934*, ed. Michael W. Jennings, Howard Eiland, and Gary Smith, trans. Rodney Livingstone (Cambridge, MA: Belknap Press / Harvard University Press, 1999), 454.

9. On the vagaries of reading such conceptual texts, see Craig Dworkin, *Reading the Illegible* (Evanston, IL: Northwestern University Press, 2003).

10. Ron Silliman, *In the American Tree* (orig. 1986; Orono, ME: National Poetry Foundation, 2001).

11. For the range of Andersen's poetic activities, see his bilingual (English/Norwegian) Facebook page. The *Audiatur* festival for *nypoesi* hold annual poetry festivals in Oslo.

12. http://www.nypoesi.net/. It is interesting that the beautiful 800+-page *Audiatur: Katalog for ny.poesi*, published in Bergen, Norway (September 2007), reproduces the works mostly in Norwegian translation (a few essays, including my own, are exceptions). Book form, it seems, demands a readership in the native language.

13. See http://sibila.com.br/. Lehto is playing on T. S. Eliot's lines "Since our concern was speech, and speech impelled us / To purify the dialect of the tribe," from "Little Gidding," the fourth of the *Four Quartets*. Eliot's passage is, in its turn, an allusion to Mallarmé's "Le tombeau d'Edgar Poe": "Donner un sens plus pur aux mots de la tribu."

14. http://www.doublechange.com. *Double Change* is published bilingually and brings together such leading U.S. poets as Rosmarie Waldrop and Cole Swensen with their French counterparts Dominique Fourcade, Olivier Cadiot, and Abigail Lang, translation and exchange playing a major role in the journal and in the group's lecture series.

15. I take these three examples from Douglas Messerli's anthology *From the Other Side of the Century: A New American Poetry, 1960–1990* (Los Angeles: Sun & Moon, 1994), 1057, 512, 997.

16. All six of these poems appear in Jahan Ramazani, Richard Ellmann, and Robert O'Clair's *The Norton Anthology of Modern and Contemporary Poetry*, vol. 2 (New York: W. W. Norton, 2003). For the original sources see Elizabeth Bishop, "The Armadillo," in *The Complete Poems* (New York: Farrar, Straus and Giroux, 1969), 122–23; Allen Ginsberg, *Collected Poems, 1947–1980* (New York: Harper & Row, 136); Sylvia Plath, *Collected Poems* (New York: Harper & Row, 1981), 191; James Wright, "A Blessing," in *The Collected Poems* (Middletown, CT: Wesleyan University Press, 1971), 135; Denise Levertov, "The Ache of Marriage," in *Poems, 1960–67* (New York: New Directions, 1983), 77; A. A. Ammons, "Corson's Inlet," in *Selected Poems*, exp. ed. (New York: W. W. Norton, 1987), 147.

17. Gerald Bruns, "The Pagans and Karen MacCormack," in *Antiphonies: Essays on Women's Experimental Poetries*, ed. Nate Dorward (Toronto: The Gig, 2006), 207.

18. Kenneth Goldsmith, "On Conceptual Writing," http://www.poetryfoundation.org/dispatches/journals/2007.01.22.html. This web manifesto is reprinted as a pamphlet, "A Week of Blogs for the Poetry Foundation" (2007), and may also be found on Kenneth Goldsmith's website (http://epc.buffalo.edu/authors/goldsmith/). Cf. Goldsmith's works posted on UBUWEB (http://www.ubu.com).

19. See Ernst Jandl, "erschaffung der eva" (The creation of Eve), 1957), in *Concrete*

Poetry: A World View (Bloomington: Indiana University Press, 1971), 21–22; commentary, 267, and figure 36. The poem is taken from Ernst Jandl, *Laut und Luise* (Stuttgart: Philip Reklam, 1976), unpaginated.

20. Cia Rinne, *archives zaroum*, 2008, http://www.afsnitp.dk/galleri/archiveszaroum. See Leevi Lehto's commentary about Rinne's work on his website, http://www.leevilehto.net.

21. The print version of the web image (see figure 1) is called *zaroum* and was printed and bound by Karisto Cy in Finland in an edition of one thousand copies. In her new *notes for soloists* (Stockholm, 2009), Cia Rinne reproduces related visual-verbal experiments, this time in book form: the printed page complements her flash works. Here is a striking short poem from the section "notes on war & god." In German, *war* means "was" (singular past tense of the verb "to be"):

> war was
> was war
> was war?
> war war
> war was?
> war was
> here.

22. Jacques Roubaud, "Introduction: The Oulipo and Combinatorial Art," in *Oulipo Compendium*, ed. Harry Matthews and Alastair Brotchie (London: Atlas, 1998), 38–39.

23. Jan Baetens, "Free Writing, Constrained Writing: The Ideology of Form," *Poetics Today* 18, no. 1 (Spring 1997): 5–6.

24. Multilingualism has also been called *xenoglossia*: see Keigo Suga, "Translation, Exophony, Omniphony," in *Yoko Tawada: Voices from Everywhere*, ed. Doug Slaymaker (New York: Lexington Books, 2007), 21–33. For further discussion of these terms, see chapter 5.

The great exophonic writer of the twentieth century is, of course, Samuel Beckett, who is also a great multilingual one. Writing in French proved to be a liberating constraint for Beckett; indeed, sentences in his English texts usually contain phrasing from three or four foreign languages: witness his recently published letters as well as the novels and plays. Beckett's multilingualism and exophony demand a full study; at the same time, he is neither a concretist nor, after *Whoroscope* and the early "Provençal" poems, a primarily citational writer, so I do not include him here.

25. For an interesting discussion of this situation, see Zadie Smith, "Speaking in Tongues," *The New York Review of Books* 61, no. 3 (February 26, 2009): 41–44. Smith points out that, like so many contemporary writers, Barack Obama weaves other languages and dialects into the fabric of his *Dreams from My Father*.

26. Leevi Lehto, "In the Beginning Was Translation," in *The Sound of Poetry/The Poetry*

of Sound, ed. Marjorie Perloff and Craig Dworkin (Chicago: University of Chicago Press, 2008).

27. See Perloff, *21st Century Modernism: The "New" Poetics* (Oxford: Blackwell, 1992), 77–120.

28. See Jasper Johns: *Writings, Sketchbook Notes, Interviews*, ed. Kirk Varnedoe (New York: Museum of Modern Arts/Harry N. Abrams, 1996), 54.

29. Craig Dworkin, introduction to *The UbuWeb Anthology of Conceptual Writing*, http://www.ubu.com/concept.

30. Charles Bernstein, "Stray Straws and Straw Men" (1976), in *Content's Dream: Essays, 1975–1984* (Los Angeles: Sun & Moon, 1986), 40–48. Bernstein brilliantly parodies the expressivist model of the 1970s:

> Or take it this way: I want to just write—let it come out—get in touch with some natural process—from brain to pen—with no interference of typewriter, formal pattern. & it can seem like the language itself—having to put it into words—any kind of fixing a version of it—gets in the way. That I just have this thing inside me . . . this flow, this movement of consciousness. But there are no thoughts except through language. (47–48)

31. Roland Barthes, "The Death of the Author," in *The Rustle of Language*, trans. Richard Howard (Berkeley: University of California Press, 1989), 49–55.

32. Michel Foucault, "What Is an Author?" (1969), in *Language, Counter-memory, Practice: Selected Essays and Interviews*, ed. Donald F. Bouchard (Ithaca, NY: Cornell University Press, 1977), 116.

33. Fredric Jameson, conclusion to *Postmodernism, or The Cultural Logic of Late Capitalism* (Durham, NC: Duke University Press, 1991), 306. Subsequently cited as *Cultural Logic*.

34. Fredric Jameson, *The Modernist Papers* (London: Verso, 2007), 4.

35. In *The Prison-House of Language: A Critical Account of Structuralism and Russian Formalism* (Princeton, NJ: Princeton University Press, 1972), Jameson singles out Tynyanov as the most "lucid" expositor of the Formalist position and one who at least understood history as dialectic, even if Tynyanov's was not a fully fledged Marxism: see 91–96.

36. Yury Tynyanov, "Literaturnyj fakt," in *Archaisty i novatory* (Leningard, 1929), as translated by Peter Steiner in *Russian Formalism* (Ithaca, NY: Cornell University Press, 1984), 107, and see 99–137. For Tynyanov's "On Literary Evolution," see Ladislav Matejka and Krystyna Pomorska, eds., *Readings in Russian Poetics: Formalist and Structuralist Views* (orig. 1971; Chicago: Dalkey Archive Press, 2002), 66–78. The essay is also available in French in Tzvetan Todorov, *Théorie de la littérature: Texts des Formalistes russes réunis, présentés et traduits par Tzvetan Todorov* (Paris: Éditions de Seuil, 1965), 120–36. For discussions of Tynyanov's theory of literary evolution and literature as system, see Viktor Erlich, "Literary Dynamic," in *Russian*

Formalism: History and Doctrine (The Hague: Mouton, 1980), 251–71; Jurij Strieder, *Literary Structure, Evolution, and Value: Russian Formalism and Czech Structuralism Reconsidered* (Cambridge. MA: Harvard University Press, 1989), 69–74.

37. Pierre Bourdieu, *The Field of Cultural Production: Essays on Art and Literature* (New York: Columbia University Press, 1993), 76.

38. Hart Crane, "Voyages, VI," in *White Buildings* (1926) and *Complete Poems and Selected Letters* (New York: Library of America, 2006), 29.

CHAPTER TWO

1. Walter Benjamin, "First Sketches," in *The Arcades Project*, trans. Howard Eiland and Kevin McLaughlin (Cambridge, MA: Harvard University Press, 1999), 840. Subsequently cited in the text as *Arcades*. For the original, see "Erste Notizen," in *Das Passagen-Werk, Gesammelte Werke*, ed. Rolf Tiedemann (Frankfurt: Suhrkamp, 1982), 5:1008. Subsequently cited as *Passagen*.

2. According to the translators, *Konvolut*, literally a bundle, derives not from Benjamin himself but from his friend Theodor Adorno, who sifted through the manuscript, which was sent to him in 1947; it had been hidden away by Georges Bataille in the Bibliothèque nationale during World War II. *Konvolut* is an awkward term in English because of its cognate *convoluted*, but the translators decided to retain it rather than to use *sheaf, file*, or *folder* (*Arcades*, xiv).

3. On the genesis and organization of the *Arcades Project*, see Rolf Tiedemann, "Einleitung des Heraußgebers," in *Passagen*, 11–41; translated as "Dialectics at a Standstill: Approaches to the *Passagen-Werk*," in *Arcades*, 929–46; Susan Buck-Morss, *The Dialectics of Seeing: Walter Benjamin and the Arcades Project* (Cambridge, MA: MIT Press, 1989), 1–7, 47–57; Ursula Marx et al., eds., *Walter Benjamin's Archive: Images, Text, Signs* (London: Verso, 2007), 251–54, subsequently cited as Marx.

4. *Paris, capitale du XIXième siècle: Le livre des passages*, trans. Jean Lacoste (Paris: Éditions du Cerf, 1989).

5. *The Correspondence of Walter Benjamin, 1910–1940*, ed. Gershom Scholem and Theodor W. Adorno, trans. Manfred R. Jacobson and Evelyn M. Jacobson (Chicago: University of Chicago Press, 1994), 580, 582.

6. See *Arcades*, 931, *Passagen*, 13. The reference is to the *N* Konvolut, note *N*2, 6; see *Arcades*, 461.

7. Richard Sieburth, "Benjamin the Scrivener," in *Benjamin: Philosophy, Aesthetics, History*, ed. Gary Smith (Chicago: University of Chicago Press, 1989), 28.

8. See http://www.wbenjamin.org/walterbenjamin.html for a very useful compendium of recent studies, conferences, and symposia. Christopher Rollason's essays, especially "The Task of Walter Benjamin's Translators: Reflections on the Different Language Versions of 'Das Passagen-Werk,'" lay out the details about the various translations and their problems.

9. For a somewhat different perspective on the poeticity of the *Passagen-Werk*, which the author sees in terms of "colportage," see Graham Lyons, "Citation as Explanation: Walter Benjamin and Louis Zukofsky as Colporteurs," *Jacket* 36 (2008), http://jacketmagazine.com/36/index.shtm.

10. The French "translation" is not quite a translation either, since the original French citations need merely be reproduced, and the German commentary is translated into French so that the text appears to be seamless. But in the French edition the reader is at least presented with the citations from Baudelaire, Rimbaud, etc., in the original, whereas the all-English *Arcades Project* undercuts the work's polylingualism completely.

11. The page (Ms 2330) is reproduced in Marx, 261.

12. See Marx, 253; the page illustrated is marked J68.

13. Cf. the similar p. 65 of the French translation.

14. According to Sieburth ("Benjamin the Scrivener,"33), Benjamin evidently "wanted to inscribe citation and commentary, the text and its interpretation on the *same plane* of the page (with the uncanny result that even his own authorial intrusions, many of which can be found in his other published works, themselves begin to sound like quotations)." I think this is often the case—commentary and citation merge—but in the manuscript the citations are regularly indented, so that Tiedemann certainly had the authority to proceed as he did.

15. According to Buck-Morss, in 1935–36 Benjamin was working in the archives of the *Cabinet des estamples* in the Bibliothèque Nationale looking for visual images that would serve as analogues to his citations. "Benjamin had copies made of relevant illustrations . . . keeping them in his Paris apartment as 'a kind of album.' The album appears to have been lost" (*Dialectics of Seeing*, 71).

16. The relation of capital to lowercase entries is equally eccentric. "Modes of Lighting" (*Beleuchtungsarten*) is assigned *T*; "Reproduction, Technology, Lithography" is under *i*, and many of the files in the lowercase sequence had not yet been filled. And in neither case do titles have anything to do with the letter of the files: "Prostitution," for example, could have been given *P* but it is *O*.

17. "Chanson nouvelle," in *Nouveaux tableaux de Paris, ou Observations sur les moeurs et usages des Parisiens au commencement du XIXe siècle* (Paris, 1828), 1:27; Arthur Rimbaud, "Solde," in *Oeuvres*, ed. Susanne Bernard (Paris: Garnier, 1960), 293.

18. *Arcades*, 31. I use the black squares of the German edition as more accurate than the empty rectangles of the English text. When Benjamin embeds French citations into his German notes, my practice here will be to give both the German and the English texts. If it is only the German, I give just the English translation.

19. Kenneth Goldsmith, *No.111 2.7.93–10.20.96* (Barrington, MA: The Figures, 1997). This encyclopedic poem collects all the phrases collected between the title dates that end in sounds related to the sound *er* (schwa), organized alphabetically by syllable count, beginning with one-syllable entries for chapter 1 and ending with the 7,228-syllable *The Rocking Horse Winner* by D. H. Lawrence.

20. The reference also sends the reader to Benjamin's various essays on his own hashish experiences, especially "Hashish, Beginning of March 1930," in *Selected Writings*, 327–30, and "Hashish in Marseilles" (1932), in *Selected Writings*, vol. 2, *1927–34* (Cambridge, MA: Belknap Press / Harvard University Press, 1999), 673–79.
21. Cf. *J22a2*, which Benjamin himself cross-references.
22. Cited by Ekke Bonk, "Delay Include," in *Joseph Cornell / Marcel Duchamp . . . in Resonance*, exh. cat., Menil Collection, Houston, and Philadelphia Museum of Art (New York: Distributed Art Publishers, 1998), 102; cf. Francis M. Naumann, *Marcel Duchamp: The Art of Making Art in the Age of Mechanical Reproduction* (New York: Harry N. Abrams, 1999), 17–18, 135–36.
23. See Naumann, *Marcel Duchamp*, 136.
24. Walter Benjamin, "One-Way Street," in *Reflections*, ed. Peter Demetz, trans. Edmund Jephcott (New York: Harcourt Brace, 1979), 66.

CHAPTER THREE

1. The program (March 6, 2001), held at the Society of the Americas on Park Avenue, also included K. David Jackson, A. S. Bessa, and Claus Clüver, all speaking on the Noigandres poets.
2. Kenneth Goldsmith, "From (Command) Line to (Iconic) Constellation," Ubuweb Papers, http://www.ubu/com/papers/goldsmith_command.html.
3. Caroline Bayard, *The New Poetics in Canada and Quebec: From Concretism to Postmodernism* (Toronto: University of Toronto Press, 1989), 24. Umberto Eco's term appears in his *Theory of Semiotics* (Bloomington: Indiana University Press, 1979), 191.
4. See Marjorie Perloff, *Radical Artifice: Writing Poetry in the Age of Media* (Chicago: University of Chicago Press, 1991), 114–18.
5. See especially William Marx, ed., *Les arrière-gardes au xxᵉ siècle* (Paris: Presses universitaires de France, 2004). Translations from this text are my own.
6. Antoine Compagnon, "L'arrière-garde, de Péguy à Paulhan et Barthes," in ibid., 99. The reference is to Roland Barthes, "Reponses" (1971), in *Oeuvres complètes* (Paris: Seuil, 2002), 3:1038: "To be avant-garde is to know that which has died. To be arrière-garde, is to continue to love it."
7. Haroldo de Campos, "The Ex-centric's Viewpoint: Tradition, Transcreation, Transculturation: Second thoughts: the dialectics of *sub*altern and *over*altern literary models," in K. David Jackson, *Haroldo de Campos: A Dialogue with the Brazilian Poet* (Oxford: Center for Brazilian Studies, Oxford University Press, 2005), 11–13.
8. Oyvind Fahlström, "Hipy papy bithithdthuthda bthuthdy," in Teddy Hultberg, *Oyvind Fahlström on the Air—Manipulating the World*, bilingual text (Stockholm: Sveriges Radio Förlag," 1999), 108–20. The manifesto, translated by Karen Loevgren, is also found in Mary Ellen Solt's classic *Concrete Poetry: A World View* (Bloomington: Indiana University Press, 1968), 74–78. Parenthetical phrases are

Hultberg's. For a detailed consideration of Fahlstrom's "Hipy papy," see Antonio Sergio Bessa, *Oyvind Fahlström: The Art of Writing* (Evanston, IL: Northwestern University Press, 2008), 3–30.

9. F. T. Marinetti, "Technical Manifesto of Futurist Literature," in *Critical Writings*, new ed., ed. Günter Berghaus, trans. Doug Thompson (New York: Farrar, Straus and Giroux, 20060), 107–19. The manifesto, originally printed as a four-page leaflet in French and Italian, is dated May 11, 1912, and August 11, 1912. For the full Italian text, see F. T. Marinetti, *Opere*, vol. 2, *Teoria e invenzione futurisa*, ed. Luciano de Maria (Milan: Mondadori, 1968), 40–54.

10. David Burliuk et al., "Slap in the Face of Public Taste," in *Russian Futurism through Its Manifestos, 1912–1928*, ed. Anna Lawton (Ithaca, NY: Cornell University Press, 1988), 51–52.

11. Kasimir Malevich, *From Cubism and Futurism to Suprematism: The New Painterly Realism* (1915), in *Russian Art of the Avant-garde: Theory and Criticism, 1902–1934*, ed. and trans. John E. Bowlt (New York: Viking, 1976), 116–35; see 126.

12. See Elizabeth Bishop and Robert Lowell, *Words in Air: The Complete Correspondence between Elizabeth Bishop and Robert Lowell*, ed. Thomas Travisano and Saskia Hamilton (New York: Farrar Straus and Giroux, 2008). Bishop is referring to Eugene Jolas's famed *transition* magazine, where *Finnegans Wake* first appeared along with other seminal avant-garde works, including, in issue 6, some of the experimental poems of e. e. cummings. D. (Dudley) Fitts was a noted classicist. Ezra Pound's *Thrones* (Cantos 96–109) had appeared in 1959, following *Rock-Drill* (Cantos 85–95), published in 1955.

13. See Robert Lowell to Ezra Pound, July 12, 1952, cited in Humphrey Carpenter, *A Serious Character: The Life of Ezra Pound* (London: Faber, 1988), 680.

14. Velimir Khlebnikov, *Collected Works*, vol. 1, *Letters and Theoretical Writings*, ed. Charlotte Douglas, trans. Paul Schmidt (Cambridge, MA: Harvard University Press, 1987), 272–73.

15. Plato, "Cratylus," in *Collected Dialogues*, ed. Edith Hamilton (Princeton, NJ: Princeton University Press, 1961), 456 (no. 421b).

16. Rosmarie Waldrop, "A Basis of Concrete Poetry" (1977), in *Dissonance (if you are interested)* (Tuscaloosa: University of Alabama Press, 2005), 47–57; see 57.

17. See Solt, *Concrete Poetry*, 119.

18. Guy Davenport, "Narrative Time and Form," in *The Geography of the Imagination* (San Francisco: North Point, 1981), 314, my emphasis.

19. See, for example, Solt, *Concrete Poetry*, 8.

20. In his essay "Brazilian and German Avant-Garde Poetry," in *Novas: Selected Writings of Haroldo de Campos*, ed. Antonio Sergio Bessa and Odile Cisneros (Evanston, IL: Northwestern University Press, 2007), 249–75, Haroldo de Campos notes that "Gomringer practiced an extremely concise poetry with a rigorous and orthogonal construction, thematically limited to notes from nature or an urban land-

scape, or instead abstract motifs of dynamic structures. . . . Brazilian concrete poetry . . . was more complex. It employed, instead of a two-dimensional (orthogonal) construction, a multidimensional, less concentrated one" (252). This book is subsequently cited in the text as *Novas*.

21. See Cornelius Schnauber, "Einleitung," in *Deine Träume, Mein Gedicht: Eugen Gomringer und die Konkrete Poesie* (Nördlingen, Germany: Greno, 1989), 5–6.

22. Ibid., 7.

23. In "How the Letters Learnt to Dance: On Language Dissection in Dadaist, Concrete and Digital Poetry," in *Avant-Garde/Neo-Avant-Garde*, ed. Dietrich Scheunemann (Amsterdam: Rodopi, 2005), 149–72, Anna Katharine Schaffner points out that in the "wind" ideogram, movement is evoked in that "the word 'wind' can be read in four directions, pairs each running the reverse course" (163). In the "O Poem" the title's circle becomes a negative presence, the two circle halves outlined by four triangles made of the container words: *show, flow, blow, grow.*

24. See Kurt Marti, "Zu Eugen Gomringers 'Konstellationen,'" and Peter Demetz, "Eugen Gomringer und die Entwicklung der Konkreten Poesie," in Schnauber, *Deine Träume,* 88–94, 151, respectively.

25. Solt, *Concrete Poetry,* 67.

26. Ibid., 68.

27. Ibid., 69–70, emphasis mine.

28. Eugen Gomringer, *das stundenbuch, the book of hours, le livre d'heures, el libro de las horas, timebook* (1965; Stamberg, Germany: Joseph Keller Verlag, 1980), unpaginated. In the English translation of Jerome Rothenberg, this page reads: "your question/my mind/your question/my word/your question/my answer/your question/my song/your question/my poem."

29. For an excellent short visual history of the Brazilian movement, see the DVD *Poesia Concreta: O projeto verbivocovisual,* curated by Cid Campos et al. (São Paulo: Academia di Cultura, 2009). This DVD exhibits many of the concrete poems as well as the *clip poemas* (in motion).

30. Ezra Pound, *The Cantos* (New York: New Directions, 1993), 89–90.

31. In the preface to his French translation of Augusto de Campos, *Anthologie despoesia* (Romainville, France: Al Dante, 2002), 7–8, Jacques Donguy has a long scholarly footnote explaining the etymology of *Noigandres.* See also Hugh Kenner, *The Pound Era* (Berkeley: University of California Press, 1971), 116. In an e-mail to me on June 26, 2002, Augusto de Campos provides further information about the term, describing his own consultation of the four-volume *Provenzalisches Supplement-Wörterbuch* (1904), where he found additional etymological data on Arnaut Daniel's use of the word. But Augusto is skeptical about the sexual theme put forward, Donguy says, by Provençalists like Julien Blaine, and he has remarked, in e-mails to me, that he thinks Donguy is also too ingenuous.

32. See "Brazilian Concrete Poetry: How It Looks Today; Harold and Augusto de

Campos interviewed by Marjorie Perloff," *Arshile*, 1994; rpt. in Jackson, *Haroldo de Campos*, 165–79; see 171.

33. Jackson, *Haroldo de Campos*, 171, emphasis mine.

34. Ibid., 173.

35. Ibid., 170, 175–76.

36. Augusto de Campos, "Lygia," first published in *Poetamenos* (1973) in Futura type-face offset, reproduced in many of Augusto's volumes—for example, *Poesia, 1949–1979* (São Paulo: Atelier Editorial, 2001), rpt. in *Noigandres* 2 (1955) in Kabel Sanserif typeface. The digital version used here is in Futura bold font; it is most easily accessible online at Augusto de Campos's official website, http://www2.uol.com.br/augustodecampos/poemas.htm.

37. Antonio Sergio Bessa, "The Image of Voice in Augusto de Campos's *Poetamenos*," manuscript.

38. See Augusto de Campos, *Anthologie despoesia*, 22, and e-mail to me on June 26, 2002. Augusto recalls how he first saw the name Solange Sohl in 1949 "signing a very beautiful poem in a newspaper," and then learned this was a pseudonym of Patricia Galvao or "Pagu," the former wife of political activist Oswald de Andade and first translator of Joyce's *Ulysses* into Portuguese. In 1983 Augusto published an edition of her work under the title *PAGU: VIDA-OBRA*.

39. See Jackson, *Haroldo de Campos*, 9.

40. In the order cited: Haroldo de Campos, *os nomes e os navios: Homero, Ilîada, II* (Rio de Janeiro: Sette Letras, 1999); Augusto de Campos, *Mais Provençais* (São Paulo: Capnhia das lettras, 1987); Augusto de Campos, *Irmaos Germanos* (Santa Caterina, Brazil: Editions Noa Noa, 1992); Augusto de Campos, *Rimbaud livre* (São Paulo: Editora Perspectiva, 1992); Augusto de Campos, *Hopkins: A beleza difiicil* (Editora Perspectiva, 1997); Augusto de Campos, *e.e. cummings 40 POEM(A)S* (São Paulo: Editora Brasiliense, 1987); Haroldo de Campos, *O Arco-iris branco* (Rio de Janeiro: Imago, 1997); Augusto de Campos, *O anticritico* (São Paulo: Companhia des Letters, 1986); Augusto and Haroldo de Campos, *Panaroma do "Finnegans Wake"* (São Paulo: Editora Perspectiva, 1971).

41. Jackson, *Haroldo de Campos*, 10.

42. The cover image of *Una rosa para Gertrude* is available online at http://www.fotolog.com/afasiadeldeseoso/50624715/.

43. Haroldo de Campos, "Poetic Function and Ideogram: The Sinological Argument." The translation here cited is that of Kevin Mundy and Mark Nelson in H. de Campos, *Novas*, 47.

44. See Haun Saussy, "Fenollosa Compounded: A Discrimination," in *The Chinese Written Character as a Medium for Poetry*, critical ed. by Ernest Fenollosa and Ezra Pound, ed. Haun Saussy, Jonathan Stalling, and Lucas Klein (New York: Fordham University Press, 2008), 1–40. Saussy notes that Haroldo, in line with the Derrida of *Of Grammatology*, came to regard Fenollosa as a pioneer in the articulation of a graphic, as opposed to a vocal or mimetic, poetics (see 36–37).

45. Haroldo de Campos, *Galáxias*, trans. Odile Cisneros with Jill Susan Levine, http://www.arts.ualberta.ca/-galaxias/; *Galáxias, 1963–1976* (São Paulo: Ed. Ex-Libris, 1984; 2nd ed., org. Trajano Vieira, São Paulo Editora 34, 2004). There is an excellent French edition prepared by Inès Oseki-Dépré and the author (Paris: La main courante, 1998).

46. "The Invention of 'Concrete Prose': Haroldo de Campos's *Galáxias* and After," in *Differentials: Poetry, Poetics, Pedagogy* (Tuscaloosa: University of Alabama Pres, 2004), 175–93. The essay is reprinted in K. David Jackson, *Haroldo de Campos: A Dialogue with the Brazilian Concrete Poet* (Oxford: Centre for Brazlian Studies, Oxford University Press, 2005), 139–61. Jackson's collection contains other important essays on *Galáxias*, including his own, "Music of the Spheres in *Galáxias*," 119–28.

47. For examples of Jandl's techique, see "Jandl" on Ubuweb, http://www.ubu.com/historical/jandl/index.html; for Bök, see especially *Tango with Cows: Book Art of the Russian Avant-Garde, 1910–1917*, proceedings of a Getty Research Center symposium, 2009, at http://writing.upenn.edu/pennsound/x/Explodity.php/.

48. Augusto de Campos, "SOS" (2000), in *Clip-Poemas*, http://www2.uol.com.br/augustodecampos/clippoemas.htm.

49. Donguy, preface, 118.

50. Augusto de Campos, "REVƎЯ" (1970), in *Equivocábulos* (São Paulo: Author, 1970); see *Clip-Poemas*, http://www2.uol.com.br/augustodecampos/clippoemas.htm.

51. The intertextual reference was pointed out to me by Odile Cisneros, April 12, 2007. On the relation of Augusto's clip poems to later digital poetry, see Friedrich W. Block, Mark Amerika, and Giselle Beiguelman, *POEsıs: The Aesthetics of Digital Poetry* (Berlin: Hatje Kanz, 2004); Christopher Funkhouser, "Augusto de Campos, Digital Poetry and the Anthropophagic Imperative," *Ciberletras*, http://www.lehman.cuny.edu/ciberletras/v17/funkhauser.htm (sic).

CHAPTER FOUR

1. Walter Benjamin, *The Arcades Project*, trans. Howard Eiland and Kevin McLaughlin (Cambridge, MA: Belknap Press / Harvard University Press, 1999), 476 (N11, 3); my emphasis; Jean Ricardou, *Pour une théorie du nouveau roman* (Paris: Seuil, 1971), 118, translation mine.

2. Jacques Roubaud, "Sables, syllabes: Préface," in *Galaxies*, trans. Inés Oseki-Dépré and Jacques Roubaud (Paris: La Main courante, 1998) unpaginated. For the original, see Haroldo de Campos, *Galáxias* (São Paulo: Editora Ex-Libris, 1984).

3. Haroldo de Campos, "Sanscreed Latinized: The *Wake* in Brazil and Hispanic America," *Tri Quarterly* 38 (Winter 1977): 56.

4. This portmanteau word is James Joyce's; see *Finnegans Wake* (New York: Penguin, 1971), 341.

5. I discuss this more fully in my "The Invention of 'Concrete Prose': Haroldo de

Campos's *Galáxias* and After," in *Differentials: Poetry, Poetics, Pedagogy* (Tuscaloosa: University of Alabama Press, 2004), 175–93. See also Inês Oseki-Dépré, "Translation as Creation and Criticism: *Galáxias* as Text as Theory of Translation," in K. David Jackson, *Haroldo de Campos: A Dialogue with the Brazilian Concrete Poet* (Oxford: Centre for Brazilian Studies, Oxford University Press, 2005), 119–28.

6. See "Pilot Plan for Concrete Poetry," in *Concrete Poetry: A World View*, ed. Mary Ellen Solt (Bloomington: Indiana University Press, 1970), 71..

7. Rosmarie Waldrop, "A Basis of Concrete Poetry" (1976), in *Dissonance (if you are interested)* (Tuscaloosa: University of Alabama Press, 2005), 49.

8. Jacques Roubaud, "Introduction: The Oulipo and Combinatorial Art," (1991), in *Oulipo Compendium*, ed. Harry Mathews and Alastair Brotchie (London: Atlas, 1998), 37–44; see 38–39.

9. See Michel Bénabou and Jacques Roubaud's set of *perverses* called "Alexandre au greffoir," in *La bibliothèque oulipienne* (Paris: Éditions Ramsay, 1987), 2:227. I discuss "Les chats" more fully in *Differentials: Poetry, Poetics, Pedagogy* (Tuscaloosa: University of Alabama Press, 2004), 208–9.

10. Jan Baetens and Jean-Jacques Poucel, "Introduction: The Challenge of Constraint," "Constrained Writing," spec. issue of *Poetics Today* 30, no. 4 (Winter 2009), 613. This special issue, which contains an earlier version of this chapter, also contains important essays on constraint by Jacques Roubaud, Richard Deming, Chris Andrewes, and Warren Motte.

11. Roubaud, "Introduction," 39.

12. Waldrop, *Dissonance*, 46.

13. *Oyvind Fahlström I etern—Manipulera världen / Oyvind Fahlström on the Air—Manipulating the World*, bilingual ed., ed. and trans. Teddy Hultberg (Fylkingen, Sweden: Sveriges Radios Förlag, 1999), 109–20; see 115, 118. The manifesto, in Karen Loewren's translation, is also included in *Concrete Poetry*, ed. Solt, 75–78.

14. Jacques Roubaud, "Poetry & Orality," in *The Sound of Poetry, the Poetry of Sound*, ed. Marjorie Perloff and Craig Dworkin (Chicago: University of Chicago Press, 2009), 20.

15. See Oyvind Fahlström, in *Oulipo Compendium*, ed. Harry Mathews and Alastair Brotchie (London: Atlas, 1998), 110..

16. Roubaud, "Introduction," 41.

17. Jacques Jouet, "With (and without) Constraints," trans. Roxanne Lapidus, *SubStance* 30, no. 3 (2001): 4.

18. Jacques Jouet, "Qu'est-ce-qu'un poème de métro?" in ibid., 10–11; for the translation by Ian Monk, see the same issue, 64. The whole issue of *SubStance* is devoted to Jouet. Jouet's book *Poèmes de metro* was published by P.O.L. Éditions (Paris, 2000).

19. Jouet, "Qu'est-ce-qu'un poème de métro?" 12.

20. Ibid.

21. Jan Baetens (with Bernardo Schiavetta), "Jugement esthétique des écritures à contrainte," paper presented at Research Conference, Paris, November 14, 2001; see Archives, Centre d'études poétiques, Paris, http://cep.ens-lsh.fr/37060428/0/fiche___pagelibre/&RH=CEP-AUTEURS; my translation. For a short statement in English by Baetens, see "Doing things that don't come naturally: A plea for constrained writing," *Drunken Boat* 8 (2006), feature "Oulipo": http://www.drunken boat.com/db8/.

22. Jan Baetens, postface, in *Slam! Poèmes sur le basketball* (Bruxelles: Les impressions nouvelles, 2006), 64–65.

23. See ibid., 64: "Mon goût de la littérature à contraintes prolonge presque directement le choix du français comme langue étrangère. . . . La découverte de la contrainte est intimement solidaire d'une approche littéraire privilégiant *l'objet* (en l'occurrence l'objet linguistique) au detriment du *sujet* (en l'occurrence le mythe de l'inspiration)." Baetens also writes in English, thus triangulating his language pool. See also Bernardo Schiavetta, "Toward a General Theory of the Constraint," *Electronic Book Review* 10, http://www.altx.com/ebr/ebr10/10sch.htm.

24. See Jan Baetens and Bernardo Schiavetta, editorial, *Formules* 1 (1997): 1, http://www.formules.net/revue/01/programme.html. Cf. "Brazilian Concrete Poetry: How It Looks Today; Haroldo and Augusto de Campos Interviewed by Marjorie Perloff" (1994), in K. David Jackson, *Haroldo de Campos: A Dialogue with the Brazilian Concrete Poet* (Oxford: Centre for Brazilian Studies, Oxford University Press, 2005), 165–79. "It was a necessity," says Augusto de Campos, "to recover the great avant-garde movements. This is why I am so critical of post-modernism. There is inside the discussion of post-modernism a tactic of wanting to put aside swiftly the recovery of experimental art and to say all this is finished!" (171).

25. Warren F. Motte Jr., ed. and trans., *Oulipo: A Primer of Potential Literature* (Lincoln: University of Nebraska Press, 1986), 18.

26. See "Brazilian Concrete Poetry," 170. Later in the interview, Haroldo de Campos quips, "Decio Pignatari has a good phrase for [surrealism]. He says that Brazil never had surrealism because the whole country is surrealist" (176).

27. See Oseki-Dépré, "Translation as Creation and Criticism," and K. David Jackson, "Music of the Spheres in *Galáxias*," in *Haroldo de Campos: A Dialogue with the Brazilian Concrete Poet* (Oxford: Centre for Brazilian Studies, Oxford University Press, 2005), 119–28.

28. Jacques Roubaud, *Quelque chose noir* (Paris: Gallimard, 1986); trans. Rosmarie Waldrop as *something black* (Normal, IL: Dalkey Archive, 1990).

29. Adelaide M. Russo, "Oulipo's Mechanical Measure: The Consequences of 'Littérature Potentielle' for Potential Criticism," in *20ieme Siècle: La problématique du discours*, Michigan Romance Studies 6, ed. Roy Jay Nelson (1986), 116.

30. See Marjorie Perloff, "The Oulipo Factor: The Procedural Poetics of Christian Bök and Caroline Bergvall, *Jacket* 23 (August 2003); rpt. in *Differentials: Poetry,*

Poetics, Pedagogy (Tuscaloosa: University of Alabama Press, 2004),, 205–26; "Vocable Scriptsigns: Differential Poetics in Kenneth Goldsmith's *Fidget* and John Kinsella's *Kangaroo Virus*," in *Poetry, Value, and Contemporary Culture*, ed. Andrew Roberts and John Allison (Edinburgh: Edinburgh University Press, 2,002), 21–43; "Screening the Page/Paging the Screen: Digital Poetics and the Differential Text," *New Media Poetics: Contexts, Technotexts, and Theories*, ed. Adelaide Morris and Thomas Swiss (Cambridge, MA: MIT Press, 2006), 143–64.

    On John Cage, see "The Music of Verbal Space: John Cage's 'What You Say . . . ,'" in Perloff, *Poetry On & Off the Page* (Evanston, IL: Northwestern University Press, 1998), 290–308.

    On Hejinian, "The Return of the (Numerical) Repressed: From Free Verse to Procedural Play," in Perloff, *Radical Artifice: Writing Poetry in the Age of Media* (Chicago: University of Chicago Press, 1991), 134–70.

31. Marjorie Perloff, "Avant Garde Tradition and the Individual Talent: The Case of Language Poetry," in "Poètes américains: Architectes du langage," ed. Helène Aji, spec. issue of *Revue française d'etudes américaines*, no. 103 (February 2005): 117–41; or in somewhat different form, as "Avant Garde Community and the Individual Talent: The Case of Language Poetry," *Foreign Literature Studies* 28, no. 4 (August 2006): 20–37; Perloff, "After Language Poetry: Innovation and Its Theoretical Discontents," in *Differentials: Poetry, Poetics, Pedagogy* (Tuscaloosa: University of Alabama Press, 2004), 155–74; Perloff, "The Pleasures of the Déjà Dit; Citation, Intertext, and Ekphrasis in Recent Experimental Poetry," in *The Consequences of Innovation: 21st Century Poetics*, ed. Craig Dworkin (New York: Roof Books, 2008), 66–89.

32. Charles Bernstein, "Stray Straws and Straw Men" (1976), in *Content's Dream: Essays, 1975–1984* (Los Angeles: Sun and Moon, 1986), 49.

33. See, for example, Barrett Watten, "Mac Low's Lexicons," in *The Constructivist Moment: From Material Text to Cultural Politics* (Middletown, CT: Wesleyan University Press, 2003), 31–42; Charles Bernstein, "Jackson at Home," in *Content's Dream: Essays 1975–1984* (Los Angeles: Sun & Moon 1986), 252–58. Ron Silliman's *Tjanting* was published by The Figures (Berkeley) in 1981, reprinted by Salt Books (London), 2002.

34. Charles Bernstein, "Hinge Picture," in *My Way: Speeches and Poems* (Chicago: University of Chicago Press, 1999), 194–96.

35. Andrew Clements, interview with Brian Ferneyhough, *The Guardian*, June 2005, http://www.guardian.co.uk/<give full URL or delete>, emphasis mine. For the libretto, see Charles Bernstein, *Shadowtime* (Los Angeles: Green Integer, 2005). All further references are to this edition.

36. Bernstein, e-mail to me, June 30, 2005.

37. For an astute review of the opera that discusses its overall linguistic as well as musical effects, see Colin Browne, "Benjamin's Angels, or Why We Sing the Lamentations," *Jacket* 28, http://jacketmagazine.com/28/browne-shadow.html.

38. Peter Demetz, introduction to Walter Benjamin, *Reflections: Essays, Aphorisms, Autobiographical Writings*, ed. Peter Demetz (New York: Harcourt Brace, 1978) , lii–liii.

39. For a seminal essay on Benjamin's use of citation, see Richard Sieburth, "Benjamin the Scrivener," in *Benjamin: Philosophy, Aesthetics, History*, ed. Gary Smith (Chicago: University of Chicago Press, 1989), 13–37.

40. Walter Benjamin, "Karl Kraus" (1931), trans. Edmund Jephcott, in *Selected Writings, Vol.2*, 433–58; see pp. 453–54.

41. Charles Bernstein, "What Does It Mean to Be a Poet in Our Time?" interview by Eric Denut," *The Argotist Online*, July-August 2004, http://www.argotistonline.co.uk/Bernstein%20interview.htm. The interview has been reprinted in more readable form on the website *All About Jewish Theatre* (2007), http://www.jewish-theatre.com/visitor/article_display.aspx?articleID=1492.

42. Walter Benjamin, "The Doctrine of the Similar" (1933), in *Selected Writings*, 2:694–98; see 696.

43. Ibid., 697.

44. See West Valley College Philosophy Home page: http://instruct.westvalley.edu/lafave/amphib.html.

45. Benjamin, "Doctrine of the Similar," 697.

46. There are two instances where the word *Jew* does not appear, "A mint bran jewel" (line 2) and "A bawl intern gem" (line 8), perhaps to suggest the stereotype of the greedy jewel-loving, gem-loving Jew.

47. Ernst Jandl, "der und die," in *Reft and Light: Poems by Ernst Jandl, with Multiple Versions by American Poets*, ed. Rosmarie Waldrop (Providence, RI: Burning Deck, 2000), 27. Cf. Karl Riha, "'der und die' im Kontext," in *Ernst Jandl, Gedichte*, ed Volker Kaukoreit and Kristina Pfoser (Stuttgart: Philipp Reclam, 2002), 61–72.

48. Benjamin, "On Semblance" (1919–20), in *Selected Writings*, vol. 1, *1913–1926*, ed. Marcus Bullock and Michael W. Jennings (Cambridge, MA: Belknap, 1996), 224. Cf. "Goethe's *Elective Affinities*," in vol. 1, 297–360.

49. Stephane Mallarmé, *Poésies* (1899), in *Collected Poems*, bilingual ed., trans. with commentary by Henry Weinfeld (Berkeley: University of California Press, 1994), and see commentary, 149–50.

50. *Constellation* is a key term in Benjamin's own writing. See, for example, "Theses on the Philosophy of History, XVII" (1940): "Where thinking suddenly halts in a *constellation* overflowing with tensions, there it yields a shock to the same, through which it crystallizes as a monad" (*Illuminations,* trans. Harry Zohn [New York: Schocken, 1968], 262–63). Again, in *Arcades* (N2a3, p. 462), we read: "It is not that what is past casts its light on what is present, or what is present its light on what is past; rather, image is that wherein what has been comes together in a flash with the now to form a *constellation*. In other words, image is dialectics at a standstill" (my emphasis).

51. Haroldo de Campos, "The Ex-centric's Viewpoint: Tradition, Transcreation,

Transculturation," in *Haroldo de Campos: A Dialogue with the Brazilian Concrete Poet*, ed. K. David Jackson (Oxford: Centre for Brazilian Studies, Oxford University Press, 2005), 3–13.

CHAPTER FIVE

1. Henry David Thoreau, *A Week on the Concord and Merrimac River*, in *Writings* (New York: Library of America, 1985); Walter Benjamin, "Karl Kraus," in *Selected Writings*, vol. 2, *1927–1934* (Cambridge, MA: Harvard University Press, 1999), 453; Richard Sieburth, *Instigations: Ezra Pound and Remy de Gourmont* (Cambridge, MA: Harvard University Press, 1978), 121.

2. Susan Howe, *The Midnight* (New York: New Directions, 2003). Subsequently cited in this essay as *M*.

3. *M* 72. I try to reproduce Howe's paragraphs just as they are, with a justified right margin.

4. See *Kino-Eye, The Writings of Dziga Vertov*, ed. Annette Michelson, trans. Kevin O'Brien (Berkeley: University of California Press, 1984), 58.

5. Susan Howe, "Sorting Facts, or, Nineteen Ways of Looking at Marker," in *Beyond Document: Essays on Nonfiction Film*, ed. Charles Warren (Middletown, CT: Wesleyan University Press, 1996), 297, 300. For Howe's own etymological definition of *documentary*, see 299.

6. Tyrus Miller, "Documentary / Modernism: Convergence and Complementarity in the 1930s," *Modernism/Modernity* 9, no. 2 (April 2002): 225–26.

7. In *The Midnight*, the verso with the stick-figure image is reproduced a second time, in reduced size. But in the earlier version of Howe's poem, the fine-press book called *Kidnapped* (Dublin: Coracle, 2002), which is about half the length of *The Midnight* and contains primarily its prose portions, there is only one image, but a more striking one—the open book, silhouetted against a black ground on the left, and, on the right, another open book beneath it, with the admonition printed in italics at the right margin (*M* 19).

8. Susan Howe commented on the passage in her reading at the Kelly Writers' House, University of Pennsylvania, Philadelphia, February 2007, http://writing .upenn.edu/pennsound/x/Howe.html

9. Susan Howe, interview by Jon Thompson, *Free Verse*, Winter 2005, 5, http:// english.chass.ncsu.edu/freeverse/Archives/Winter_2005/interviews/S_Howe .html. The passage in question comes from Thoreau, *A Week on the Concord and Merrimac Rivers*.

10. See Jahan Ramazani, *Poetry of Mourning: The Modern Elegy from Hardy to Heaney* (Chicago: University of Chicago Press, 1994); see also Marjorie Perloff, "The Consolation Theme in Yeats's 'In Memory of Major Robert Gregory,'" *Modern Language Quarterly*, Fall 1966, 306–22; Perloff, "Robert Lowell's Winslow Elegies," in *The Poetic Art of Robert Lowell* (Ithaca, NY: Cornell University Press, 1973), 131–60.

11. See Princess Grace Irish Library (Monaco), http://www.pgil-eirdata.org/html/pgil_datasets/authors/b/Bennett,Louie/life.htm.

12. In the expensively produced *Kidnapped*, there is a real tissue interleaf.

13. Stephen Collis, "Drawing the Curtain on Midnight," *Jacket* 25 (February 2004), http://jacketmagazine.com/25/collis-s-howe.html. See also Collis's *Through Words of Others: Susan Howe and Anarcho-scholasticism* (Victoria, BC: English Literary Studies Editions, 2006). *Bed Hangings* was originally a separate book with pictures by Susan Bee (New York: Granary Books, 2001). It encompassed what was to become "Bedhangings I."

14. According to the Granary catalog, http://www.granarybooks.com/pages.php?which_page=product_view&which_product=75&search=bed hangings howe &category=, "This series of poems explores the themes of colonial America and its decorative arts, religion and Puritanism through a visual and verbal investigation of the metaphysics of beds, curtains, and hangings. The poems and pictures play off each other in a humorous, mystical and occasionally mischievous manner."

15. Robert Louis Stevenson, *A Child's Garden of Verses* (London: Longman's, 1885), 5. This is a Google book.

16. E-mail to me, July 14, 2008. Emphasis added.

17. *The Collected Works of W. B. Yeats*, vol. 1, *The Poems*, rev. ed., ed. Richard J. Finneran (New York: Macmillan, 1989), 233, 243. Called *Poems* in later references.

18. In *Letters to the New Island*, ed. Horace Reynolds (Cambridge, MA: Harvard University Press, 1934), 103–4, Yeats declares, "Allingham had the making of a great writer in him, but lacked impulse and momentum, the very things national feeling could have supplied."

19. Yeats, *Poems*, 78. The fourteen-line poem begins, "One that is ever kind said yesterday / Your well-belovèd's hair has threads of grey," and concludes "O heart! O heart! if she'd but turn her head, / You'd know the folly of being comforted."

20. W. B. Yeats, *Autobiographies* (New York: Macmillan, 1966), 74.

21. For an excellent discussion of Howe's early visual poetry vis-à-vis such poets as Ian Hamilton Finlay and the artist Ad Reinhardt, see Kaplan Page Harris, "Susan Howe's Art and Poetry, 1968–1974," *Contemporary Literature* 47, no. 3 (Fall 2006): 440–71.

22. See Susan Howe, "The End of Art," *Stereo Headphones* 8, 9–10 (1982): 40–43. Finlay's "Homage to Malevich" is reproduced on 43.

23. *M* 118. The biography in question is Christopher Fitz-Simon, *The Boys: A Biography of Micheál MacLíammóir and Hilton Edwards* (Dublin: New Island, 2002); Howe draws especially on material on 24–29.

24. For an earlier discussion of Howe's page, see Perloff, *Differentials: Poetry, Poetics, Pedagogy* (Tuscaloosa: University of Alabama Press, 2004), xxx–xxxii.

CHAPTER SIX

1. Walter Benjamin, "Translation: For and Against," in *Selected Writings*, vol. 3, *1935–1938*, ed. Howard Eiland and Michael W. Jennings, trans. Edmund Jephcott and others (Harvard, MA: Belknap Press, 2002), 250.
2. Yoko Tawada," "An der Spree," in *Sprachpolizei und Spielpolyglotte* (Tübingen: Verlag Claudia Gehrke, 2007), 12. Translation of this and the other Tawada passages is mine unless indicated.
3. T. S. Eliot, *The Waste Land*, in *The Complete Poems and Plays, 1909–1950* (New York: Harcourt, Brace and World, 1962), 37–55.
4. Craig Raine, *T. S. Eliot* (Oxford: Oxford University Press, 2006), 87. Not everyone, of course, has admired this "exoticism": see chapter 1 for Edgell Rickword's objections to the citational method of *The Waste Land*.
5. T. S. Eliot, "Burnt Norton," III, lines 1–9; in *Complete Poems and Plays*, 120.
6. Ibid., 117.
7. In "'Mature poets steal': Eliot's Allusive Practice," in *The Cambridge Companion to T S. Eliot*, ed. A. David Moody (Cambridge, 1994), James Longenbach points out that in the *Quartets* the allusions no longer have a structural function; rather, Eliot adapts passages (without using quotation marks) when it suits his purpose. In *East Coker*, for example, lines 137–39 come from St. John of the Cross ("In order to arrive there, / To arrive where you are, to get from where you are not, / You must go by a way wherein there is no ecstasy"), and lines 32–35 come from Sir Thomas Elyot's *The Boke Named the Governour* ("Two and two, necessarye coniunction, / Holding eche other by the hand or the arm / Which betokeneth concorde." The latter lines, Eliot explained to his friend John Hayward, give the passage in question an early Tudor setting (185). Such allusions are, in any case, presented in English.
8. *The Cantos of Ezra Pound* (New York: New Directions, 1993), 41. All further references are to this edition.
9. See Carroll F. Terrell, *A Companion to the Cantos of Ezra Pound* (Berkeley: University of California Press, 1980), 48.
10. Horace, *The Odes and Epodes*, trans. C. E. Bennett (Cambridge, MA: Harvard University Press, 1978), 178–79. Cf. Lawrence Rainey, *Ezra Pound and the Monument of Culture: Text, History, and the Malatesta Cantos* (Chicago: University of Chicago Press, 1991).
11. See http://www.carolinebergvall.com. Bergvall's website, regularly updated, has links to most of her work. In this case, the *Say: 'Parsley'* project can be both heard and seen, the video documenting the Antwerp production where the English source words were given to Flemish/French speakers, who recorded what they heard or seemed to hear.
12. See Perloff, "The Oulipo Factor: The Procedural Poetics of Caroline Bergvall and

Christian Bok," *Textual Practice* 18, no. 1 (2004): 23–45; rpt. in *Differentials: Poetry, Poetics, Pedagogy* (Tuscaloosa: University of Alabama Press, 2004), 205–26.

13. By "differential," I mean a text that exists in various states (e.g., print and digital, or print and recorded voice) without any one variant being *the* authoritative text. See my "Vocable Scriptsigns: Differential Poetics in Kenneth Goldsmith's *Fidget* and John Kinsella's *Kangaroo Virus*," in *Poetry, Value, and Contemporary Culture*, ed. Andrew Roberts and John Allison (Edinburgh University Press, 2002), 21–43.

14. In its print version, the title is "Say: 'Parsley.'" See Bergvall, *Fig* (London: Salt, 2005), 51.

15. It is interesting to compare Bergvall's treatment of the parsley shibboleth to Rita Dove's 1983 poem on the same incident: "Parsley," in *Museum* (Pittsburgh: Carnegie Mellon University Press, 1983), recently reprinted on the Poetry Foundation website, http://www.poetryfoundation.org/archive/poem.html?id=172128/. Dove writes a narrative poem in which "El General" (Trujillo) searches for a word that can kill; the poem concludes with the lines "The general remembers the tiny green sprigs / men of his village wore in their capes / to honor the birth of a son. He will / order many, this time, to be killed / for a single, beautiful word." This mimetic account, in which the lyric poet assumes she can enter the mind of the evil dictator, allows for no real reflection on an important issue. It is merely histrionic.

16. See http://en.wikipedia.org/wiki/Engrish#cite_note-0.

17. Stills from *Say: Parsley*, 2008, a data piece conceived for the siting of Bergvall's installation at MuHKA, Museum of Contemporary Arts (Antwerp, May 28–August 17, 2008), as presented on Bergvall's website, http://www.carolinebergvall.com/.

18. Bergvall discusses the significance of typos, misspellings, and the like in her essay "Typose Translove: Mina Loy, Erin Mouré, Lisa Linn Kanae, Paolo Javier": see http://www.carolinebergvall.com/. An earlier version of this essay appeared as "Truncated/Troncated: Mina Loy's misspellings," *Open Letter* (Toronto), June 1999.

19. See Urban Dictionary, http://www.urbandictionary.com/define.php?term=Turgle.

20. http://www.carolinebergvall.com/#downloads/.

21. In a recent essay called "A Cat in the Throat: On Bilingual Occupants," *Jacket* 37 (2009), http://jacketmagazine.com/37/bergvall-cat-throat.shtml/, Bergvall meditates on what it means to be, like herself, a bilingual writer: "It is not about having a 'voice' (another difficult naturalizing concept), it is about siting 'voice,' locating the spaces and actions through which it becomes possible to be in one's languages, to stay with languages, to effect one's speech and work at a point of traffic between them, like a constant transport that takes place in the exchange between one's body, the air, and the world." In French, one must spit out "the cat in one's throat"; but in English, it's a frog—a distinction worth pondering.

22. Yoko Tawada, *Ekusophonii: Bogo no soto e deru tabi* (Tokyo: Iwanami Shoten, 2003), partially translated by Keijiro Suga in "Translation, Exophony, Omniphony," in *Yoko Tawada: Voices from Everywhere*, ed. Doug Slaymaker (Lanham, MD: Lexington Books, 2007), 27–28.

23. Ibid., 30; my emphasis.

24. Yoko Tawada, "Artist Books and Migration: A Conversation with Yoko Tawada," interview by Bettina Brandt, *Comparative Literature Studies* 45, no. 1 (2008): 19–20.

25. Yoko Tawada, *Sprachpolizei und Spielpolyglotte* (Tübingen: Verlag Claudia Gehrke, 2007), 8.

26. *Sprachpolizei*, 11. Translations here and elsewhere are mine, unless otherwise noted.

27. Ludwig Wittgenstein, *Philosophical Investigations*, ed. and trans. G. E. M. Anscombe (New York: Macmillan, 1958), no. 32 (15–16e).

28. J. W. von Goethe, *Werke: Erster Band, Gedichte, Faust* (Wiesbaden: Insel, 1945), 174.

29. "The Wild Roses," sung by Herman Weng in Japanese; You Tube, Heidenr#3299C4.

30. See, for example, David Wellbery, *The Specular Moment: Goethe's Early Lyric and the Beginnings of Romanticism* (Stanford, CA: Stanford University Press, 1996), 225–33; Lawrence Kramer, *Musical Meaning: Towards a Critical History* (Berkeley: University of California Press, 2001), 55–60.

31. I have translated this essay, in slightly abridged form, for *Lyric* (9 [2006]: 55–63), but the version used in the Jandl homage, *Volltext: Zeitung für Literatur*, Sonderausgabe no. 1/ 2005, 14–15, is slightly different from the book version, and hence I have retranslated the citations here.

32. Eliot, *Complete Poems*, 140; Pound, *ABC of Reading* (New York: New Directions, 1960), 32.

CHAPTER SEVEN

1. Hart Crane, "Proem: To Brooklyn Bridge," in *The Complete Poems and Selected Letters and Prose*, ed. Brom Weber (New York: Anchor Books, 1966), 46.

2. Kenneth Goldsmith, *Traffic* (Los Angeles: Make Now, 2007), 78 ($4.21). Digital reading edition on *Eclipse*: http://english.utah.edu/eclipse/projects/TRAFFIC/Traffic.pdf, 51. Subsequently cited in the text as T.

3. http://www.poetryfoundation.org/harriet/2008/06/conceptual-poetics-kenneth-goldsmith/.

4. Kenneth Goldsmith, "Kenneth Goldsmith and Conceptual Poetics," ed. Lori Emerson and Barbara Cole, special issue, *Open Letter: A Canadian Journal of Writing and Theory*, ser. 12, no. 7 (Fall 2005): 98; see also http://www.ubu.com/papers/kg_ol_goldsmith.html/.

5. Sol LeWitt, "Paragraphs on Conceptual Art," *Artforum* 5, no. 10 (June 1967): 79–83, and widely reprinted: see http://radicalart.info/concept/LeWitt/paragraphs.html/. In "American Trilogist: An Interview with Kenneth Goldsmith," *Rain Taxi*

(Fall 2008), Kareem Estefan refers to the "stealing" of LeWitt's paragraphs (http://www.raintaxi.com/online/2008fall/goldsmith.shtml), but most readers, including the editors of the special issue of *Open Letter* who published it (see note 4), seem unaware that it is not an "original."

6. Kenneth Goldsmith, *73 Poems*, with Joan Le Barbara (1994; repr. New York: Permanent Press, 2000); for the "singings through," see Goldsmith's author page at PennSound, http://www.writing.upenn.edu/pennsound/x/Goldsmith.html.

7. Kenneth Goldsmith, "Being Boring," delivered at Red Cat Symposium, 2004; see http://epc.buffalo.edu/authors/goldsmith/goldsmith_boring.html.

8. Ron Silliman, http://ronsilliman.blogspot.com/2006_02_01_archive.html, February 27, 2006;http://epc.buffalo.edu/authors/goldsmith/silliman_goldsmith.html.

9. Kenneth Goldsmith, *Day* (Great Barrington, MA: The Figures, 2003); *Fidget* (Toronto: Coach House Books, 2000); http://archives.chbooks.com/online_books/fidget/applet.html; *Soliloquy* (New York: Granary Books, 2001), http://www.epc.buffalo.edu/authors/goldsmith/soliloquy/days.html.

On *Fidget*, see Perloff, "'Vocable Scriptsigns': Differential Poetics in Kenneth Goldsmith's *Fidget*," in *Poetry, Value, and Contemporary Culture*, ed. Andrew Roberts and John Allison (Edinburgh: Edinburgh University Press, 2002), 21–43; Rubén Gallo, "*Fidget*'s Body," in "Kenneth Goldsmith and Conceptual Poetics," special issue, *Open Letter: A Canadian Journal of Writing and Theory*, ser. 12, no. 7 (Fall 2005): 50–57.

10. Walter Benjamin, *H* Konvolut 1–3, in *The Arcades Project*, trans. Howard Eiland and Kevin McLaughlin (Cambridge, MA: Harvard University Press, 1999), 203.

11. Kenneth Goldsmith, interviewed by Marjorie Perloff in "A Conversation with Kenneth Goldsmith," *Jacket* 21 (February 2003), http://jacketmagazine.com/21/perl-gold-iv.html. The interview has been reprinted in *Sibila*, http://www.sibila.com.br/2/index.php/sibila-english/303/.

12. Goldsmith, *No. 111.2.7.93 — 10.20.96* (Great Barrington, MA: The Figures, 1997). "The Rocking-Horse Winner" is reprinted on 588–606.

13. Goldsmith interview by Perloff, *Jacket* 21.

14. See Molly Schwartzburg, "Encyclopedic Novelties: On Kenneth Goldsmith's Tomes," "Kenneth Goldsmith and Conceptual Poetics," special issue, *Open Letter: A Canadian Journal of Writing and Theory*, ser. 12, no. 7 (Fall 2005): 30–31.

15. An excellent recent study is Tom Vanderbilt's *Traffic: Why We Drive the Way We Do (And What It Says about Us)* (New York: Alfred A. Knopf, 2008).

16. This designation was first given the trilogy by D. J. Huppatz in an essay posted on his blog Critical Cities in August 2008: "Kenneth Goldsmith: The New York Trilogy." The complete illustrated essay may be found on Goldsmith's own web page: http://epc.buffalo.edu/authors/goldsmith/huppatz-goldsmith-trilogy.pdf. It is forthcoming, in slightly different form, in *Critical Inquiry*.

17. The parallel is drawn by Craig Dworkin on the back cover of the MakeNow edition. Dworkin also cites Guy Debord's "Positions situationnistes sur la circulation" as a model to be parodied here.
18. F. T. Marinetti, "The New Ethical Religion of Speed" (1916), in *Critical Writings*, ed. Günter Berghaus, trans. Doug Thompson (New York: Farrar, Straus and Giroux, 2006), 256.
19. J. G. Ballard, "Introduction 1995," in *Crash* (1983; London: Harper Perennial, 2008), unpaginated.
20. On a witty assessment of metaphor in *Traffic*, see Huppatz, "Kenneth Goldsmith."
21. See, for example, Cage, *Silence* (Middletown, CT: Wesleyan, 1973), 93.
22. On the back cover of *Traffic*, Craig Dworkin notes that *Traffic* "proves the last of Guy Debord's 'Situationist Theses on Traffic,' 'Revolutionary urbanists will not limit their concern to the circulation of things, or to the circulation of human beings trapped in a world of things. They will try to break these topological chains, paving the way with their experiments for a human journey through authentic life'" (Dworkin's translation). This is a suggestive connection, but I would argue that *Traffic* submits these political notions, like Godard's, to a playful and disillusioned deconstruction.
23. http://www.1010wins.com/pages/7792.php.
24. Sina Queyras, *Expressway* (Toronto: Coach House Books, 2009), 43.
25. F. Scott Fitzgerald, *The Great Gatsby* (1925; New York: Scribners, 1953), 182.
26. The richness of the link was first pointed out to me by Craig Dworkin, e-mail message, July 12, 2009. I am grateful to Dworkin to this and other special insights into *Traffic*.
27. Kenneth Goldsmith, "Flarf and Conceptual Writing," *Poetry*, July/August 2009, 315–16. This talk was originally delivered at the Whitney Museum of American Art, April 17, 2009, on the occasion of a "debate" between Conceptualist and Flarfist poets. See http://epc.buffalo.edu/authors/goldsmith/whitney-intro.html. The term *Flarf*, invented by the poet Gary Sullivan to define a new aesthetic of the "inappropriate" in all its guises, has as its stated method "to mine the Internet with odd search terms and then distill the results into often hilarious and sometimes disturbing poems, plays, and other texts" (Wikipedia).
28. Silliman's Blog, http://ronsilliman.blogspot.com/2009_07_07_archive.html, July 7, 2009, and cf. the dozens of comments, responding to Silliman's strictures, made by other, mostly angry, bloggers. But for the opposite position, one close to my own, see K. Silem Mohammed on his blog Lime Tree (http://lime-tree.blogspot.com/<date/title of the post you're quoting?>), with reference to Craig Dworkin's long conceptualist poem *Parse* (2008).

At nearly 300 pages, even the most diehard conceptualist might balk at the prospect of actually reading *Parse* front to back, and in fact Kenny Goldsmith has used it as an example of *conceptual texts that don't actually need to be read:* the *idea is enough.* As appealing as I find this notion in many ways, I don't ultimately find it fully adequate to an assessment of Dworkin's work (or Goldsmith's, for that matter). What I think books like this do is ask us to reconsider *what it means to read*, and to find ways of actualizing new reading practices. This might mean something as simple as flipping around here and there throughout the book rather than reading straight through. It might mean reading one or more sections in an intense state of attention, and generalizing outward from such readings to a larger engagement with the total work. It might mean submitting for extended periods of time to the monotony of the governing structure, so that when there is some kind of variation in the pattern, it takes on an added value of surprise. (my emphasis)

29. Pierre Cabanne, *Dialogues with Marcel Duchamp*, trans. from the French by Ron Padgett (New York: Viking, 1968), 48, 16, and passim.
30. Ibid., 43.
31. Ibid., 38–39.
32. On the Munich interlude, see *Thierry de Duve, Pictorial Nominalism: On Marcel Duchamp's Passage from Painting to the Readymade*, trans. Dana Polan (1984; Minneapolis: University of Minnesota Press, 1991), 19–56.
33. The phrase is Jasper Johns's: see "Sketchbook Notes" in *Jasper Johns: Writings, Sketchbook Notes, Interviews*, ed. Kirk Varnedoe (New York: Museum of Modern Art, distributed Harry N. Abrams, 1996), 54.
34. The split, extending from at least Donald Allen's *New American Poetry* (1960) to the present, is well documented by Cole Swensen in her introduction to *American Hybrid: A Norton Anthology of New Poetry*, ed. Cole Swensen and David St. John (New York: Norton, 2008), xvii–xxi. For Silliman's terminology, see Silliman's Blog, passim.
35. On Craig Dworkin and Jan Baetens, see my "The Pleasures of the Déjà Dit: Citation, Ekphrasis, and Constraint in Recent Experimental Poetries," in *The Consequences of Innovation: 21st Century Poetics*, ed. Craig Dworkin (New York: Roof Books, 2008), 255–82. This essay was reprinted in *Another Language: Poetic Experiments in Britain and North America*, ed. Kornelia Freitag and Katharine Veeter (Berlin: Lit Verlag 2009), 125–48. On Bergvall, see chapter 5 above and my "The Oulipo Factor: The Procedural Poetics of Christian Bök and Caroline Bergvall," in *Differentials: Poetry, Poetics, Pedagogy* (Tuscaloosa: University of Alabama Press, 2004), 205–26.
36. Goldsmith, "American Trilogist," 3.
37. Gallo, "Fidget's Body," 50–51, 53.
38. Goldsmith's technique in *Fidget* is anticipated by David Antin's *Talking at the Boundaries* (New York: New Directions, 1976) and many subsequent collections of "talk pieces"; like Goldsmith's, these transcribe the poet's own speech, producing a written simulation of speech rhythms in a continuous unpunctuated low-

ercase prose that uses space between phrases to indicate pauses. But Goldsmith's strenuous minimalism creates an artifice that recalls the Beckett of *How It Is* rather than such Antin pieces as "Who's Listening Out There?" Antin, moreover, is not primarily an appropriative poet.

AFTERWORD

1. (Evanston: Northwestern University Press, 2010). The anthology originated in Dworkin's *Ubuweb Anthology of Conceptual Writing* on Ububweb (http://www.ubu.com), but it has been substantially changed and Dworkin has supplied an entirely new introduction.

2. Vanessa Place, *Statement of Fact* (Los Angeles: Blanc Press, 2010). In an earlier form, the book was published as no. 42 in the Publishing the Unpublishable series (Ubu Editions, 2008). Place, a criminal defense appellate attorney for the state of California in Los Angeles, has based *Statement of Fact* on her own cases. See also her nonfiction book *The Guilt Project: Rape, Morality, and Law* (New York: Other Press, 2010).

3. Craig Dworkin, *Parse* (Berkeley, CA: Atelos, 2008).

4. Craig Dworkin, "Dure," in *Strand* (New York: Roof Books, 2005), 75.

5. I discuss this poem at length in "The Pleasures of Déjà Dit: Citation, Intertext and Ekphrasis in Recent Experimental Poetry," in *The Consequences of Innovation: 21st Century Poetics*, ed. Craig Dworkin (New York: Roof Books, 2008), 255–79; see esp. 264–69. This essay appeared in slightly different form in *Another Language,: Poetic Experiments in Britain and North America*, ed. Kornelia Freitag and Katharine Veeter (Berlin: Lit Verlag, 2008), 125–48.

6. Jan Baetens, *Vivre sa vie: Une novelisation en vers du film de Jean-Luc Godard* (Paris: Les Impressions nouvelles, 2005). I discuss this text in "Pleasure of Déjà-Dit," 258–64.

7. Letter to the author, November 4, 2009.

8. In describing the method of *Roaratorio* (1985), for example, Cage writes, "Do not permit for a single appearance of a given letter the repetition of a particular syllable. Distinguish between subsequent appearances of the same letter. Other adjacent words from the original text . . . may be used *according to taste*, limited, say to forty-three characters to the left and forty-three to the right." See John Cage, afterword to *Roaratorio: An Irish Circus on "Finnegans Wake"* (Königstein, Germany: Athenaeum, 1985), 173.

9. Antoine Compagnon, *La seconde main, ou Le travail de la citation* (Paris: Seuil, 1979), 17. My translation.

Index

Numbers in boldface indicate pages on which main treatments of subjects can be found; numbers in italic refer to pages with illustrations.